D1194167

DISCARDED

THE boat improvement BIBLE

THE boat improvement BIBLE

PRACTICAL PROJECTS TO CUSTOMISE AND UPGRADE YOUR BOAT

ADLARD COLES NAUTICAL

BLOOMSBURY

LONDON · NEW DELHI · NEW YORK · SYDNEY

Published by Adlard Coles Nautical
an imprint of Bloomsbury Publishing Plc
50 Bedford Square, London WC1B 3DP
www.adlardcoles.com

Copyright © Adlard Coles Nautical 2015
First edition 2015

ISBN 978-1-4081-5419-9
ePub: 978-1-4081-5898-2
ePDF: 978-1-4081-5590-5

All rights reserved. No part of this publication may be
reproduced in any form or by any means – graphic,
electronic or mechanical, including photocopying,
recording, taping or information storage and retrieval
systems – without the prior permission in writing of
the publishers.

This book is produced using paper that is made from
wood grown in managed, sustainable forests. It is
natural, renewable and recyclable. The logging
and manufacturing processes conform to the
environmental regulations of the country of origin.

Produced for Adlard Coles Nautical by Ivy Contract.

Managing editor: Judith Chamberlain-Webber
Project editor: Sarah Doughty
Project designer: Lisa McCormick
Consultant: Barrie Smith

Typeset in Veljovic Book and Bliss
Printed and bound in China by C&C Offset Printing Co

Note: while all reasonable care has been taken in the
publication of this book, the publisher takes no
responsibility for the use of the methods or products
described in the book.

Contents

Welcome to boat improvement   **8**

Setting up   **10**
Safety and tools   12
Types of tools   14
A working toolkit   18
Setting up a portable workshop   20

Hull and deck   **22**
Woodworking skills   24
Cockpit grating   26
Nameplate   28
Dorade vents   30
Passarelle   32
Cockpit table   36
Grab rails   38
Faced-ply cabin sides   40
Faux decks – floor   44

Faux decks – fore and sidedecks   46
Replacing aluminium fittings   48
Pulpit and pushpit   50
Gantries and goalposts   52
Roll reducer   56
Lightweight tiller   58
Bathing platform   62
Davits   64

Canvas and upholstery   **66**
Care and repair   68
Cockpit cushions   70
Bimini   74
Low profile windscoop   76
Hatch covers   78
Dodgers   82
Lee cloths   86

Domestic   **90**
The ideal galley   92
Gimballing the stove   94
Galley straps   96
Deck handholds and footholds   98
Fiddle rails   100
Simple veneers   102
Charcoal heater   106
Hot air diesel heating   108
Diesel cooker   112
Fridge and cool box   116
Air conditioning   120
LED interior lighting   122
iPod   124
Domestic tips   126

General mechanics	**128**	Bow thruster	172
Mechanical skills	130	Stern thruster	176
Manual water pumps	132	Trim tabs	178
Pressurised water	134	General mechanics tips	180
Hot water	136		
Shower	138	**Electrical**	**182**
Electrically operated heads	140	Electrical skills	184
Bilge pump and alarms	142	Radar	186
Engine-driven bilge pump	144	Navtex/AIS	190
Watermaker	146	Inboard autopilot	192
Ventilation	150	LED navigation lights	196
Gas alarm	154	Underwater lights	198
Generator	156	Lightning protection	202
Fuel capacity	160	Battery-charging inputs	204
Tank level gauge	162	Battery capacity	208
Windlass	164	Shore power	210
Chain counter	166	Inverters	212
Wheel steering	170	Electrical and systems tips	216

Mast, rigging and sails   **218**

Rigging and sail-mending skills   220
Lazy jacks   222
Headsail furling   226
Additional forestay   230
Backstay adjuster   232
Jackstays   234
Deck gear   236
Leading halyards aft   238
Sheeting points   242
Single-line reefing   244
Cruising chute   248
Spinnaker   250
Mast steps   252
Pop-riveting   254
Windvane self-steering   256
Tiller pilot   260
Electric winches   262
Sails and rigging tips   266

Eco upgrades   **268**

Solar energy   270
Wind power   274
Go electric   278
Fuel cells   282
Better insulation   284
Holding tank   288
'Greener' antifouling   292

Glossary   294
Index   300
Acknowledgements   304

Welcome to boat improvement

Many boatowners enjoy working on their boats, especially when they are improving the boat or making life easier, safer and more comfortable for everyone on board. Most have a 'wish' list of jobs they would like to do – anything from upgrading the galley to installing an autopilot. With this book, arranged in sections outlined below, those who like to turn their hand to DIY will gain the guidance needed to achieve a satisfying result.

Essential tools

What tools do you need to get the jobs done on the boat, and how do you organise your working area? Start here for advice on basic tools and how to set up a portable workshop.

Hull and deck

Here are some practical ideas for the exterior of your boat, from laying a faux (synthetic) teak deck to improving the pulpit and pushpit. You might want to make life easier for your crew with grab rails, a passarelle and a cockpit table. And if you enjoy swimming or like to access your boat from the stern, try creating a bathing platform. If you'd just prefer to have a quiet few hours on board, make a simple roll reducer to keep you upright while at anchor.

Above **Upgrade the appearance of your deck by laying faux teak on a fibreglass deck.**

Below **Consider the options for a bimini to provide shade from the sun in warm climates.**

Canvas and upholstery

Keeping your boat's upholstery in good condition is part of general maintenance, but have you ever thought of creating your own bunk cushions, hatch covers, dodgers and lee cloths? With a few simple tools you can save yourself an expense if you can make them yourself. A bimini is a more ambitious project that is useful in warm climates, while a windscoop is simple to make and effective in providing cooling ventilation on board in hot weather.

Above left **The ease and convenience of a cockpit electric winch can be very beneficial.**

Above right **Fit a solar panel onto your boat for maintenance-free renewable energy.**

Domestic

The appearance, practicality and safety of the galley is important to anyone who spends time on a boat. More ambitious projects include revising the heating, cooking and refrigeration facilities when updating the galley area. Easy projects include changing to LED lighting, which can save precious battery power on board. Straightforward changes to your on-board stereo system can make playing your iPod through it a reality.

General mechanics

Water systems, including heads, pumps and showers are all ideal areas for upgrade and improvement. You might consider upgrading the ventilation and fuel systems, too. To make life easier for the crew, you could install an electric windlass and chain counter on your boat. Bow and stern thrusters are helpful additions in today's crowded marinas.

Electrical

A few electrical skills are key to many boat improvements that will bring your boat up to date, such as installing radar or Navtex. Understanding on-board electrics also helps improve fundamentals such as battery charging and capacity. With the high demand for shore power today, it simply makes good sense to know how to connect the mains power to your boat safely. However, if you have all the everyday electrics you could want, why not go one step further and fit some dramatic LED underwater lighting?

Mast, rigging and sails

Your sails and the ease and efficiency of their use are key aspects of sailing. You can make hoisting sails easier, or adjust the rig to add sails and improve performance. If you are short-handed on board you may benefit from lazy jacks, plus you can make sheets and reefing lines easier to handle by altering their configuration. If you intend going long distance, windvane self-steering gear may be an alternative to long stretches of time on the helm. For the ultimate easy handling of sheets, electric winches may be the answer!

Eco upgrades

This section explores some of the green approaches to upgrading a boat, including power from solar panels and wind-powered generators, clean electric engines and the trend towards using fuel cells on board. Modern technology can also be one step ahead on traditional antifouling methods, with alternatives that are longer lasting and kinder to the environment.

With tips to guide you on other ideas for improvements, we hope this book will help you plan your next steps and cater for your aspirations, however simple or ambitious you want your improvements to be.

Setting up

Safety and tools

When undertaking any boat improvement project it's vitally important to create a safe and efficient working environment. If done properly it will not only minimise the risk of injury, but will speed up the workflow and help you produce a neat and professional job.

A hazard assessment is key to creating a safe working environment. At sea, all skippers are accustomed to being constantly on the lookout for hazards, and this is a skill that can be easily transferred to the boatyard. Before starting each project identify all the potential risks, and ensure you're prepared to handle each one.

Below **Kitted out for self-protection, this boatowner is wearing coveralls, safety glasses and a dust mask. The belt sander he is using on the hull has an extractor bag to collect the dust.**

Personal safety

When working on a boat you must first remember to protect yourself – physically from dirt, chemical and paint splashes by wearing overalls and stout gloves if handling rough materials. Wear safety glasses if there is a possibility of something getting in your eyes. They are also essential for jobs such as grinding metalwork, power sanding, woodwork and painting in general. Use skin protection if you are working with antifouling paint.

Dust is the largest health hazard arising from boat improvements. Whatever the construction of your boat, it's inevitable that you will be exposed to harmful particles at some stage, so buy the best dust mask you can find – and make sure it's the right mask for the job. You should also use a sander with an effective vacuum extraction system.

Don't forget about others if you are working in a boatyard – ensure that you don't cause trip obstructions for others when setting up your

Above **Don't cut corners if you need to work above ground level when the boat is ashore. There is no substitute for proper staging.**

Left **Ensure the ladder is secured to a rail or stanchion and placed at an angle of 15 degrees to the vertical.**

workspace, and if you intend to carry out grinding, sanding or painting jobs, make sure you are not going to damage another person's property or cover their boat in dust.

Ladders and staging

Many boatyard accidents occur when unsafe ladders or temporary staging are erected to allow you to work on your boat's topsides. Ladders should be placed on level ground, at an angle of 15 degrees to the vertical, and should be tied to a strong deck fitting to prevent them capsizing or slipping away from the boat. If the ladder footing is on sloping ground, wedge the bottom by packing pieces of plywood underneath it to form a level foundation.

When working your boat's topsides, staging should be laid on substantial trestles, again on level ground. The minimum safe width for such staging is 60cm (2ft) and a

toe board on the outer edge should be included. Make sure the boards are tied to the platform framework securely. For bigger yachts use a scaffold or ladder.

Don't be tempted to carry items weighing more than 10kg (22lb) on a ladder. Instead, use a rope to lower items to the ground or heave them on board. Extra heavy items can be lifted on board yachts using the boom and mainsheet or, on a powerboat, with the davits.

Paints, solvents and resins

Many boat interiors are small spaces that are poorly ventilated, so a build-up of noxious fumes from these products is a very real possibility, and you could consider using a fan to disperse fumes. In addition to the health hazards, some solvents pose a risk of fire or

explosion. This should be considered when storing these products, so make sure they are kept well clear of heat sources.

Below **Disposable gloves are essential when working with paints, solvents or resins. Make sure they are suited to the job by checking the specifications on the packet.**

Types of tools

If you're doing improvements on your boat, you'll need a variety of tools and products. Over the past couple of decades tools have become significantly cheaper. Many can now be found second-hand, too, so there's no excuse for not having the best tools for each job.

Hand tools

The starting point is a set of hand tools. It's possible to do any job with these, they will never break down and they won't run out of power. But be aware that with hand tools a 'one size fits all' philosophy never works – a wide range of sizes and types of screwdriver and spanner, for example, are typically needed so that you have one to fit every size and type of fastening on the boat, engine and electronics.

It is worth having your own set of 'boat tools' so that you are not always moving all your tools between locations. However, unless you are a professional who uses tools every day, there is no need to aim for professional quality tools to keep on board. For the occasional boat improvement project, budget tools will be fine as long as you keep them in good order.

Proper maintenance of your tools on board, whatever their quality, is vital. Make sure you keep your boat's interior as dry as possible, either through good ventilation or by using a dehumidifier if mains power is available. And don't keep tools in a damp locker. It can be a good idea to keep them in stout plastic boxes with a lid, as they will tend to get thrown around when out in a rough sea.

Right **Keep a bag of essential tools you might need for home and work to carry with you while keeping a main set stored on your boat.**

In addition, all moving parts should be lubricated with a light oil to prevent them seizing up; this will also help to keep rust at bay. Tools should be kept sharp, too – chisels and planes benefit from being kept super sharp, although in today's throwaway society we tend not to sharpen drill bits or handsaws.

General safety

When working with hand tools make sure you have thoroughly familiarised yourself with the tool first. Ensure that the material you are working with is held firmly, ideally in a vice or clamped to something that won't move. Here are some tips for using hand tools:

Hand tools with sharp blades:
- Keep both hands behind the blade at all times.
- Keep the blade sharp – a sharp blade is much safer when working than a blunt one.
- Work away from your body, not towards it.
- Always ensure that a sharp tool is put away safely so that you don't cut yourself searching for it. Retract the blade if possible as

soon as you have finished with it or wrap a protective cover around it.

Hand tools with blunt blades:
- Even tools with blunt blades, such as screwdrivers, should be treated with caution.
- Keep your hands behind the 'blade' or tip.
- Use the tool only for the purpose for which it was designed.

Top left and right **Keep tools in plastic boxes on your boat for easy removal when needed. Keep them dry rather than storing them loose in a locker that may be damp.**

Bottom left and right **It is essential to keep your chisels sharp, so ensure you have a good sharpening stone and use it frequently. If possible, use a workbench when there's chiselling or similar work to be done. In either case, ensure the item can't move while you're working on it.**

Types of tools 2

Power tools

Powered tools help speed up progress enormously, as well as removing much of the physical effort required when using hand tools. However, it is important to be aware of the inherent dangers of using mains power tools outdoors.

Safe handling of tools should quickly become second nature, yet many people take potentially dangerous shortcuts. In particular it's vitally important to keep hands behind and clear of any cutting blade, whether it's a chisel or an electric saw. Make sure that any item you are working on is held securely before you start drilling, cutting or planing. A portable workbench incorporating a vice, and three or four clamps, should be sufficient for this.

Here are some tips for using power tools:

- ✪ Read the manual supplied with the tool and observe all the safety instructions.
- ✪ Ensure the mains supply has circuit breakers so that the current can be cut off immediately should any fault occur.
- ✪ Try not to work in the rain or over water. Extension leads should have all-weather connections to keep them dry.
- ✪ Extension leads should be fully unwound so as not to act as a heater element by being coiled up.
- ✪ If the trigger can be locked 'on', think carefully before you do so. In the event of an accident it will keep running, possibly with dire results.

- ✪ If the tool has a safety guard, always use it, even if it seems inconvenient. If you can't do the job with the guard in place, it is the wrong tool for the job.
- ✪ Take care with mains-powered tools to ensure you don't cut or entangle the power lead.
- ✪ When you release the trigger, let the tool stop rotating before you lay it down. High-speed rotation can cause a strong gyroscopic effect on the tool as you move it, and you may drop it while it is still rotating.

Below left **A mains powered drill is a powerful tool and well suited for heavy or repetitive jobs.**

Below right **A battery-powered drill is useful for light jobs.**

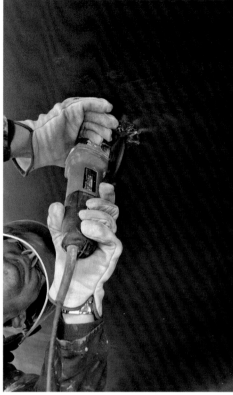

Above **Angle grinders are useful for working on a fibreglass hull.**

Left **A power planer is one of the most useful power tools for working with wood. Be sure to wear eye and ear protection when using this tool.**

Other options

It's also worth considering cordless power tools – most are now available for a modest price from DIY stores. The tools you need will vary according to the type of improvement work being undertaken, but by far the most useful on-board electric tool is the cordless drill/screwdriver. They are low voltage and do not have cables to hinder operations.

Indeed for many projects it's worth having one for drilling holes, and the other to use as a screwdriver – as this eliminates the time needed to repeatedly swap between drill and screwdriver bits. For a big project consider getting a model that's sold with two batteries so that you never need to wait for one to recharge.

Next on the list for most boatowners are electric sanders. A good starting point is a standard random orbital sander; although many boatowners eventually collect a range of models, including a triangular detail sander for work in intricate corners. Beyond this, serious fibreglass repairs often require an angle grinder, while jigsaws and circular saws are useful for projects involving woodwork.

A working toolkit

You always need to carry some tools on board your boat for maintenance, and a toolkit is essential if you are undertaking boat improvements. The more jobs you carry out yourself the larger your toolkit needs to be, but here are some of the basics.

General tools

An assortment of tools for jobs on board, both handheld and powered.

Spanners

You can choose between open-ended spanners or ring spanners (or a combination spanner has one of each). Alternatively an adjustable spanner might be the right tool, but may not grip the nut so well. A socket spanner is a deep ring spanner with an extra ratchet handle, allowing more force to be exerted.

Screwdrivers

You will need both crossheaded and flat-blade screwdrivers. The correct type of head should be used to avoid damage to the screw.

Pliers and mole grips

Used to grip a metal objects, which a spanner cannot grip because it has no 'flats'. Although useful, they can cause damage to the metal surface when in use so should be used with caution.

Pop-riveting tool

Attachments to masts and booms are often made using tubular rivets, which need to be worked with a pop riveter.

Electrical or cordless drill/ cordless screwdriver

Rechargeable tools are probably the most useful power tools on the boat. For heavy duty work mains-powered would be a more practical option than battery tools.

Drill bits

A set of twist drill bits is all you may need. Go for good quality bits that won't need to be sharpened very often.

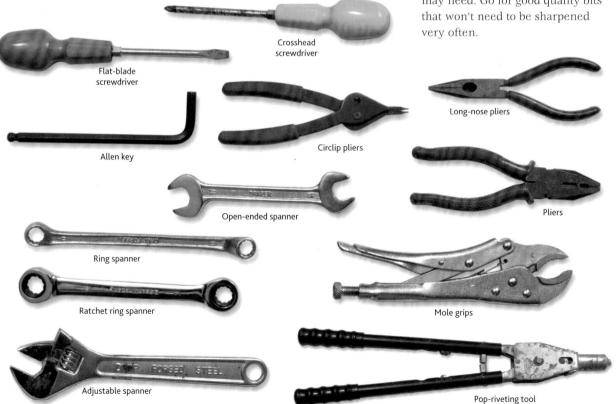

Crosshead screwdriver

Flat-blade screwdriver

Long-nose pliers

Allen key

Circlip pliers

Open-ended spanner

Pliers

Ring spanner

Ratchet ring spanner

Mole grips

Adjustable spanner

Pop-riveting tool

Electrical

A basic set of tools is required for installing and improving electrics on board.

Wire cutters

A pair of wire cutters is useful to cut the size of wire to the length you need.

Gas soldering iron

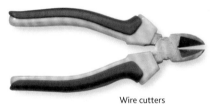

Wire cutters

Wood chisel

Spokeshave

Electrical screwdrivers

Designed to be safer than ordinary screwdrivers to use on electrical jobs because they are insulated against the possibility of touching a live wire.

Long-nose pliers

These are useful for holding things in awkward places where ordinary pliers are too big.

Crimper

Used to fit cable connectors to electrical wire. The ratchet type makes a more secure connection.

Soldering iron

Soldering irons come in many different wattages and may be mains-powered or powered from a 12-volt system. For soldering small wires a 25-watt iron will be fine.

Woodworking

Woodworking tools will be useful for many projects. Stow them in a strong waterproof box so they don't become damp and rusty.

Saws

A tenon saw is used for more accurate cutting and it has a rigid spine and small teeth. A rip saw has long flexible blades for fast cuts.

Chisels

For most jobs a set of bevel-edged chisels will be adequate, but they need to be kept sharp.

Spokeshave

Used for rounding off edges on a piece of timber, although a plane can be used on longer pieces of wood.

Planes

Rasp planes and smoothing planes are used to improve surfaces on sawn timber. A longer jack plane is used when you are working on larger surfaces.

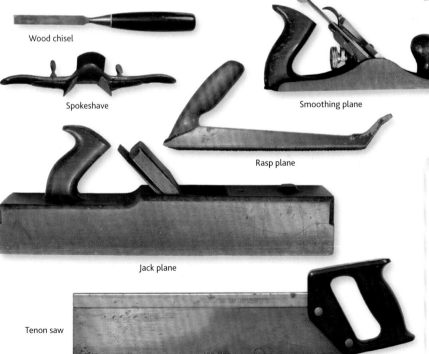

Smoothing plane

Rasp plane

Jack plane

Tenon saw

OTHER TOOLS

Also useful:

Bolt cutters	Vernier gauge
Hole saw	and micrometer
Bradawl	Multimeter
Oil stone	Jigsaw
Multi tool	Circular saw
Sanding block	Set square, bevel
Mastic gun	and clamp
Tape measure	Polisher
Torque wrench	

Setting up a portable workshop

A well-ordered workspace is essential to be able to work quickly and safely, so the time spent organising your tools and materials for each project is often repaid many times over.

Few boatowners have the luxury of being able to work on their vessels at home, with full workshop facilities available. For most, creating an efficient work area is therefore a major challenge. Don't be tempted to skimp on this stage, though.

A decent workshop makes a huge difference to the time it takes to complete a job and to the quality of the finish that can be achieved.

A proper on-site workshop

Most well-funded racing yachts have shipping containers fitted out as fully equipped workshops and stores, enabling their crews to fix almost any type of damage overnight. Not many boatowners have the resources for this kind of facility, but for a big project it's worth looking at ways to create a proper workshop. With a bit of

Above **A portable workstation on deck speeds up repair work and reduces the dangers associated with repeatedly ascending and descending a ladder.**

Below **A large wheeled tool chest facilitates the organisation and transportation of tools.**

Right **Erecting a shelter over the boat is well worth the effort, but never tie tarpaulins to the shores supporting the vessel.**

planning, it's possible to create space for labour-saving items such as table saws, bench drill presses and even lathes.

The easiest option for this is a 'tow a van' type trailer, which can be fitted out with workbenches, power tools and storage. Much of the capital cost of buying a trailer can be recovered by selling it at the end of the project, although fitting out an inexpensive old caravan in a similar manner might reduce the upfront costs. Similarly, the cost of parking the trailer in a boatyard is often recouped through finishing the project more quickly.

Creating a shelter

Unless the boat is in a shed it is also worth spending time building a decent shelter around it. In hot climates this will give protection from the sun, allowing you to work with more energy, and in the case of wooden boats it helps to prevent them drying out too much. In cooler regions a shelter will keep the rain off and the wind out, and allow the work area to be heated in cold weather. Another alternative, if using staging, is to build a shed on a scaffolding platform – this has the advantage of the workshop being on the same level as your work, which can save an enormous amount of time.

For a smaller project, it's possible to create a portable yet practical workstation based around a folding workbench, which can even be set up on deck if necessary.

Transporting tools to and from your boat can, however, be a headache – it's all too easy to find you've left a crucial item at home – so it pays to keep them well organised. Fortunately, large toolboxes on wheels are now readily available, and this makes it much easier to travel with a complete set of tools, and even by public transport if necessary.

Above **Many raceboats use containers or trailers as a workshop and a store – ideal when close to hand and properly organised.**

Above **For a big project it's worth building a free-standing and all-encompassing shelter that can double as a workshop.**

Hull and deck

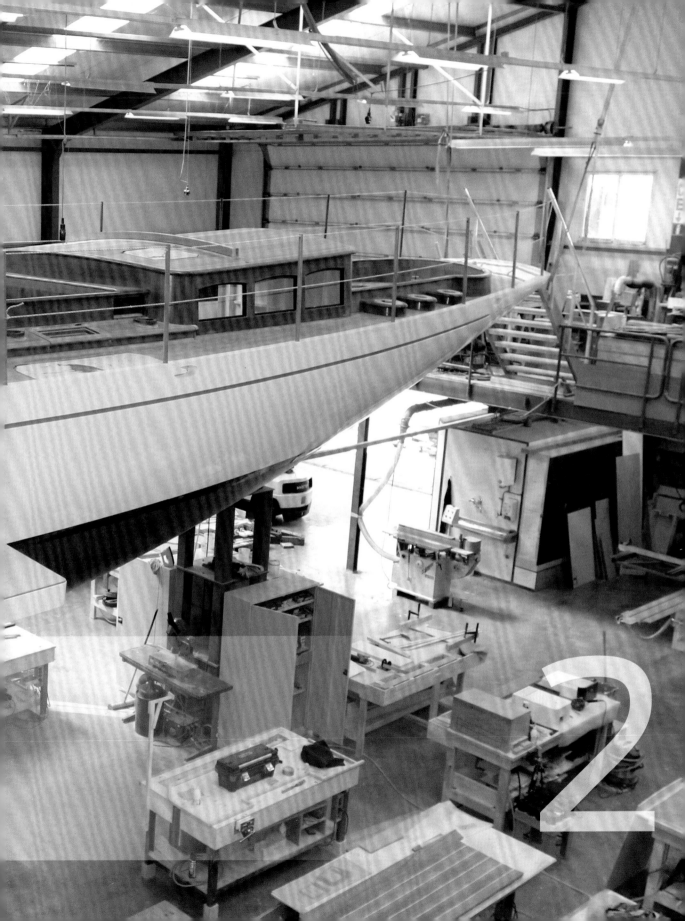

Woodworking skills

The ability to use a basic selection of hand tools will enable a boatowner to carry out most of the woodworking repairs needed to keep their vessel shipshape and to make improvements.

Sharp edges

Working with sharp edges requires constant attention to achieve the best results and avoid any unnecessary injury. It is always better to sharpen a blade before it becomes blunt, so aim to sharpen your tools at regular intervals.

If you have time, a tool should be sharpened before it's put away so that it can be used immediately when it's needed again. If you don't maintain a sharp edge, you'll find that more effort is required to drive the tool through the wood, which in turn will undermine the quality of the final result, as well as increasing the risk of an injury caused by the tool slipping.

When it comes to sharpening a blade, there are a variety of methods and sharpening materials available, including diamond, oil and water stones. Deciding which method to use will probably be determined by personal preference because they are all effective – although keep away from cheap stones as they are invariably too soft, they wear quickly and unevenly, and are generally a poor investment.

Above **For final trimming work use the chisel with the flat edge down.**

Using a chisel

To achieve the best results with a chisel it should be 'driven' whenever possible by a mallet, rather than 'pushed' by hand, as it's less likely to slip. If there is a lot of material to be removed, use the chisel with the bevel edge down, because this will lift the material away from the surface. Use the chisel with the flat edge down to carry out the final trimming work; this will produce a flatter surface. Once you have finished using the chisel, protect the tip with either a plastic guard or by putting it in a canvas tool roll.

Below **When using a plane, 'follow through' by keeping the plane flat and level until the end of the stroke to avoid leaving a rounded surface.**

Using a plane

Before using a plane, it must be set up correctly. Having checked the blade is sharp, make sure it's parallel to the base of the plane, using the lever to adjust its angle. If this is not done properly, the plane will leave 'tramlines' (lines with raised edges) on the planed timber surface. Once the blade is parallel, set the depth by which the blade projects below the plane's base.

Depending on the type of wood you're working on, a plane's blade will start to cut when it projects below the base by up to 2mm ($^5/_{64}$in). You should therefore begin with the blade projecting almost flush with the base and gradually increase its depth until it cuts. If you want a smooth finish, it's always better to take off lots of fine shavings than a few coarse ones.

Your posture is also important. Stand comfortably; do not overstretch, and ensure your weight is over the top of the tool. Try to 'follow through' by keeping the plane flat and level until the end of the stroke to avoid leaving a rounded surface. When the plane is not in use it should always be placed on its side to protect the base.

Using a spokeshave

The spokeshave should be set up along the same lines as a plane – although the adjustment mechanism for the blade tends to be more basic. When it comes to holding a spokeshave, do so lightly with the thumb and first finger of each hand, while wrapping the remaining fingers around the handles. It's important not to grasp the spokeshave too tightly and to simply direct it with your hands. Best results can usually be achieved by using a spokeshave at a slight angle to its direction of cut.

Above **A Japanese backsaw gives a clean cut, though the teeth are more vulnerable.**

Saws

The majority of cutting tasks can be carried out using one of the two main types of saw. A tenon saw is ideally suited for finer work, whereas a panel (or 'hand') saw should be used to cut larger pieces of timber when a coarse cut is acceptable. A Japanese backsaw gives a nice clean cut; however, the teeth cannot easily be resharpened and are vulnerable to hidden nails and screws.

Above **For a smooth finish it is always better to take off several fine shavings.**

Above **Hold a spokeshave lightly and guide it with your hands. Try not to force it.**

TIP

Sharpening a Japanese saw is a specialist job. Files for sharpening these saws have a very flat diamond profile, allowing them to reach into the bottom of the narrow, deep gulleys.

Cockpit grating

Adding a bespoke hardwood grating not only makes the cockpit safer underfoot, especially in the wet, but it also greatly enhances the look of the boat. Low maintenance materials can provide a good alternative to using hardwoods.

Cockpit gratings are designed to allow water to drain away quickly while still giving a warm and non-slip foothold, which is why they are also commonly used in domestic showers.

As a boat's cockpit can often represent a cold shower when hammering into a head sea, gratings can be designed to add a whole new dimension to the cockpit's functionality. They can either be custom-made or assembled from kits.

The most striking and popular form of cockpit grating is made from interlocking teak strips, typically 22mm (⅞in) thick and suspended in a 28-mm (1⅛-in) outer frame to give additional strength. This deeper outer frame raises the majority of the grating above the deck, therefore allowing any water to escape underneath.

Although appearing quite complex to make, the actual assembly of an attractive grating is well within the realm of a competent DIY enthusiast, although professional suppliers will be happy to make one to your templates.

Grating options

The cheapest option is called a 'single castle', where a flat section of wood is locked into a 'castle' section underneath. A sturdier, and more costly, design is the 'double castle', which, as the name implies, locks two castellated strips together.

TIP

Because a grating is made of wood, it could float in a fully submerged cockpit. Each section needs a set of securing clips to hold it in place. The grating needs to be secured to the cockpit by wooden turnpegs or brass barrel bolts, neither of which need to be very big.

Other designs of cockpit grating involve single strips of thick hardwood, usually teak or mahogany, screwed to a basic frame. Longitudinal runners underneath raise the whole assembly clear of the cockpit sole.

Several boatowners also use a mass-produced rubber or plastic mat often found in swimming pools, as this is easy to cut and trim. While not as attractive as wood, and much slower to drain, it won't need any maintenance either. A number of gratings have even been made out of plastic pipe, and given a slight camber for better grip as the yacht heels.

By using strips of wood set into the edges of the seats, some gratings can be temporarily raised to form the base of a bed for sleeping in the cockpit. Gratings can also be used for bathing platforms, companionway steps and attractive gangways for passarelles.

Left **A cockpit grating can be made from kits to fit into most shapes of cockpit. The wood provides a strong and reliable foothold while enabling the water to drain away quickly.**

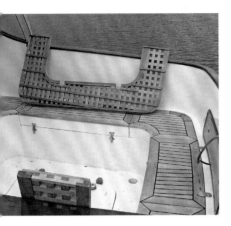

Choosing a grating

When designing a grating, the key is not to make it too big and heavy. This is usually achieved by breaking the design up into two or three smaller pieces.

The first task is to create a template out of paper, cardboard or hardboard on which you can sketch the desired shape and mark in important items such as cockpit drains, emergency steering access or inspection hatches. It is quite possible to have the outer frame follow any sweeping curves in the cockpit to give a more refined finish.

Some suppliers will create a custom frame for home completion. A grating kit can be supplied so you can assemble the gratings yourself, although these are usually the simpler rectangular designs. Gratings with smaller holes are available for shower or for more decorative applications.

Once fitted, a grating must be expected to weather, as it will be exposed to sunshine, sea water and tread underfoot. Most gratings are allowed to weather to grey, as varnishing inside each square will prove tricky and time-consuming.

Above left **On large gratings, additional strips of hardwood keep each section clear of the cockpit sole, allowing water to drain freely.**

Above **A cockpit under construction. When making a hardwood template, try to make it as accurate as possible, with a slight gap between each panel. Mark in any slots or apertures, such as access points.**

The weathered teak also gives better grip in the wet, whereas oils and varnishes are more slippery. Despite the upkeep, some gratings are maintained in pristine condition.

MAKING A GRATING FROM A KIT

① The kit supplied will consist of interlocking castellated strips of teak and a frame that are easy to cut and shape to suit your cockpit.

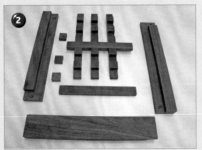

② The grid is held in a frame, which is slightly deeper than the grid (for drainage). The parts of the grid are fitted and glued together, then clamped while the glue is drying.

③ When complete, the grating is ready to fit on board. Don't be tempted to add slippery varnishes to your grating, but simply allow the teak to weather to grey.

Nameplate

At one time the only way of applying a name to a boat was to use the services of a signwriter. This is still an option, and for the most complex designs it may well be preferable. Today, however, it has become much easier to make your own nameplates and a number of choices are available, including carved timber nameboards as well as vinyl or stainless steel lettering.

Carved timber nameboards look especially good on classic wooden vessels and can be produced using a sharp chisel or, alternatively, can be freehand cut using a router or Dremel-type multitool. The design can be printed off full sized on any computer and traced onto the timber. Either method is within the scope of the competent DIY owner.

Vinyl lettering

The least expensive method is probably vinyl lettering and, unless the name is for a new boat, the first job is to remove every trace of the old name. A hot air paint-stripping gun is a good start to lift the old letters so that they can be peeled off. Any sticky residue can be washed away using methylated spirit, although when finished, make sure you allow any leftover meths to evaporate for a few minutes.

Wipe the surface with a weak mixture of washing-up liquid and water to prevent the new letters sticking immediately, allowing time to make any final adjustments to their position. Peel off the backing sheet from the name letters in preparation for placing into position. Align the name and touch it lightly onto the surface. This becomes more difficult to do with increased size and complexity of the letters.

Once in position and with no air bubbles behind the letters, press each letter down firmly using a finger for narrow letters or a cloth

pad for larger letters. Peel off the front spacing paper that keeps the name properly spaced, align and individually place each letter, this time using a clean cloth. Small air bubbles can be removed by pricking them with a pin and squeezing the air out, while continuing to press the letters down.

Above **A carved wooden nameboard in the seatback of a skiff.**

The finished name should be left for a few hours to allow the soapy water to dry out.

Stainless steel lettering

Applying stainless steel lettering is somewhat easier than vinyl as all that is required is to roughen the backs of the letters to give them a key and then stick them to the hull using an adhesive sealant. These letters can be obtained from local stainless steel fabricators.

You can choose your grade of stainless steel but expect to pay more for higher grades. As laser cutters are computer-guided, almost any style and size of font are available for you to choose from. More complex script styles are also available, although this becomes more expensive as the amount of metal in the design increases.

LETTERING IN VINYL

Methylated spirit removes the residue from the surface, which is then wiped clean.

The backing paper is removed, and the name is carefully placed into position.

Above top **Fabricated metal lettering gives a distinctive look to the name of a boat.**

Above **For stainless steel lettering, choose a font and provide the fabricator with the details of your choice. The thickness of the letter can also be specified.**

A finger is ideal for smoothing out narrow letters into place.

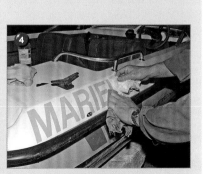

The spacing paper is carefully peeled back and the job is done.

Dorade vents

The dorade vent, also known as a 'collector box', is basically a self-draining cover designed to sit over a deck vent opening and prevent any water from finding its way down below. If well designed, these boxes can greatly complement a deck while enhancing ventilation.

The dorade vent took its name from the first yacht to use them, the American-built ocean-racer *Dorade*. Her original ventilation system had air scoops that fed directly into the cabin, but this did little to limit water entering in bad weather. Her designer realised that a cover with a series of baffles set in front of the deck vent would deflect the water through drainage holes while allowing the air to continue on down below.

The dorade box can be substantial, so over the years they have been sculpted to match the lines of the superstructure and topped off with polished or painted cowls. Nowadays, a dorade vent can be bought as a ready-to-fit item, either as a simple circular base over a mushroom-style closing vent or as a kit. This can comprise three main components – a deck box made of wood, plastic or steel (which can be customised to the deck camber), an attractive cowl and a metal deflector guard to protect the cowl from damage.

A dorade vent relies on the natural flow of air over the deck to ventilate the cabin. To improve this flow, some boxes have a second position allowing the detachable cowl to be relocated directly over the deck vent, temporarily bypassing the baffles. The vacated hole is filled with a blanking plate. The cowls can also be rotated by hand through 360 degrees to make the best use of any breeze. The dorade vents work best mounted vertically, and are most often fitted in matching pairs.

Fitting a dorade

The best location for a dorade vent is anywhere where it will provide maximum ventilation below without interfering with any bulkheads, wiring conduits or deck equipment. The key component is the box, which is usually twice as long as it is wide. As most decks have some kind of camber, the top of the box ideally needs to be horizontal. A mock-up of the box can be made from cardboard or MDF, and a line scribed on the leading and trailing edges using a pair of compasses.

The box itself can then be made from hardwood, moulded from GRP, or purchased as a ready-made item. As water tends to drain aft, the cowl is normally at the rear of the box, with the raised deck vent at the front, but a variety of combinations is possible. The drain holes can be any shape, usually half rounds or long ovals. The baffle plate is usually half the height of the box and is also cambered at the base.

With the box now trimmed to fit, the vent hole is cut in the deck using a jigsaw or hole saw. Take care to seal the exposed edges of any balsa core material with epoxy. If the deck vent is to have a sealable mushroom top, ensure that it doesn't touch the inside of the box when fully open.

Left **Dorade boxes are often made from hardwood, as on this classic Dutch yacht. Form meets functionality in a very pleasing way.**

The box can be attached either by using through bolts, or screwing it to an inner frame already fastened to the deck. The box should be easy to remove for maintenance. The inside of the box should be sealed with epoxy prior to fitting, and bedding compound used along the bottom.

The cowl guardrails can be bought pre-made and trimmed with a cutting disc prior to attaching to the base plates, which are screwed or bolted either side. They can also be custom-made with either a single loop or, alternatively, with a forward or aft-facing third arm.

Below (inset) **The simplest form of retrofit dorade is a cylindrical cowl over a sealable mushroom vent.**

Above **Cowls can be doubled up into one larger dorade box, often as part of a hatch housing or cabin-top arrangement.**

Below **How a full-sized dorade box works. The vent itself can be rotated to face aft in bad weather or away from the prevailing wind when in a marina or on a mooring.**

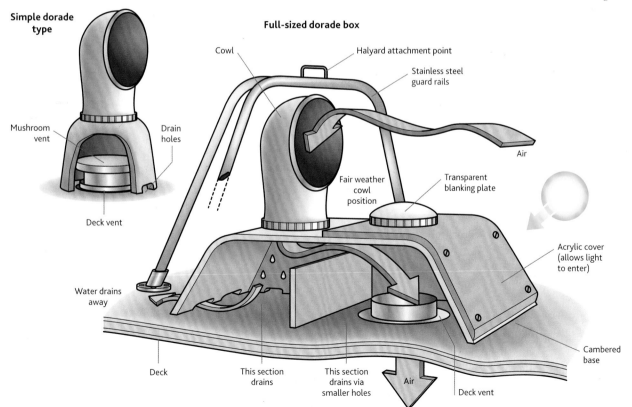

Simple dorade type

Mushroom vent

Drain holes

Deck vent

Full-sized dorade box

Cowl

Halyard attachment point

Stainless steel guard rails

Air

Fair weather cowl position

Transparent blanking plate

Acrylic cover (allows light to enter)

Water drains away

Cambered base

Deck

This section drains

This section drains via smaller holes

Air

Deck vent

Passarelle

Climbing on and off a modern yacht, especially for the less athletic, can be a challenge. An elegant solution is a passarelle. These range from a simple gangplank to a hydraulically articulated walkway, but each design solves some common boarding problems.

The passarelle has undergone some ingenious developments over the years, making it easier than ever to join or leave a yacht, especially when it is moored awkwardly with its stern some distance from a raised quayside. In the Mediterranean, where stern-to mooring is common practice, a passarelle is seen as essential.

The term itself is usually associated with articulated gangways that can be either hinged or telescopic, or both, and are designed to stow away into the fabric of the yacht. However, even the simplest of gangplanks are sometimes referred to as passarelles.

Types of passarelle

Leading the development has been the luxury yacht sector, where space is less of a problem. The passarelle is frequently custom built, and often colour matched to complement the aesthetics. Some hydraulic passarelles remain on the outside of the yacht, pulled up like a drawbridge or folded back in some way, whereas others disappear completely into the hull. Many of these stowage solutions can be scaled down for smaller craft, which often find storage space difficult to find.

Below **Passarelles can be quite complex, electro-hydraulic affairs that complement the yacht, as seen on the back of this 18m (60ft) Swedish yacht.**

TIP

When finding the ideal place to attach a passarelle, don't forget about access to and from the boat. On some designs it may be necessary to modify the pushpit rail to allow easy access.

Above **Simple rigid passarelles can be tricky to stow on smaller yachts. This 2.5m (8ft) aluminium version on deck has a single pivot point at the inboard end, and two nylon castors. Stowing against the stanchions is a good option.**

Above **A robust hull attachment like this allows a great range of movement.**

Right **Aluminium is favoured as a gangway material as it is light and easy to customise. Note the hinge in the centre to allow the passarelle to fold for stowage, the wheels at the end to allow for movement and the detachable hand rails.**

Passarelles also need to be sturdy enough to handle anything from a crate of bottles to a crewman carrying a heavy outboard. Certain designs can also be lowered down in the form of self-levelling stairs, allowing the crew to disembark to a pontoon or even a dinghy alongside.

The materials used for a passarelle vary considerably, but generally aim for a high strength-to-weight ratio, so aluminium, fibreglass and composite (including carbon fibre) are common, with the more complex hydraulically operated passarelles featuring added stainless steel and teak trim. They can be bought as a production item from chandlers, home built to suit the yacht, or custom-made by specialist suppliers, with plenty of choice for every budget.

Left **A passarelle has to be easy to deploy and stow. This one has a stainless steel attachment to the hull, and is designed to fold back on itself for a snug fit into its bracket. Note the rope supports, working via a bridle to a single halyard, and the slatted treads.**

Basic designs

A passarelle will be bridging a gap over deep water, so it's important that the gangway can be firmly attached to the boat, and yet remain flexible without feeling unsafe. In addition, it has to have a dependable, non-skid surface. A deep toe rail and even collapsible railings are also desirable features, depending on the stowage constraints.

The simplest passarelles are either a single span of lightweight material, often with a slight upward curve for strength, or a folding design. On some smaller yachts, the outboard end attaches to a bridle that runs to a masthead halyard to raise it at night. The inboard end is usually connected to a robust stainless steel fitting bolted to the deck, topsides or transom.

The average length of a passarelle is around 2.4–3m (8–10ft), and many of the fixed type are supplied with a bag to aid stowage. Passarelle planks, even of the simplest design, should be able to float if they are lost overboard. Combinations of a foam core and a composite shell have made some models of passarelle particularly light and strong, so they are very easy to manoeuvre into place.

Passarelle 2

Self-levelling stairs

Fitting a set of self-levelling stairs is a useful way to overcome several problems at once. A number of visitors may find climbing up a steep incline quite difficult, whereas stairs will prove easier. Some passarelles have a set of stairs incorporated into the gangway itself, jutting up more proudly as the angle increases due to tidal fall. Other designs attach a set of stairs to the end of a self-supporting gangway, held level by a hydraulic arm. The stairs also add some useful extra length.

Stairs can also be used to board a tender alongside. Some drop into a float, but generally they simply drop down to just above water level, usually with a railing on the outboard side.

More complex arrangements

On larger yachts, there are a number of options for powered passarelles, mostly electro-hydraulically operated. Powered passarelles tend to be found on yachts and motorboats over 12m (40ft), and while some are factory fitted as an option, others are usually custom-built by a yard.

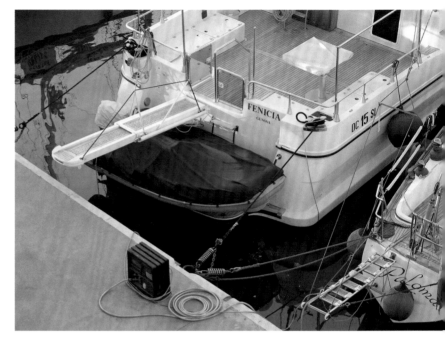

Above **Contrasting solutions. The complex electro-hydraulic passarelle on the motorboat will telescope back and fold upwards when the vessel is under way. Note the raised hand rail on the stern deck.** The sailing yacht has a simple, low maintenance gangway. Note the cross-bracing ropes on each corner, to stop any sideways swing, the design of the halyard bridle, and the opening in the pushpit rail.

Right **Passarelles that can stow inside the boat will be less prone to the ravages of the elements, but may also be compromised in flexibility. When designing your passarelle, try to give it the biggest range of movement and angles to cope with all eventualities.**

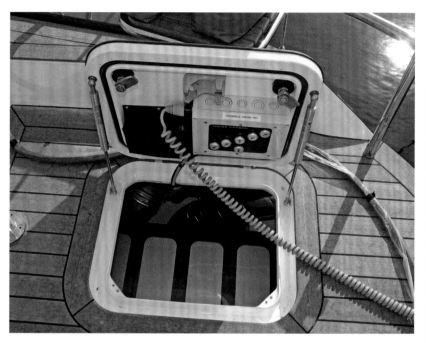

Above left **The control box of an electro-hydraulic passarelle is hidden away under a lazarette hatch, but has a remote control (on the umbilical cord) that can be used to view and direct the deployment from the aft deck.**

Above right **Attractive, folding passarelles can be bought through most good chandlers, and are supplied with a choice of brackets to fit the deck, topsides or transom. Customised brackets can also be made by a good stainless steel fabricator.**

Fabricators will measure the available space and decide how compact a unit can be made. Because many types of passarelle actually stow into a void in the hull, this has to be made watertight, so a hydraulically operated door is fabricated from a section of the hull.

Owners can purchase complete external systems in a wide range of designs for self-installation, and some companies will supply them as a kit. The hull may need strengthening or modifying to take the extra weight, but the systems themselves are often self-contained and relatively straightforward.

Additional features

On larger yachts, the passarelle becomes much more of a statement, although it can often be adapted for various other uses, too. Security plays an important part, with the passarelle featuring motion sensors on the end, triggering cameras that

cover the approach. The passarelle can also be something of an art form, with a self-levelling floating end and welcoming courtesy lights. Wi-Fi remote control allows the owner to retract the passarelle when away from the yacht.

Some designs lift out a section of the bathing platform to become a floating dock, complete with access stairs. Others, usually on a raised deck, swing upwards to form a diving board, again with self-levelling steps. A few can also be adapted to carry a lightweight canopy. When designers have some room to play with, plenty of hydraulic power available and an unlimited budget, it is remarkable what they can do with a versatile pivoting gangway.

But even those of us with more modest means can emulate the principle of a safe and welcoming walkway for guests, painting the structure to match the yacht's colour

scheme, adding its name and some LED courtesy lights, and having a smart non-slip surface with detachable stainless steel hand railings. However, if you'd rather buy a passarelle off the shelf, then some very well made folding versions are available as kits.

Cockpit table

The cockpit is a great social area, so a strategically placed table enables family and friends to make the most of this versatile outdoor space. Even if the cockpit is an awkward shape, there is usually a practical solution.

Many modern yachts have a cockpit table fitted as standard, especially those destined for the charter market, but buying a ready-assembled retrofit kit is also a possibility. Some cockpit tables are free-standing, allowing them to be folded away and stowed below, while other designs even drop down to form the cockpit grating, fulfilling a dual role.

Cockpit tables can be made from attractive hardwood, complete with brass or stainless steel hinges and built-in fiddles, or from more functional, low maintenance GRP or composite. Many prefer the

latter as they are easy to clean and can be left exposed to the elements all year round. The usual type, often seen semi-permanently attached to steering pedestals, is made up of a three-leaf design. When stowed away, this results in a very slim piece of furniture that swings down

vertically and locks in place to avoid cluttering the helm station. Everything needed to deploy the table is neatly stowed within it, so the supporting leg drops down, two crossbars pull out and two leaves unfold to triple the surface area for a large crew.

Right **A high-quality cockpit table in its stowed position, safely out of the way of any crew working on the deck.**

Below **The same cockpit table, fully deployed. This table is detachable so it could be removed for winter storage, preserving the varnished surface for the next season.**

TABLE IDEAS

This free-standing table has a pair of removable tubular supports. When not needed, it can be stowed against an interior bulkhead and the base used as a footrest.

The most versatile form of cockpit table is the swing down type, shown here in its stowed position. It is easily detachable, and can be retrofitted to most modern pedestals.

This design is on telescopic supports, so it can be dropped down to the level of the side seats and form the basis of a full-width sunlounger, or outdoor berth.

When at sea, the table can be deployed with only a single leaf exposed, formed of the underside of the two outer ones, and surrounded by fiddles. This design allows drinks and snacks to be to hand while only taking up a small amount of room when under sail. When the boat is at rest, the table can be fully deployed and, although the fiddles are now on the underside, they aren't really needed.

Choosing a table

When planning a cockpit table, there are two main considerations: how big should it be and where will it stow? Certain yachts only need a small table with a set of built-in cup holders and some permanent fiddles, as the table will only be used when under way. Others want full dining for six under the bimini, so there is a wide choice of options in the retrofit market.

Because a table is a relatively simple item, a number of yachtsmen in smaller, tiller-steered boats simply trim a sheet of plywood and add some collapsible camping legs. The tiller itself, locked amidships, is often used as a central support. Covered with a tablecloth, these simple tables are perfectly adequate. Another solution is to buy a pre-made three-leaf table, which requires only a tubular stand. With a mounting plate set in the underside of the table and a base set in the sole, this type of table is easy to use and can be secured to a bulkhead when not needed. Scissor-support versions are also available and can be used for picnics ashore.

Many retrofit tables are supplied as just the tabletop (with or without leaves), allowing the owner to decide on the best fitting method. Pedestal manufacturers will often make provision for attaching a table and have their own attachment kits available.

For maximum comfort, the table height is important – it should be clear of guests' legs and not too wide. The position of the supports is important, too, especially if you want to avoid spectacular table collapses mid-meal when they are accidentally kicked out or slide inwards. Make sure the supports are resistant to clumsy knocks as they will be unavoidably close to legs and feet. Some consist of a single arm that drops down to the base of the pedestal to avoid this problem. A pin enables the entire table to be removed from the pedestal for winter storage.

A pleasing final touch is to have the yacht's name engraved or inserted by marquetry on a wooden table. Use a transfer for a composite or GRP version.

TIP

If you plan on creating your own table for use by the steering compass when under way, ensure there are no magnetic catches or ferrous screws used in its construction, which might interfere with the compass.

Grab rails

The grab rail is an essential part of the boat to help you move around in a seaway. Although it is a safety item, it can also be designed to enhance the interior look of a yacht.

Grab rails, also referred to as handholds, come in many forms, but all have one primary purpose – to keep you on your feet in a moving yacht. The bigger the yacht, the more important the placing of grab rails, as there is further to travel if you lose your footing.

You will usually find a wide range of types and lengths of grab rail in your local chandlers, but DIY or custom solutions are also relatively inexpensive. The most common are those made from teak or stainless steel, but even rope has been used, slung between two anchor points.

A good test is to see if you can 'swing' yourself from one end of a boat's accommodation to the other, rather like a monkey through a forest canopy. If you find a dead spot where both hands need to be free

before you can reach the next secure contact, then you need to place more handholds.

Usually grab rails are located overhead, away from the centreline of the boat to preserve headroom, and consist of a series of loops with several anchor points. Hardwood varnished grab rails to match the boat's interior joinery is a pleasing solution, but polished stainless steel also looks good, as does any stout material painted to match the trim. Grab rails can also be mounted vertically and are particularly important in the often overlooked areas of the galley and heads. The area around the companionway is particularly important for safety in heavy weather, as this mini staircase isn't normally fitted with a banister.

A very clever solution adopted by boatbuilders is to incorporate as many handholds into the actual structure of the boat and its furniture as possible, from the outside edges of tables to the corners of partitions.

Choosing and fitting

The big challenge for any grab rail is how securely it can be attached. Grab rails may have to take the sudden weight of a heavy crewman if the yacht lurches. Stout anchoring is essential. In smaller boats, a good solution is to through-bolt the interior grab rail to its external counterpart using stainless steel

Left **This Dutch-built 11.2-m (36-ft) Winner has grab rails everywhere, and they are clad in suede for a warmer and better grip by wet hands. Note the vertical holds by the galley, the long rails in the roof, and shorter ones inset into the chart table and both ends of the saloon table. Handholds are needed in all parts of a boat where you might need a good purchase in a seaway.**

Below **A wide base helps to spread the load and, if held with several stainless steel screws, is easy to remove for access behind the headlining.**

FITTING BACKING PADS

To secure a handhold to a single-skinned GRP cabin inside, first attach plywood pads behind the headlining to match the handrail's fixing points. Cut and shape each pad and apply adhesive sealant. Degrease the deckhead with acetone and apply hot glue to the back of the pad.

Push the pad quickly into place, and support it for a few seconds while the glue cools and hardens. The sealant cures to form a tougher bond. This pad will act as the anchor for the self-tapping screws that will hold the handrail in place. Note the bevelled edges to aid fibreglassing.

After the sealant has cured, apply a layer of fibreglass over the wood to secure it and bond it into the immediate area. Paint on activated resin, push the fibreglass cloth onto it and wet it out with dabs of a brush. Once cured, drill the screw holes to depth through the replaced headlining.

screws or bolts, but this relies on the deck fittings to allow this alignment. More usually, grab rails will secure to an interior wooden batten, glassed, screwed or, on alloy boats, welded to the deckhead.

When adding a new handhold, check you can secure it with bolts rather than screws as a preference. The substrate behind the handhold's anchor points will be the decider,

and some may need the addition of reinforcement pads. If you have to use screws, then self-tapping versions through multiple attachments will help to spread the load.

Positioning of handholds

Areas where vertical handholds will be useful are: in the heads compartment, beside the door (both inside and out), in the galley

area, beside the chart table and either side of the companionway. With vertical designs, the longer the rail can be the better, to allow its use by people of all heights, especially children. Horizontal rails can also be fitted so they protrude out from the cabin sides, rather than drop down from the ceiling. This also enables them to be used as hanger rails in port.

Custom handholds can be made from kits, using stainless steel supports that take a length of polished stainless tube. This allows a curving design to be made by having the tube gently bent. The rail is then assembled and the anchor points bolted or screwed down. Small grub screws or sealed end caps stop the tube from moving. A teak dowel can be used instead or, alternatively, strips of wood can be laminated together to create a sculptured rail.

Below **Effective handholds can actually be sculpted into the fabric of the yacht, such as the sides of these companionway steps on this Hallberg-Rassy.**

Below **Fiddle rails can also become handholds. This one has been made very deep, and with a recessed groove for fingertips to grip.**

Faced-ply cabin sides

Using faced ply is a straightforward means of renewing the appearance of timber cabin sides that are beyond being revarnished. This may have come about due to a number of reasons, such as the removal of certain fittings, deep water staining or perhaps where an isolated area has rotted and needs to be replaced.

Faced ply is available with many different veneers, so using something akin to the original will dramatically improve the appearance of the vessel. Teak-faced ply is about three times the price of any other, so if you need to economise, anything other than teak would be a good choice! Similarly, marine ply is substantially more expensive than exterior ply, so it may be preferable to go with the latter option.

The main difference between marine and exterior ply is that marine is guaranteed to have no voids between the plys, but they both use the same adhesives and construction methods. However, the quality of exterior ply can vary greatly, so it is essential to use very good quality ply.

A further point to consider is that the veneer on faced ply is usually 0.6mm ($^{1}/_{32}$in) thick, which doesn't leave much scope for sanding,

especially when revarnishing in years to come. Teak decking ply often comes with a slightly thicker veneer of 1mm ($^{3}/_{64}$in) or more, but this is generally only available as marine ply, so it becomes very expensive again. If you decide to use exterior ply, then many builders merchants offer 4mm ($^{5}/_{32}$in) faced ply at reasonable prices.

Left **Fitting one of the new side panels in position. Using faced ply can renew the appearance of worn or damaged cabin sides.**

Below **A finished side panel, with a trim strip of matching timber fitted at the top of the panel to give a smart edge to the faced-ply cabin sides.**

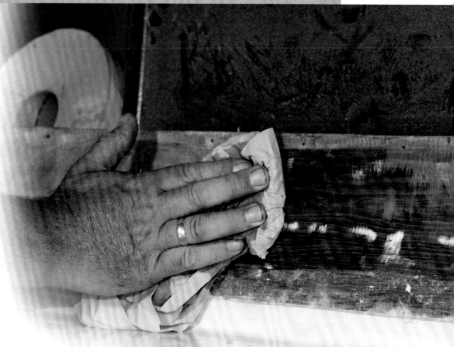

Preparing the ply

First remove the windows, along with any fittings liable to get in the way, then prepare the surface of the cabin sides by removing all the paint and varnish, and then sanding back to clean, dry timber. Then wash down with acetone to remove any remaining contamination, and wipe dry with paper towelling.

Hardboard is ideal for making templates since it is cheap to buy and easy to cut. First cut the sections slightly over-sized for each part, as this is easier than trying to handle an entire sheet of hardboard. Then offer them up and accurately mark the outer edges where the new ply will finish and where the window cut-outs will be.

It makes life easier if you clamp these sections into place before marking them. If the boat was accurately built, one set of templates should do for both sides. But carefully check this before making any final decision and, if necessary, make templates for both sides.

Once completed, the templates are ready for transferring the measurements to the faced ply. Back at the bench, lay the ply face down to allow all cuts to be made from the back. Once you are absolutely certain that the ply is the right way round, it is time to start cutting.

With a jigsaw, this gives a much cleaner cut on the face side. Place the template onto the ply, ensuring it is also face down, otherwise the finished panel will end up with the face on the inside, which is quite annoying to say the least!

Above **After sanding, remove any remaining contamination with acetone.**

Left **Place the hardboard on the cabin sides and accurately mark the outer edges and the cut-outs for the windows.**

Below left **Transfer the marks and measurements to the faced ply, ensuring that you are working from the correct side of the pattern.**

Faced-ply cabin sides 2

Cutting and fitting the ply

A jigsaw with a new fine-cut blade is the best bet for cutting pieces out of full sheets of thin ply. If the blade starts wandering and needs forcing through the ply, it means it has become blunt and should be replaced. To ensure that the cuts are perfectly straight, cut slightly outside the line and finish the cut using a small plane with a sharp blade to trim accurately down to the line.

If all the lines are straight, then a router with a trimming bit and a straight edge clamped over the marked line is even better. Any slight mistakes in the cutting shouldn't be a problem. When it comes to the window cut-outs, the frames will cover 12mm (½in) or more of the edge of the panel. For the outer edges, timber trims can be used and these can be any size, within reason, to cover cutting errors.

Once all the panels are satisfactorily cut and trimmed, the fitting can start. The first step is to coat the back of the first panel with adhesive. Epoxy adhesives are preferable for this type of work. Similarly, coat the timber face of the cabin side and position the new panel in place.

Using multiple clamps, hardboard pads and lengths of scrap timber beneath the clamp feet, secure the panel firmly into position. You must ensure the panel is in proper contact with the cabin side at all points. 'One-handed' clamps are ideal for this purpose as they are much easier to clamp on than old-fashioned 'G' cramps and they can often be bought cheaply.

Right **Finish the cut by trimming with a small woodworking block plane.**

Below **Use a jigsaw with a new fine-cut blade and change the blade once it starts to become blunt.**

Protecting the panels

Once all the panels are bonded into position, you need to decide what the final protective coat will be. Varnish is the obvious choice, but it may be better to consider using an epoxy resin to seal the surface and offer a more durable coating. Epoxy resins are not UV-resistant, so after being applied they must be protected against UV rays by adding coats of varnish over the top. Although it is an extra task, the protection is much greater and should last far longer than varnish alone.

With the final finish decided, the panels can be very lightly sanded and given their first coats of the chosen finish to protect the surface from dirt while the last bit of trimming is done. The joint between the coachroof and the panel can be completed using a timber finishing strip, while the joint at the deck is best sealed by first using a polyurethane sealant and then adding a quadrant or beading.

FITTING THE PANELS

Coat the rear face of the first panel with epoxy adhesive.

Coat the cabin side with epoxy adhesive.

Carefully position the new panel onto the cabin side.

Clamp the panel securely to the cabin side, ensuring it is tightly in contact over the whole area.

Faux decks – floor

Modern teak-effect deck materials have several advantages over real teak-laid decks, including a lack of maintenance once it is fitted. However, installing it requires a good deal of care and attention to detail, making it very time-consuming, which is why labour costs for a professional installation are so expensive.

When it comes to replacing a cockpit floor, it is worth considering teak-effect decks. Apart from the basics of getting the surface properly prepared and using adhesives correctly, there are no set rules as to how to lay the deck, although it is best to follow certain guidelines.

Materials

A number of companies supply synthetic teak. The supplier will usually provide it in various sections, normally made up of four elements: a king plank (centreline plank); a caulking strip; an intermediate decking strip, with a tongue on one side and caulking on the other; and an outer margin strip, which is finished on one side, with caulking on the other. The caulking is usually supplied in black, although it may be possible to obtain it in other colours such as cream.

You will need a polymer-based waterproof seal for bonding the deck material down and for caulking. This may come supplied as a 'sausage', so you should also acquire an appropriate sealant gun to administer it. In addition, you will need a contact and solvent adhesive for bonding the strips of deck together.

Cockpit floor replacement

When working on the cockpit floor panel, the first job is to remove the worst of the old paint and varnish by scraping them off. Coarsely sand the surface to give a key to the primer coat of epoxy. Once this has been applied and cured, coarsely sand the epoxy to provide a key for the polymer sealant.

Lay a length of margin deck along one edge of the first panel and mark the corner using a 45-degree marking bevel. Cut the corner using a craft knife and straight edge. Lay a short length of caulking strip at the cut end of the decking.

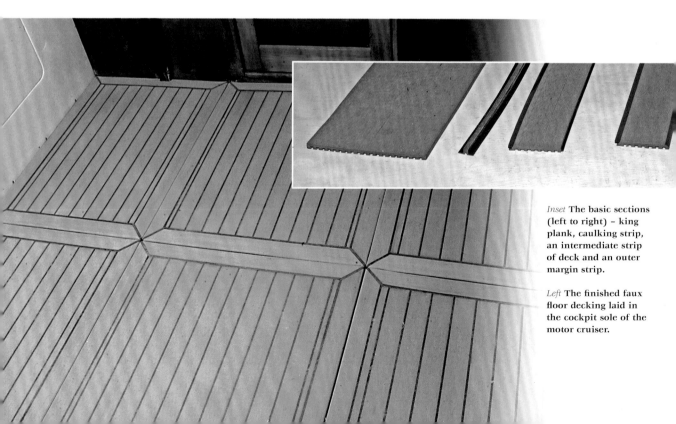

Inset **The basic sections (left to right) – king plank, caulking strip, an intermediate strip of deck and an outer margin strip.**

Left **The finished faux floor decking laid in the cockpit sole of the motor cruiser.**

Repeat the process for the rest of the margin decking on the panel. Trim each caulking strip to length and ensure everything is ready to be bonded to the panel. Mark the position of the strips onto the panel to allow the polymer-based sealant to be accurately applied all round using the sealant gun. 'Comb out' this sealant using the tile comb supplied with the product. Lay the strips in position and carefully align before rolling to ensure the polymer sealant has squeezed up into the grooves under the decking.

To begin the infill, measure the centre point to work out the best layout for the strips to give an even finish on both edges. The two outer strips need to be cut lengthways to allow them to fit. When satisfied with the fit, draw a straight line across the whole set as a guide for gluing the strips together.

The strips now need to be pulled together, keeping them in the correct order. Place a thin bead of adhesive along the tongue of each strip to bond them together into a mat. Use a pencil line to ensure they are all still correctly aligned.

LAYING THE PANEL

A length of margin is cut to 45 degrees and a caulking strip laid into the corner.

Polymer-based sealant is applied with a sealant gun and is 'combed out'.

Adhesive is applied to the strip edges.

The strips are fitted and glued together before the cured 'mat' is lifted out.

Polymer-based sealant is applied and is 'combed out' before the mat is replaced.

The strips are rolled out before the panel is finally cleaned.

TIP

One of the advantages of modern synthetic teak decking is the lack of maintenance it requires once fitted. The surface is durable and non-porous, so water, oil and dirt do not penetrate, and it should look like a newly installed deck for many years to come.

Once the adhesive has cured sufficiently (after ten minutes or so), lift the mat out to make way for the polymer sealant to be applied over the entire area. It is then 'combed out' and the mat laid back in place. It should then be rolled using plenty of pressure on the roller. The whole of the panel should be cleaned up using 60-grit paper. Repeat this process for as many panels as are needed to lay the cockpit area.

Faux decks – fore and sidedecks

Laying long lengths of deck and fitting the king plank on fibreglass deck fore and sidedecks, as shown on this small motor cruiser, is a more complex task than laying cabin or cockpit soles.

There are no rules with regard to the style of the deck layout. You can do exactly as you please so long as you carefully prepare the surface and use the adhesives properly by following the instructions.

Laying the deck

The first job on a fibreglass deck is preparation. The fibreglass must be cleaned back to the original gel coat. (Epoxy or two-pack finishes can remain if securely adhered.)

Once the deck is clean, begin by laying the inner margin and mark its position so you can apply a polymer-based sealant. Mark and cut the corner joints, allowing room to fit the caulking strip. Use anything as a weight to keep the corner joint in position while the rest of the corners are cut. Trim around any obstructions on the deck, allowing space for caulking with the polymer-based sealant later on. Prepare the outer margin in the same way. Lift the completed inner and outer margins, and apply polymer-based sealant, but leave the forward 150mm (6in) of the outer margin unglued to enable it to be cut into the king plank later on. Then roll both glued sections down.

Moving to the foredeck, the first piece to be fitted is the king plank. This is the most interesting, but also

Above **Clean off any previous coatings back to the gel coat.**

Below **The finished fore and sidedecks on the motor cruiser.**

Above **The outer margin is fitted and both margins are then glued and rolled down. The forward end of the outer margin is left unglued as it will eventually run into the king plank.**

LAYING THE FOREDECK

The king plank is cut to shape, glued and rolled into place.

The foredeck mat bonded together and ready for laying.

The unglued forward end of the mat strips being cut to shape and bonded down.

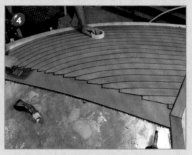

The foredeck section cleaned off and ready for masking, prior to caulking.

the most complex part of the job. The aft end is cut to the angle of the joint on the inner margin before the forward end can be cut to fit. In this case it also has to fit around the central mooring bollard. Once it is cut to shape, you need to glue it down and roll it out.

Now to deal with the infill strips. On this boat, the small area of the deck means that the two margins touch as they pass the forward corner of the cabin. This enables the foredeck planking to be completed in short lengths rather than running the whole length of the sidedecks.

Cut each strip to length and then bond it with its neighbour to form a mat. Bond down the mat with polymer-based sealant and roll down while leaving the front 150mm (6in) of the piece unglued.

Once the sealant has cured, mark the forward end of each strip and cut to shape into the king plank. The ends of the planks can be any shape you like, or you can follow the manufacturer's instructions. After all the strips have been cut into the king plank, clean off the strips and mask, ready for final caulking with a polymer-based sealant.

For the sidedeck, strips are prepared in the same way, although inner margins obviously use the longest lengths. At some point you will need to cut a long length and this is easiest to do using a small circular saw or a bandsaw.

Alternatively, you can make accurate cuts using a craft knife (although this can be very time-consuming on a long length) or a standard jigsaw. Clean up the edges using a small, sharp woodworking plane.

Replacing aluminium fittings

Many production boats were originally fitted with aluminium deck furniture such as cleats and bow rollers. Unfortunately, they are usually attached to the boat with stainless steel bolts or screws, and consequently can suffer from galvanic corrosion over the years.

Aluminium fittings are lighter and cheaper than stainless steel ones, and often match the rest of the fittings and deck furniture such as spars, hatch frames and toe rails. They look very smart when new but, over time, galvanic action between the stainless steel bolts and the aluminium fittings will take place, causing corrosion and eventually locking the two metals together. As this happens, you will notice a white powder oxide around the join of the dissimilar metals. The aluminium itself will also begin to pit and discolour, making it look tired. In extreme cases, the corrosion can lead to failure under load.

Although proper marine-grade 316 stainless steel is expensive, it will retain its good looks indefinitely. It is also harder wearing and, of course, fully compatible with marine-grade stainless steel bolts, so will not suffer from corrosion.

TIP

If you lightly coat the threads of stainless steel bolts with a non-metallic grease or zinc chromate paste, it will make them easier to undo at a later stage. It will also act as a barrier and help limit the effects of corrosion, especially if you are still using some aluminium fittings on deck.

Below **Cheaper production boats often have basic aluminium fittings. This one is being replaced with a much more functional, and striking, stainless steel bollard.**

Above **A plywood backing plate. Note how the edges have been bevelled to allow for GRP reinforcement to be added.**

Left **The new bollard position is lightly marked with a drill, dead centre of the bolt holes, prior to drilling through.**

During a refit, or at the same time as doing a repair, it is a good idea to swap old aluminium fittings for new stainless steel ones. Removing the fittings should be straightforward, although you might find the bolts have corroded firmly onto the body of the fitting. This can make removing them tricky, but if the nuts themselves come undone it shouldn't be too much of a problem as the whole assembly will pull vertically out of the deck. If not, the bolts may have to be cut off.

Replacing old fittings

✪ Remove the old fitting, allowing for the fact that the bolts may also come away. If the fitting is not too badly corroded, it may still have some value on the second-hand market, so it is worth trying to remove the bolts at a later stage.

✪ Reappraise the fitting's position, and consider replacing it with a more substantial fitting in stainless steel, especially if the yacht is to be used for long-distance cruising.

✪ Clean up the area and re-bed the fitting on polyurethane sealant, taking care to circle each bolt hole.

✪ Select a wide backing pad, either in wood, fibreglass or mild steel. Nyloc nuts, which have a nylon collar insert in them to increase friction between the screw and the nut threads, will prevent the fitting from vibrating loose if it is near an engine bay.

Right **To fill old screw holes, use a countersink drill bit to widen them, and then apply some epoxy filler. Stick some electrical tape on the other side to prevent the epoxy falling through.**

Pulpit and pushpit

The solid safety rails around each end of the boat can be modified to become more useful than just being there for safety. Here are some great ideas to make them contribute more to your cruising pleasure.

Designers of pulpits and pushpits can see a great deal of functionality in these structures, creating versatile attachment points for additional deck equipment and better access for boarding and anchoring.

Pulpit

Access ashore can sometimes be difficult, so you can modify the bow to form a step-through arrangement, which enables a ladder to be attached to get on and off. This sometimes means removing the wraparound part of the rail, although a gated section can be added instead.

A step-through design can help with anchoring too, and some owners add an additional bow platform to take a pair of anchors. The pulpit rail is extended, allowing the crew to walk out directly over the water.

It is now common to have seats in the bow area. They are usually made of teak, attached to a cross member, positioned literally above the bow wave, but within the security of the wraparound rail. Similarly two seats

can be set inside the pulpit and raised above the mooring cleats.

You may be able to buy a different type of pulpit from the original manufacturer that will exactly fit your boat and give you additional functionality. Some after-market outlets also offer suitable substitutes fairly cheaply. But if you want to do modifications to the pulpit,

a standard 25mm (1in) or 38mm (1½in) of stainless steel 316 tubing should be used. You will require the services of a fabricator who will need an accurate set of measurements, a pattern and a clear idea of what you want.

Below **Opening the bow into a step design helps with anchoring and disembarking.**

Above **The rails can be extended to allow the attachment of swing-up solar panels.**

Above **A step-through arrangement on a pulpit. Note the small seat on the cross member and the safety wire that can be used when under way.**

Above **These dolphin-watching benches can seat two adults side by side. Note the clearance from the deck gear.**

Above **The bow can be extended and widened for twin anchors with this anchoring platform. The pulpit rails are also extended outboard.**

Pushpit

Extra seating can be added to the corners of the pushpit, but this requires a horizontal middle bar to work. The corners of the top rail can be bowed outwards, and an angled seat attached to the middle rail beneath. This seat is usually shaped to complement the cockpit design. It can be made from GRP, or cut from a 40-mm (1⅝-in) sheet of white polyethylene.

A more traditional option is to use hardwood in a stainless steel frame. Some of these seats tip up to give better access to the cleats, or to any corner lockers set into the deck. A wider seat will need additional support from a central leg, set inboard. You will need to support the seat properly with load-bearing pads under the deck, secured with large bolts with wide washers. Making the feet relatively large will also help to spread the downward load.

Sometimes, when adding a bathing platform to a boat, the pushpit will have to be opened with a gateway. If the pushpit relied on an unbroken crescent shape for its supportive strength, then this gateway will introduce a weakness, so additional cross bracing of the legs will be needed. The pushpit normally carries important items such as a Danbuoy and lifebuoy, GPS antennas, outboard brackets and dodgers. Pushpits can also be extended forward with solid rails, where you could mount swing-up solar panels.

> **TIP**
>
> Making your own corner seats for the pushpit is very easy and rewarding, but remember that the rails are rarely entirely symmetrical. Create a pattern for each corner for the fabricator, and mark it clearly to avoid confusion.

Above **This neat stern arrangement has a sociable seat with a removable backrest integrated into the pushpit. Note the stowage bracket for the spare anchor.**

Above **A smart stainless steel BBQ suspended outboard, ruggedly attached to the pushpit rail.**

Above **A detachable, hard-wearing GRP seat set into an outward curve of the pushpit rail.**

Gantries and goalposts

With so much extra equipment to carry, from solar panels to radars, the use of a gantry helps to place this equipment in its optimum position, while also keeping it safely out of the way. Gantries can range from a single mast arrangement to a custom-built 'goalpost' design.

The stern of a yacht, clear from the majority of the rigging, is the ideal place to erect a set of supports for all the equipment that helps with navigation and safety. Items such as radio aerials, radar scanners, GPS antennae, solar panels, dinghy hoists and wind generators can all be lifted clear of the deck to interact more efficiently with the sea and sky.

There are two main ways to make the best use of this space – a single pole gantry or a more complex 'goalpost' design.

Single pole gantry

A quick and practical method is to buy a retrofit pole (a 'radar mast'), specifically designed for this task. Several companies can supply kits in lightweight aluminium alloy or GRP/carbon composite in a choice of finishes, with a cylindrical tube fitted with lugs for the attachment of collars, supports and ancillaries.

These poles are usually located on one corner of the stern, attached to a substantial base plate and well braced against the rolling motion of a boat at sea. They come in a range of popular lengths, with some being telescopic, so no cutting is required. Custom kits can also be provided. All the wiring enters the pole through pre-located waterproof glands, before running through another gland in the base plate and into the hull.

These proprietary systems are robust and very well made, with the option to add a whole range of modules such as a gimballed radar bracket, an articulated solar panel support or an outboard-lifting crane.

Left **A well-made gantry can complement a yacht, while also positioning essential items where they can work most efficiently.**

TIP

Some owners fit two gantry poles, one on each corner, linking them together with cross brace bars to support additional equipment such as rigid solar panels.

While not cheap, these single pole gantries are versatile in design, and enhance the functionality of a boat. A DIY solution would be to use a length of discarded tubular mast or spinnaker pole, or buy an extrusion from a manufacturer.

Planning a radar mast

Fitting a single radar mast is fairly straightforward. The biggest consideration is where the base plate will go, and whether you want it flush-mounted or through deck to a base plate fixed to the inside of the hull. The position of the cross braces also needs to be considered, as they mustn't interfere with any of the rigging, such as the backstay, and must not prevent the opening of any hatches on the aft deck.

Ideally, the electronics should all be just above head height, and wind generators as high as possible for safety, but also to catch the best breeze. A simple mock-up using plastic wastepipe and lengths of timber will highlight any problems.

It is tempting to fit a wide array of electronic receivers and transmitters onto the same pole, but take care that these devices don't interfere with each other. Powerful VHF transmissions can corrupt GPS signals, and radar output ideally needs to be above head height. Wind generators can also give off electromagnetic radiation that interferes with some signals. Get advice about which devices will cause problems in close proximity and how they should be placed, so you can consider alternative positions if there is a clash.

MAST IDEAS

A radar mast can be robustly braced into the corner of the pushpit rail and carry a wide range of accessories. This custom-made mast includes a wind generator and a crosstrees for GPS antenna.

For greater strength, the radar mast base can go through the deck and attach to a plate in the bilge area. This will remove the need for cross braces. Note the outboard davits, and stern light raised above the deck.

Shorter masts can simply be used for antennae. This one is mounted outboard, and the right-angled branches minimise interference. The polished stainless steel structure complements other deck fittings.

Two poles can be connected together to form a goalpost gantry. The wind generator is as high as possible, and the GPS aerials are above the radar transmitter. The whole framework supports a bathing platform.

Gantries and goalposts 2

The second method is to build a full-sized gantry, capable of taking a more substantial array of equipment, such as large, rigid solar panels. These 'goalpost' gantries are usually made from tubular stainless steel, but can also be made from carbon fibre, GRP/composite and even from laminated strips of wood.

By taking into account the lines of the hull and superstructure, the gantry can become a stylish addition to a cruising yacht, while also providing a robust and versatile platform for electronics and other useful hardware.

Planning a gantry

Before designing your gantry, you'll need to ask yourself exactly what you want it to carry, bearing in mind that it will put significant weight quite high up and also add to the windage. The most critical part of any gantry system is the attachment points to the deck. These have to be able to support a substantial burden, while not interfering with any of the deck fittings or the boat's interior structure.

The role of the pushpit rail also has to be considered. Some designs actually use the pushpit as part of the structure, whereas others will stand free of it.

The position of the backstay on a yacht will be a critical factor too, as will the reach of the boom, or the position of the mizzen mast on a ketch. This is why it is best to design your gantry when the yacht is fully rigged, so you can experiment.

Right **Some gantries can become very substantial affairs, adding significantly to weight aloft. This French cruiser has created its own power station with angled solar panels and two powerful wind generators. Note also the two small davits.**

Points to consider are:

✪ Any design should be able to keep radars and other antennae above head height, with as clear a view of sea and sky as possible.

✪ The gantry shouldn't impede anyone climbing on and off the boat over the stern.

✪ Give consideration to weight, windage and cross bracing.

✪ Can any wind-operated self-steering gear function without being blanketed? (This is why tubular stainless steel is often the preferred material, due to its low windage profile.)

✪ Will the gantry be a permanent or a semi-permanent fitting? (Important for yachts that may be trailed or stored undercover.)

GANTRY FITTING IDEAS

The fabricator will need to know the exact position of the feet. This yacht has cleverly used a large base plate to support displaced deck gear such as the cleats, samson post and pushpit feet.

On motorboats that may have to negotiate low bridges, the gantry can be made to fold, as shown here. Note the strong hinges and simple release arrangement.

Some designs, such as on Hunter Yachts, have even used the gantry as an anchor point for the mainsheet, a move that has uncluttered the cockpit very effectively.

A good design can also rake the gantry to complement the lines of the boat, but thought has to be given to the extra strain placed on the feet beneath the overhang. If you own a popular model of yacht, you might be inspired by the solutions from like-minded owners.

Some designs use different thicknesses of stainless steel at the base, thinning towards the top to reduce weight higher up. Extra strength is added where needed with cross bracing. When itineraries have included venturing through inland waterways, a number of owners have designed the gantry to either fold in half or be easily detachable, plus provide support for the unstepped mast. Some bridge heights on smaller waterways would otherwise prove a problem.

Commissioning a design

Designs are usually commissioned from specialist stainless steel fabricators, who can work to accurate measurements or to a mock-up. Because of the weight the gantry will have to carry, on boats above 10m (30ft) in length, the structure is usually made from 40-mm ($1^5/_8$-in) stainless steel tubing, and a popular design is for two hoops set slightly apart. This gives a double rail at the top to support any solar panels.

Right **While it is best to design the gantry with the rigging in place, allowances can be made for when the yacht is derigged for winter storage. Use scraps of wood or lengths of water pipe to check angles.**

TIP

If you are having a gantry custom-built, make sure to add a number of strategically placed lugs or welded attachment points throughout the structure. These may prove useful for attaching gear for long-distance cruising.

Roll reducer

One of boating's most uncomfortable experiences is to be in a windless anchorage with a swell surging in from some meteorological disturbance beyond the horizon or the wash from passing vessels. Given a bit of wind, a boat will tend to lie with its head into it. When there is none, and in the absence of a tidal stream, most boats will just roll at anchor.

Fortunately, a practical remedy is possible. You need a flopper-stopper – a somewhat inelegant term for what could more tastefully be described as a 'roll reducer' or, more pretentiously, a 'roll attenuation device'.

There are a few proprietary products on the market but they are often mechanically complicated, bulky and expensive. Here's one you can make yourself that has the considerable virtues of mechanical simplicity, a conveniently stowable flat shape and is low cost. Once you've laid your hands on the materials, you should be able to make one within a couple of hours.

How it works

An equilateral triangular plate, weighted in one corner, is suspended underwater as far outboard as possible – typically from the end of the boom or spinnaker pole.

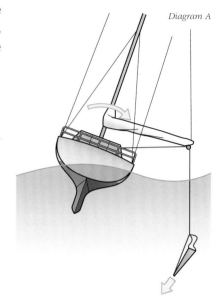

Diagram A

- When the boat rolls towards the roll reducer, the weighted corner drops and the plate dives, almost edge on (diagram A).
- Then, as the boat begins to roll upright again, the three-legged harness snaps the plate horizontal and the sudden increase in drag dampens the rolling. Comfort improves considerably (diagram B).

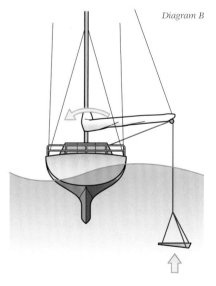

Diagram B

Above The roll reducer is rigged on a spinnaker pole or boom perpendicular to the boat. Place the topping lift at the end of the pole to take the heavy snatch load as the boat comes upright.

Left Exposed anchorages are often prone to incoming swell. When this occurs, it's time to deploy the roll reducer.

Making the roll reducer

Although it would be possible to use plywood, ideally the plate should be non-buoyant. For example, it could be cut from a sheet of fibreglass about 8mm ($\frac{5}{16}$in) thick, laminated especially for the purpose. Equally practicable would be aluminium or steel. Whatever you use must be thick enough not to flex under load. The construction details are simple enough but below are a few points worth noting:

⚙ While there is no real formula for size, the roll reducer plate shown here has sides 700mm ($27\frac{1}{2}$in) in length before the corners were rounded off to help protect the topsides if it ever clattered against them. Experience tells us that this would suit a boat of about 11m (36ft) or less.

⚙ Any type of weight will serve but it needs to be fairly heavy if the plate is to dive without delay. The one shown here is a 2kg (5lb) lead dive-belt weight but a zinc anode, even a partially depleted one, would do.

⚙ Don't skimp on the rope harness. The one here is of 10-mm ($\frac{3}{8}$-in) three-strand polyester, which is easy to splice. Note that the strand ends have not been trimmed and melted, leaving them long and soft to handle. This is a matter of personal choice. You could even use knots if you prefer. The three legs of the harness attach to stainless steel pad eyes bought at the local chandlers. Folding eyes would have made it even easier to stow.

Rigging the roll reducer

Ideally, the plate should be suspended below any surface wave action. However, this is often impractical since boats tend to anchor in relatively shallow water. But do try and get it as deep as you can. It helps to lead the attachment line back to the cockpit so depth adjustments can be optimised, particularly in tidal waters.

Right **The roll reducer's construction is very simple and it can be made from a variety of materials. Note the weight that is attached, which makes the plate dive.**

Below **The roll reducer needs deep water to be really effective, but even at a shallow depth there will be an improvement in the motion of the boat.**

If using a spinnaker pole, the topping lift should be rigged to the pole's outboard end, not the usual mid-length point. The vertical snatch loads can be fierce and you wouldn't want to bend or break the pole.

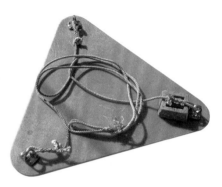

Lightweight tiller

For centuries, timber has been considered the traditional material of choice for tillers but the development of synthetic resins, foams and fibreglass reinforcements has opened the door to other options. Here's how to make an ultra-lightweight tiller, which is low maintenance and should never need varnishing.

Items needed to make your tiller

- A non-stick work surface into which you can drive screws. You could use a workbench covered in polyethylene film. In this case we're using a sheet of melamine-faced chipboard.
- A number of shelf brackets to form the jig. The more elaborate the tiller's shape, the more you will need, along with as many clamps as you can lay your hands on to hold it all in position. You may have to scrounge some extras from friends.

Below **To laminate a curved tiller you will need a simple jig, some clamps and some polyurethane glue.**

- Closed-cell PVC foam sheet. The foam used here is 10mm ($^3/_8$in)-thick Herex H60, but anything similar – Corecell for example – will work fine. Don't use polyurethane foams, which will break down in time.
- One-pot polyurethane wood glue. Make sure it's not too fast a grade as you will need plenty of time to assemble the laminate stack.
- Epoxy resin – again not too fast a grade. Err on the slow side, if in doubt, allowing for a pot life of at least two hours.
- Unidirectional and woven or biaxial glass rovings. The lighter weights are much easier to work with. Also woven glass tape, about 75mm (3in) wide. Don't

be tempted to use chopped strand mat, which relies on the styrene contained in polyester resins to dissolve the binders that hold the fibres together.
- Heat-shrink plastic tape 30–40mm ($1^1/_8$–$1^5/_8$in) wide – and a hot air gun to make it work.
- Assorted tools and accessories.

How to proceed

Start by designing your tiller, by deciding on its curves and then establishing the width necessary to match the rudder head. The tiller described here was made narrower than necessary, before adding phenolic laminate packing plates (a composite material in flat plates suitable for shaping) to bring it out

TIP

When using epoxy resin don't fall for the idea that you can slow a fast grade down by adding less hardener. Epoxies involve a coactivation process that requires exact proportions to reach full strength. To change the proportions will weaken the resin considerably

to the desired width. From your working drawings, plot the curved profile onto your work surface and screw shelf brackets to it, to act as a jig. It helps to lightly wax the surface to prevent sticking.

Cut the foam into fairly generous over-width strips, keeping the edges as straight as possible. A bandsaw would be ideal, but a razor knife and straight edge would suffice.

Next, glue and clamp the foam core. The glue's curing process relies on moisture, which, of course, occurs naturally in timber but not in synthetic foams. To compensate for this deficiency, spread the glue on one surface and moisten the other with a damp rag. Not much, though. It shouldn't be visibly wet. Stack the various layers one on top of the other, before flexing the whole structure around the jig. Tighten the clamps lightly; very little pressure is required.

After leaving it overnight, remove the foam blank from the jig (you'll be astonished how light it is) and cut away the irregularities on each side where the edges of the foam strips don't quite coincide.

Again, a bandsaw is the best tool for this but, with care, a handsaw (preferably a Japanese-type pull-stroke saw) can also work well. Now parallel from end to end, it is a somewhat brutal object, desperately in need of some shaping.

Mark the tapers on the top and sides and the hatched areas shown here. Now cut away the excess by whatever means you used before. Also round off the blank's square edges, either with a router or by hand with coarse (60-grit) abrasive paper.

Above **Don't overtighten the clamps when gluing up. Too much pressure will damage the foam.**

Below **To taper the tiller, it helps to mark the material to be cut away before you start shaping it.**

Lightweight tiller 2

To hold it clear of the surface and provide access all round, impale the now recognisable tiller on a couple of stiff wires clamped in a workbench.

Note the grey circles on the fat end. These are cores of lightweight epoxy filler passing through holes drilled right through the foam. Their purpose is to resist the compression loads where the tiller is attached to its associated hardware.

Mix up a small quantity of epoxy resin and apply a primer coat to the core. Allow it to cure just enough to become tacky. From here on, the work must proceed in a continuous operation – there's no going back! Mix up the main batch of resin. The laminating process should take about one hour, so make sure you are using a grade of epoxy with a pot life at least that long.

Below **The tiller ready for action, well after its construction was recorded. It has never needed to be varnished.**

Forming the layers

The first layer of unidirectional (or woven) glass roving forms around the blank. The tacky resin effectively grabs the rovings and prevents them slipping off.

However, you should be able to tease out the creases. Once the top is done, turn the tiller over, spiking it the other way up. Apply more rovings on the bottom. You now have the rovings in place top and

Above **After laminating and shaping, the tiller must be primed with epoxy resin.**

bottom, with the overlaps at each side where the double thickness will be the most structurally efficient. Use polyester thread to run a series of half hitches along its length, to make the whole package more handleable.

Cover it over with epoxy. It's important that no dry patches remain so you will need to be quite generous with the resin. This is a spectacularly messy job so wear old clothes and, of course, gloves! The latter are essential since epoxy resins are potentially allergenic.

With the unidirectional rovings thoroughly covered over, a 'bandage' of woven glass tape is wound on next – maybe three or four layers. The tape should absorb the resin you applied earlier, so you shouldn't need more. To stop the tape unwinding, secure each end with a rubber band.

Wind shrink-film tape on in much the same way as the glass tape, pulling it as tight as you reasonably can and ensuring there are no gaps between turns. Again secure the ends with rubber bands.

You now need to shrink the plastic tape with a hot air gun. This will have two fairly immediate effects: it will both reduce the viscosity of the resin and draw the tape down tight around the tiller, consolidating the laminate and driving out air bubbles; it will also kick in the curing process, so there are only a few minutes for this part of the job.

Finish the tiller

And that's about it. Once fully cured – a couple of days later – peel off the tape to behold your new tiller! You should have a good quality laminate, which only needs fairing and painting to finish the job. The

MAKING THE LAYERS

The first layer of glass roving is wrapped around the blank.

The surface is wetted with epoxy, covering it thoroughly.

A bandage of woven glass tape is wound on in three of four layers and secured.

Shrink-wrap film is wound around the tiller and secured.

The plastic tape is shrunk with a hot air gun, drawing it in more tightly.

After curing for a couple of days, the tiller is ready for completion.

ends can be tidied up by carefully hollowing out the foam to a depth of about 20mm (³⁄₄in) or so, before filling the void with lightweight epoxy filler. Naturally, the after end of the tiller must be adapted to fit the specific attachment joining it to the rudder. Since there is no

standard configuration, modify this to suit whatever is needed, although the same applies to tillers made from any other material.

Bathing platform

What better way to enjoy the heat of summer than with a dip in the water from a bathing platform fitted to the stern of your boat? Installing a bathing platform is a straightforward task for which you will require a suitable supply of wood, the ability to use a jigsaw, a plane and a router – along with the services of a stainless steel fabricator.

Choosing the wood

For the stainless steel frame you need to supply the fabricator with a pattern and measurements in order to make up the structure. Once the fabricator has supplied the metal frame, the first task is to decide what type of wood to use for the platform. While teak is frequently used, it is becoming increasingly difficult to source long teak boards that are wide enough to allow for the desired curve of a platform's planking for larger motor cruisers or yachts. In these circumstances, iroko is an economic and equally durable alternative.

Making the planks

Having selected the type of wood you want, choose a potential width for the individual planks to create the desired effect and then divide the available width within the stainless steel frame by this measurement to determine the required number of planks. Remember that there should be a gap between the planks for drainage, and it may be necessary to adjust the chosen figure for the width of the planks if the gaps are going to be too big or small. Once the planks' dimensions have been established, each one can be marked out on the

Below **A neat platform made by employing the services of a professional welder combined with some basic woodwork.**

INSTALLING THE PLATFORM

Mark the planks on the board one at a time, and cut them out using a jigsaw.

Mark the position for each groove, then use a router to cut the treads.

Use plywood offcuts to set the gap between the planks to achieve a consistent look.

Clamp the planks in place before fastening, using the plywood spacers.

Drill the screw holes and secure the planks to the frame with stainless steel screws.

Secure the platform using stainless steel bolts through-bolted into the transom.

board and cut out using a jigsaw, before the edges are trimmed with a plane. The appearance of the planks' upper surface is a matter of personal choice. Some people like a smooth finish, while others prefer the improved grip that is provided by the addition of grooves with a router. The number of grooves will be determined by the width of the plank. However, they should be equally spaced and situated at least 10mm (⅜in) apart to minimise the chances of the raised wood between the grooves breaking off. Having cut the grooves, use a router to bevel the outer rim of the plank to ensure there are no sharp edges to catch barefoot swimmers.

Fitting the wooden planks

For a smart appearance, it is vital to ensure there is an even gap between the planks. This can be achieved by placing four pieces of wood that are the same width as the planks within the bathing platform's metal frame and using plywood offcuts of various thicknesses to establish the size of an appropriate gap.

Attaching the platform

At least two people will be required to fit the platform, depending on its weight and size. Having secured the planks to the metal frame, place the bathing platform on a set of wooden supports to determine the correct position for it.

When it looks right, mark out the holes on the hull, drill them out and apply a ring of sealant around each hole. If all of the holes are above the waterline a silicone sealant can be applied, otherwise a polyurethane-based sealant should be used.

When all of the stainless steel nuts and bolts have been secured in place, the excess sealant should be removed. To avoid damaging the gel coat of a GRP boat, use either a wooden or Perspex scraper. Any remaining sealant can then be wiped away using white spirit on a soft cloth.

Davits

Davits are the structures used to support a dinghy or tender on the stern of a boat. They enable the dinghy to be lifted out or lowered into the water easily, using pulleys or winches.

Choosing suitable davits for a vessel can be a straightforward task, but there are certain points to consider:

- The position on the boat where they are to be fitted must be substantially stronger than the davits themselves.
- The weight and distribution of the load: if an outboard is to be permanently installed on the tender, then the davit nearest the motor will carry 90 per cent of the total weight of the tender and motor. It is therefore essential to select a pair of davits that each have the strength to support the total weight.

There are generally two mounting positions for davits; on the deck or on the transom. On a steel vessel, the hull and deck may be strong enough to take the weight of the loaded davits, but it is still good practice to strengthen the area as, unless the original hull/deck design allowed for the extra strain, flexing of the metal may eventually lead to failure.

Above A pair of transom-mounted lightweight davits, each capable of carrying a safe load of 60kg (132lb).

Below When carrying a heavy tender and outboard motor, the davits must be strong enough to take both the weight and the forces exerted on them in rough weather.

TIP

A common problem when fitting heavy-duty davits is that they encroach on the lower guard rail. This can be overcome in a smart and practical way by cutting the rail and making up end fittings that cap the rail and then bolt onto the davit body, thus retaining the strength of the rail and adding to the rigidness of the davit.

Reinforcement

A simple, mild steel bracket, ground off clean and epoxy coated, will make a very strong, cheap and corrosion-resistant reinforcement for all types of boat. Stainless steel can be used, although it is more expensive. In either case the metal for the bracket should ideally be over-specified with 6mm (¼in) being the minimum thickness. The bracket, which is formed to suit the angle between deck and transom, will ideally be bolted through both the deck and transom to provide a very strong base for the davit.

If you are working on an older boat, the vessel may already have an immensely strong hull due to the hefty lay-up of early GRP vessels, so therefore it may not require additional reinforcement.

Weight

When the davits carry both an outboard motor and a tender, their weights need to be established. If together they weigh 60kg (132lb) for example, then the davits would need to be rated for over 120kg (264lb) as a pair and over 60kg (132lb) individually. You could test each davit with a 100kg (220lb)

man swinging from the outer end. The davits may show signs of flexing, but if the transom remains unmoved, the structure is stable. So while it is good practice to follow the reinforcement recommendations, there will always be instances where these can be modified.

Mounting pads

Where the deck or transom doesn't allow the davits to sit squarely with each other, it is a simple job to mould mounting pads to attach them to, although it is essential to use a polyester fibreglass filler to provide

Above **Fixing bolts over a moulded knuckle and a spacing pad of ply below the knuckle provide a strong mount. Inside the boat, the only reinforcement needed comprises three stainless steel strips, one behind each pair of mounting bolts.**

Inset **A mounting pad on a sloping deck made from polyester fibreglass filler allows the davits to sit squarely with each other.**

enough strength for the load. Ensure you don't confuse these fillers with ordinary body fillers, which have no strength at all!

Canvas and upholstery

Care and repair

Boat upholstery can last many years. However, over time, upholstery can become tired, frayed and misshapen. The good news is that you don't always have to replace it at great expense – quick repairs can do much to revive it.

There are two distinct types of material used in boat upholstery: waterproof vinyl, which is usually used for cockpit cushions, and a softer polyester-type fabric that is used for interior bunk cushions. Some older boats may have vinyl seat covers down below, too.

Waterlogged foam

A common problem with vinyl cockpit upholstery is that the foam can become saturated when water finds its way in through the stitching. In most cases the cover can be removed, and the foam squeezed out so it can dry naturally, or be replaced. A waterproofing agent should then be applied to the cover's stitching to seal up the holes and reduce further water ingress.

Un-seizing corroded zips

Seized zips as a result of corrosion are more difficult to repair, because the evaporated salt water leaves behind hard carbonates, and may also have eaten away the metal parts of the zip mechanism. Use very hot water, or even steam from a kettle, to dissolve the hard deposits and un-seize the zip. Acetic acid (vinegar)

> **TIP**
>
> If a zip is so badly damaged that it needs replacing, specify a large tooth plastic replacement zip, as this will give fewer problems with salt water corrosion in the future. Make sure it is smeared with plenty of silicone lubricant after it has been fitted.

or lemon juice can also be effective. Use an old toothbrush to work the fluids into the zip, and with a bit of effort it should free up, although it may take some time. Once the zip is running again, smear the teeth with a silicone lubricant, and work the zip a few times so that all the parts are well covered.

Repairing vinyl seat covers

If a vinyl seat becomes stained or torn, or cracked due to ultraviolet radiation, use a vinyl repair kit, which can be colour-matched to your existing upholstery. Entire seats can be painted with a specialised, hard-wearing paint system to extend the life of your vinyl. To make a repair:

- Thoroughly clean the area with warm water and detergent.
- Allow the area to dry, before gently abrading it to remove the shine.
- Glue a vinyl patch over the damage, and paint it for a complete colour match.

Left **Boat upholstery will last many years, but suffers from the effects of salt water and mildew in the harsh marine environment.**

Right **Stretching stockinette over the foam of a cushion will help the foam keep its shape and make it easier to fit the covers.**

Bolstering your cushion foam

It is usually not cost effective to replace the foam in a cushion, as it is unlikely that it will fill out the cover properly again. Over the years both the foam and the fabric stretch, taking on a different shape. The ultimate solution is to invest in a new set of cushions, so that both the cushion and the foam are an exact match.

However, a temporary solution, which can be very effective, is to use an additional piece of polyester matting to bolster the old foam.

MAKING A CUSHION FILLING

A layer of polyester material is put over the foam cushion and cut to length.

The surface of the foam is sprayed with a spray tack adhesive.

The polyester is pressed onto the adhesive and patted all over for a complete bond.

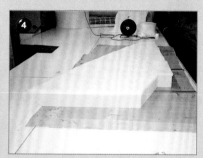

The excess is then trimmed to shape, before being covered in stockinette.

- Remove the cushion cover and then cut a layer of polyester wadding to fit over the top of the existing foam. This material is readily available from most fabric shops, and is inexpensive.
- Cut some stockinette material to the length of the bunk. Pull the stockinette over the foam and the polyester to hold the two parts together.
- Reinsert the foam back into the cover. With a little manipulation, you will find the new layer will fill out the cover again and give a bit more spring to the cushion.

Cockpit cushions

Comfort afloat has become a big issue. Gone are the times when cruising sailors were content to spend hours at the helm, their sterns parked on unyielding cockpit seats that became harder and harder with every passing minute.

Cushion requirements

So, what makes for good cockpit cushions? Well, there are only a few essential requirements:

- They should be comfortable.
- They should be non-slip when stood upon.
- They should dry out quickly and not remain waterlogged.
- They should be buoyant so they can be heaved overboard as an instant response to that direst of emergencies – an MOB situation.

These seem easy aims to fulfil. However, it's not until you review the various commonly employed materials that you realise that none satisfy all demands:

- **Polyurethane foam:** cheap, cheerful and readily available, but lacks any significant buoyancy.

It will soon become waterlogged and will take days to dry out. You can, of course, cover them with a waterproof fabric such as reinforced PVC. But this is quite slippery underfoot and, anyway, the seams and zips will still leak. Also it's heavy and can be unpleasant to sit on, particularly in hot climates.

- **Closed-cell foam:** it doesn't absorb water and it floats, but it lacks springiness, being little more resilient or comfortable than the original cockpit seats.
- **Reticulated foam:** meaning 'net-like', forming a structure of open galleries (as opposed to cells), which drain rapidly and can't hold large quantities of water, like a conventional sponge. However, reticulated foams are non-buoyant, which doesn't fit one of the criteria.

Above **The top (yellow) foam is the reticulated variety, the white beneath it is buoyant closed cell.**

However, by combining the closed-cell and reticulated foams together as a laminate and then covering the whole in acrylic canvas, you end up with a cushion that is comfortable to sit on, and has good non-slip properties.

The feature that makes this type of homemade cockpit cushion unique lies in the foam core. The cushion resembles, at least visually, a layer cake. It comprises a laminate of two different foams glued together. The bottom layer is 25mm (1in) of closed-cell foam topped by 75mm (3in) of reticulated foam. The thicknesses aren't critical, but they do work well together.

Left **The cockpit cushions in place. The foam core and top layer of reticulated foam make an ideal combination for cushions.**

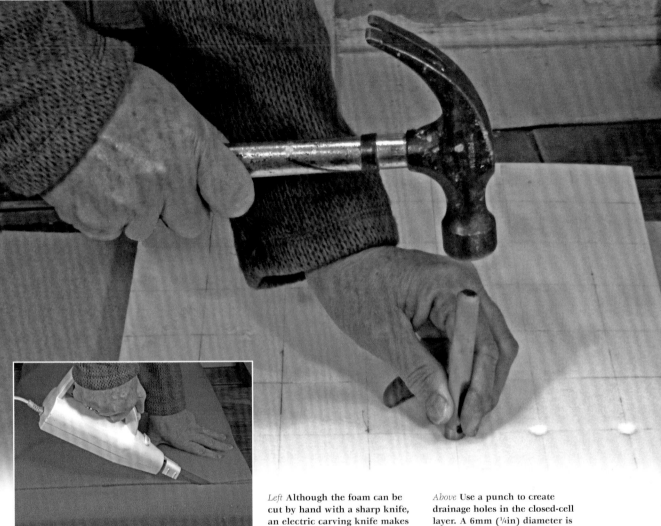

Left **Although the foam can be cut by hand with a sharp knife, an electric carving knife makes the job a lot easier.**

Above **Use a punch to create drainage holes in the closed-cell layer. A 6mm (¼in) diameter is ideal for the holes.**

Making the cushions

Start by making a template of the seat you intend upholstering – perhaps out of plastic sheeting or wrapping paper. Also check that both the port and starboard sides are the same. Surprisingly, dimensional symmetry can't always be relied upon on yachts.

Lay the template over the closed-cell sheet and draw around its perimeter and cut out the shape. A domestic electric carving knife cuts foam cleanly, quickly and without tearing. Be accurate. If possible, lay the shaped foam in its actual place on the boat to confirm that it fits. Being closed-cell makes this a rather incompressible material, so the footprint of the bottom layer will determine that of the whole cushion.

Water will drain quickly through the reticulated foam, but will face an impenetrable barrier when it reaches the bottom layer. Some form of drainage must be provided; the simplest being to make a number of holes through the closed-cell foam. What works surprisingly well is a hammer and 6mm (¼in)-diameter punch. The neatest way to do this is to mark a grid with lines about 50mm (2in) apart and drive the holes through at the intersections.

The next task is to cut out the reticulated foam. Use the closed-cell layer as a template and draw a cutting line about 25mm (1in) outside it. This excess is to allow for any inaccuracies when you glue the two layers together.

Cockpit cushions 2

The next job requires an aerosol sprayed contact adhesive, available from a commercial upholstery materials suppliers or carpet shop. When applying the glue there are two options, depending on the size of the cushion. One way is to spray both joining surfaces, allowing them to dry (about 4 minutes), then bringing the two pieces together for an instant bond. A safer option for larger cushions is to spray just the upper face of the closed-cell foam, then press the reticulated layer onto it as soon as you can.

It's possible to do this in stages, bending the reticulated foam up to allow you to spray adhesive underneath it as you work your way along. The bond between the two layers isn't very critical anyway,

since it will all eventually be held together by the fabric cover. Whichever method you choose, you will need a flat surface that is large enough to move the cushion around as you bring the two layers together. An uncarpeted floor space, protected by plastic sheeting or strewn newspapers, is ideal.

Once the two layers are joined, all that remains is to trim off the excess reticulated foam, again with the electric carving knife, and you are ready to make the cover.

The best material to use for this is acrylic canvas, which has good resistance to UV light, holds its colour well and doesn't fray easily. The traditional method is to make 'boxed' cushions. This is a very apt term to describe a cover that has a

top, bottom and sides, the last of which is a narrow strip that runs continuously around the perimeter without seams in the corners.

The original template is used to mark out the top and bottom panels, allowing an extra 25mm (1in) or so all round for the seam. It's best to use a chalk marker that will not permanently stain. The side strips should be made a little narrower (by 6mm/$\frac{1}{4}$in) than the total depth of the cushion. If, say, the uncompressed foam filler was a total of 75mm (3in) thick, make the side strips just 70mm (2$\frac{3}{4}$in) wide, plus 25mm (1in) each side for the seams – a total of 120mm (4$\frac{3}{4}$in). Having the cover slightly too tight will help remove creases from the finished cushion.

Above **The two layers of foam are now glued together to form a single laminate.**

Left **An aerosol-type adhesive makes applying the glue a very easy task.**

Right **A domestic sewing machine is well able to sew acrylic canvas but make sure you have the right needles for heavy material on your machine.**

Using an ordinary domestic sewing machine, the seams are stitched with the cover inside out. It's common to fit a zip into the hidden side so the filler can be stuffed in. But zips and seawater are not happy bedfellows, so some people prefer to close the cover by making the last seam by hand. It's easy to pull the seam tight with a needle and thread and the tension helps pull out any creases.

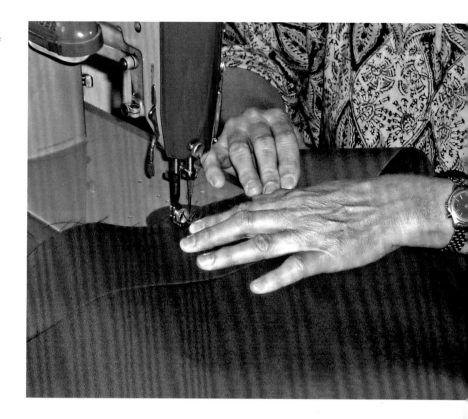

TIP

You may need some form of attachment to prevent cockpit cushions blowing away. There are several methods you can use. One of these is fitting snaps into the cushion and the boat surfaces, such as the corners of seats.

Right **A sailmaker's palm and needles close the final seam. Zips could be used for the seam but in time are likely to corrode and seize.**

Bimini

A well-designed bimini can make a huge difference to crew comfort. Apart from providing protection from the elements, particularly the sun, it can also create extra sleeping space on board, support solar panels and even channel rainwater for drinking.

Very few boats are supplied with a bimini as standard, so being able to design your own retrofit version can be very rewarding. Many blue water cruisers list a bimini as one of their most essential items, especially in the Mediterranean and Tropics.

A bimini is universally accepted as being a temporary fabric awning that can be pulled over the cockpit to provide shade. Add some detachable side panels, and it can form the backbone to a complete cockpit tent. On some smaller boats, this can provide the equivalent to an extra sleeping cabin, usually with full standing headroom. A bimini

shouldn't be confused with a cockpit awning, as this tends to be draped over the boom and can't be used with the mainsail hoisted.

There are several ways to support a bimini, the most usual being on a series of stainless steel hoops or 'bows' set on running tracks. When not in use, the bimini is slid back and tied against the radar arch, or folded forward under the sprayhood.

Size and location

A bimini needs to be useful without getting in the way. On a yacht, it is usually designed to completely cover the helm area, affording the

helmsman the most protection. A bimini can reach as far forward as the sprayhood, where it can be secured to the deck, and the sprayhood dropped to promote a through draught. To provide shade when sailing, a bimini has to be lower than the boom and yet still afford standing headroom. The supports will also have to be sturdy enough to withstand the unexpected squall or, if fitted to a motorboat, the effects of wind speed when planing.

Below **A sturdy bimini will give welcome shade from the sun when out sailing, at anchor or in a marina. It is regarded as essential in hot climates.**

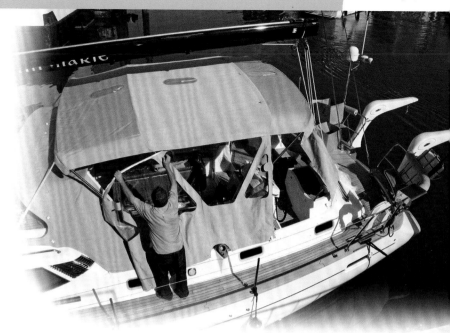

Right **A custom-made bimini on a Discovery 67 with full headroom. Note the closable vents on the roof, the detachable side panels and the zip on the front to attach the bimini to the sprayhood.**

Before fitting a bimini, decide how much of the cockpit (and sidedecks) you want to cover. The biggest challenge will be the location of the framework's anchor points, ensuring that they don't foul any winches or clash with other fixtures on the coaming. Usually, careful planning and the use of mock-ups using plastic wastewater pipe will highlight any potential problems.

A bimini can be bought off the shelf as a kit, but ordering a custom-made one will be a good investment. Although this will cost more, it will fit the boat exactly and can be made multifunctional. Many blue water sailors use detachable panels as additional sun protection, especially when the sun is low or the yacht is heeled. The side panels can also be partly rolled up to collect water for drinking. In addition, the bimini's top can have attachment points for flexible solar panels and the frame can be modified to accept temporary interior lights.

Which material?

Although providing shade is the prime concern, biminis also need to be weatherproof, so choosing the right material is important. A UV-resistant acrylic or polyester is usually best, as they are lightweight and flexible, as well as easy to wash. Vinyl is a heavier alternative. Owners like to match the colour of the fabric to the boat, although a white bimini will reflect more sunlight away, and also reflect sunlight from the water back down into the cockpit. Large plastic zips, tape tiebacks and corrosion-resistant poppers are used to hold a deployed bimini in place. The quality of these fittings normally indicates how trouble-free the bimini will be.

KEY ELEMENTS FOR A BIMINI

A running track each side of the cabin allows spacing of the anchor points, so the hoops can be more easily tensioned and stowed.

It is best to use the high quality, UV/corrosion-resistant fixtures and straps for trouble-free extended use.

Biminis should be able to stow securely in heavy weather, with a UV-protective cover to extend the life of the fabric.

Low profile windscoop

In hot weather, windscoops are wonderful aids to ventilation, but some are better than others, at least in certain circumstances.

The conventional windscoop is an impressive object, a sort of puff-chested spinnaker hoisted high above the deck, usually hovering over a forehatch, although it can be rigged elsewhere. In terms of scooping the wind, these devices are certainly efficient, but they also bring problems. Namely...

- ✪ They will direct rain below as well as wind. It isn't a big problem if the hatch can be closed without lowering the windscoop, but this isn't always possible.
- ✪ In order to keep 'flying' (in the same way as a spinnaker does), they are made of very light fabrics, typically nylon spinnaker cloth, which is susceptible to UV light degradation. Spinnakers are not usually deployed day after day, but windscoops certainly are. Sailors in sunny climates struggle to get a couple of seasons' use from nylon scoops.
- ✪ They obstruct the view forward, making them difficult or even impossible to use while under way.
- ✪ They present significant windage.

So you may like to consider making a low-profile windscoop. It won't draw quite the volume of air below as the conventional spinnaker type, but it wins hands down on practicality and convenience.

TIP

Although there is some variation between brands, the most popular size of deck hatch is somewhere around 600 x 600mm (2ft^2), and the windscoop described here would suit such a hatch. However, the dimensions aren't critical and can be adjusted easily to suit your own circumstances.

Unrigged, the panel is perfectly flat, with no seams apart from those that run around its edge to reinforce it and prevent it fraying. For anyone interested in getting into canvaswork, this is an ideal first project.

Below **The windscoop rigged over a forehatch, providing useful shelter from the rain and shade from the sun.**

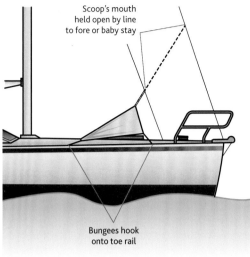

Scoop's mouth
held open by line
to fore or baby stay

Bungees hook
onto toe rail

Above **Eyelets could be used instead of the webbing loops shown here.**

Left **Note the shockcord (bungee) lines used to tension the windscoop, which hook onto the toe rail.**

Above **The mouth of the windscoop is held open by a line tied to a forestay. This allows a breeze to enter the cabin.**

Windscoop make-up

Laid flat, the windscoop is nothing more than a trapezoid of acrylic canvas, some 1,100mm (43in) fore-and-aft, 1,400mm (55in) at the mouth and 1,110mm (43in) at its trailing edge. Of course, this is the finished size, so you should allow extra material for the hems – let's say another 50mm (2in) all round.

From each corner, run shock-cord (bungee) tensioners that hook either onto the toe rail or to pad eyes, which are fitted to the deck to receive them. The mouth of the scoop is held open by a light topping lift that attaches to a stay, possibly the baby stay or forestay. Much depends on the rig and, of course, the position of the hatch.

An attachment loop can be made in less than an hour using a domestic sewing machine.

The polyester webbing loops are hand stitched and take perhaps another hour at most. If you have the facilities to fit them, brass eyelets would have done just as well.

The advantages of a low-profile windscoop

- ❂ It covers the hatch, keeping nearly all the rain out. Further protection can be gained from having the hatch half-closed under the scoop. No rain gets in and you still get a decent breeze.
- ❂ The scoop also shades the hatch, keeping out most of the sunlight. The white acrylic still allows useful illumination. Choose a darker colour if you would like more shade.
- ❂ The view ahead is pretty much unobstructed so the windscoop can be kept rigged, even at sea if conditions permit. This is useful under power, when the improved ventilation helps disperse the heat generated by the engine.
- ❂ Acrylic is much more resistant to UV degradation than nylon spinnaker cloth, so you can confidently expect many years of service.
- ❂ It can be rigged and taken down in an instant.
- ❂ The windage it adds is negligible.
- ❂ It looks neater than the billowing variety.

Hatch covers

The simplest way to prevent leaks and protect varnishwork is to fit a hatch cover. To anyone inexperienced in canvaswork, these covers can look extremely complicated and hard to design and make. However, with careful patterning, they are straightforward.

Before you start making your hatch cover, consider how it will be attached. There are three options: it can be fitted with an elastic drawstring to hold it snugly in place, it can be attached via snap fasteners to the hatch frame, or by turnbuckles on the deck. All three options are relatively simple to do and follow the same principles of construction.

Left **Lay a piece of lightweight cover material over the hatch to make a pattern.**

Below **Fold the material around the hatch, and mark the edges and sides of the hatch with a permanent marker.**

Patterning up for a cover

The key to making a well-fitting hatch cover is the pattern. If you make a good pattern in the first place then your hatch cover will fit first time; if you don't then there will be plenty of to-ing and fro-ing between your work area and your boat to readjust it. You can buy specific patterning material online, but all you really need is a piece of lightweight tarpaulin material, of the type often used for all over winter boat covers, which can be picked up fairly cheaply. White is the best colour, as it will show up your pen marks. You will also need a black permanent marker.

To make a pattern for a square hatch with 90-degree corners and snap fasteners:

- ✪ Roughly cut a piece of patterning material that is big enough to cover the entire hatch top, the hatch sides and allow enough for the hems (50mm/2in all round).
- ✪ Drape the material over the hatch and then crease it along the top edges, drawing round it to show where the edges are.

- ✪ Fold the corners of the material diagonally, and mark where the corners of the hatch frame are on both sides of the diagonal folds. When the material is laid out, you should see a cross in each corner. Once the seam allowance has been added, these will be sewn together to form darts, which give the hatch cover its shape.

TIP

When marking out the pattern on your piece of canvas, use chalk instead of pens and markers. Chalk can be rubbed out easily, whereas ink will seep into the material, making the lines permanent, and you'll end up with your smart new canvaswork covered in pen marks.

Transferring the pattern and cutting out

Once you have made the pattern for the hatch cover, you can transfer the marks to your canvas.

✪ Cut out a piece of canvas to the same size as your pattern, remembering to allow an extra 50mm (2in) on all four sides to leave enough canvas for a hem, and more if you want to fasten the cover to the deck with turnbuckles.

✪ To transfer the corner marks at the top of the hatch, place a pin through the patterning material and the canvas, and then gently pull its head through the patterning material so that it is left in the canvas. Large-headed pins such as glass-headed dressmaking pins or map pins are good for this, although if the patterning material is very strong you may need to assist by cutting it first. Mark where the pins are with a chalk or soapstone pencil.

✪ Now transfer the hatch frame corner marks by measuring in from the outer corners, checking that all the sides are exactly the same size.

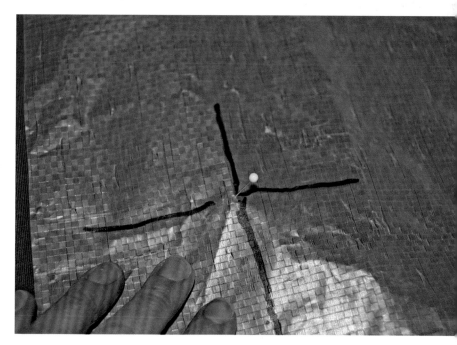

Above top **Once you have made the pattern, lay it out on a piece of canvas. Don't forget to allow for the hem.**

Above **Use a pin to help transfer the marks from the patterning material to the canvas.**

Hatch covers 2

Sewing the hatch cover together

When you have transferred all your marks, make the darts to give the cover its shape.

- Carefully pinch one corner of the canvas together, so that the two lines marking the corners of the hatch frames are on top of each other, with a triangle of canvas to one side.

- Sew the two sides together, about 6mm (¼in) away from this line, on the side that the triangle falls.
- Repeat with the three remaining corners, and then place on your hatch to check the fit. If it is ok, trim the excess dart material (the triangles).

- You now have a hatch cover that needs to be hemmed. To do this, fold 38mm (1½in) under and crease along its length. Sew it together, 6mm (¼in) away from the crease line. If you prefer the look of a double-rubbed seam, then fold the raw edge under and then sew it together, 6mm (¼in) away from the crease line.

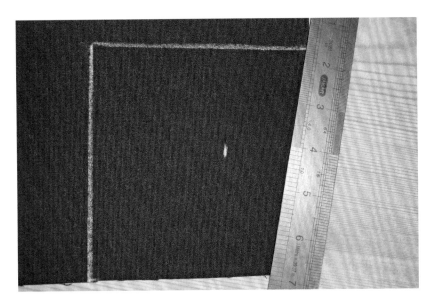

Left **The marks that you made on the patterning material should be transferred to your canvas using chalk.**

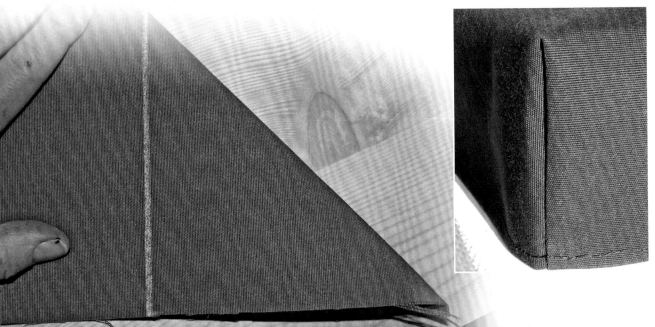

Bottom left **Pinch the corners of the canvas together to form the darts that give the canvas its shape.**

Bottom right **The corners of the hatch cover once they have been sewn together.**

Attaching the hatch cover

If you are going to attach the hatch cover to the hatch via snap fasteners, it is easier to attach them to the boat first, before sewing the corresponding part onto the cover.

Screw the snap fasteners at equal distances around the hatch frame and then put the hatch cover in place. By pressing hard on the snap fasteners, you should be able to make a mark in the canvas where the other half needs to go, or if you prefer, you can make a mark with a chalk pencil.

Below **The finished cover should sit snugly over the hatch.**

Variations

If your hatch incorporates a decklight and you don't want it to be obscured when the hatch cover is on, then make a corresponding one out of clear PVC. If using acrylic canvas, make the hatch cover as usual, and then sew on a piece of PVC that is the same size and shape as the decklight.

Once it is sewn in place, carefully cut the canvas away so that you are left with a PVC-covered aperture. You will need to seal the cut edges with a hot knife or glue gun to prevent fraying. If you have used canvas, however, you will need to cut out the hole first, before attaching the PVC. Hem the canvas to prevent fraying, and then sew on the PVC panel.

Drawstring hatch covers

To make a hatch cover that is fastened using a drawstring:

- Cut off the excess dart material before sewing the sides together, remembering to leave enough to make a seam.
- Turn up the corners and stitch in place.
- Next, turn up the bottom edge of the hatch cover and hem it, with the raw edge tucked under. Make sure the hem is wide enough to take a length of elastic or light line, as this will be what holds the hatch cover in place.
- Sew the cover's side seams and then turn it round the right way out.
- Feed a length of elastic or light line through the hem, and once on the hatch, tighten it so that the cover fits snugly.

Dodgers

There is nothing worse than getting soaked by spray coming over the side when you are sitting in the cockpit. With a smart pair of dodgers, however, the risk of this can easily be reduced.

Above **Measuring for the dodger. Measure the distance between the forward and aft stanchions, and the height between the top guard wire and toe rail or deck.**

Spray dodgers, or weather cloths as they are also known, are one of the easiest canvaswork projects to do on a boat. Essentially a hemmed rectangle of material, they can be laced to the guard wires around your cockpit and will provide instant protection from cold winds and spray coming over the side.

Although usually only fitted in pairs, one either side of the boat, provided you have guard wires (lifelines) around the stern, a whole cockpit can be enclosed to increase privacy and/or security – useful if you are sailing with small children.

Below **Spray dodgers or weather cloths provide instant protection from the elements for the crew in the cockpit.**

Measuring up

Dodgers are generally made up of one length of canvas, so there are only three measurements that are needed: the height from the top guard wire to the toe rail; the distance from the top of the stanchion to which the forward end of the dodger will be laced, and to the top of the stanchion to which the aft end of the dodger will be laced; and the same measurement for the bottom edge between the two stanchions.

These last two measurements are usually the same, but if the aft stanchion forms part of the pushpit and is sloping rather than vertical,

then they will obviously be different. Ignore any stanchions that may be in the middle of the dodger, as it will just pass around these. However, you should make a note of the location of any cut-outs that need to be made at deck level, as these will also need to be hemmed to prevent the material fraying.

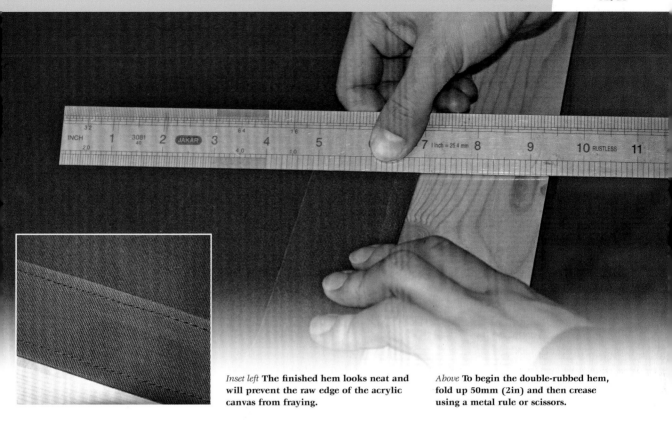

Inset left **The finished hem looks neat and will prevent the raw edge of the acrylic canvas from fraying.**

Above **To begin the double-rubbed hem, fold up 50mm (2in) and then crease using a metal rule or scissors.**

Making the dodgers

Acrylic canvas is the best material to use for dodgers. Not only is it resistant to UV rays and water, but it is also relatively hardwearing and less susceptible to mildew than other types of canvas. Polyester thread is also recommended.

Before cutting out your canvas, don't forget to add an extra 50mm (2in) all the way around the outside edge to allow for the hem. It is also a good idea to cut out both dodgers at the same time, to make sure they are the same size.

Once the dodger has been cut out, you can begin hemming it. To give it a neat appearance, double-rubbed hems are recommended, as the cut or selvage edges of the canvas can then be hidden within the hem. To create a double-rubbed hem:

✪ First, fold up 50mm (2in) of one side of the canvas, carefully creating a hard crease along its length by rubbing over the fold.

✪ Next, sew along the length of the hem, about 6mm (¼in) from the edge that has been folded. Most domestic sewing machines should be able to cope with this, although the heavier the canvas, the larger the needle you will need. The majority of polyester threads require a 90 or 110 needle size. Don't forget to start and finish your stitching by double sewing over the first 18mm (¾in) to prevent if from unravelling later.

✪ Now turn 12mm (½in) of the cut or selvage edge of the canvas underneath the fold, so that it is hidden within the hem, and again sew along its length, about

6mm (¼in) away from the folded edge. Repeat this process on all four sides. You may find that your sewing machine struggles at the edges when you sew over other hems, so take it slowly.

✪ Before starting your second dodger, make sure you have it the right way round. Rectangular dodgers can go either way round, but it will matter with odd-shaped dodgers, as you want the hems to be on the cockpit-side to give a smarter appearance.

Dodgers 2

The eyelets

Once the canvas has been hemmed, it is time to fit the nickel-plated brass eyelets or grommets, through which the dodgers will be laced to the guard wires. Eyelet or grommet punches are relatively inexpensive to buy from a hardware store and can produce very neat results. They are basically made up of a steel die in several parts and an eyelet made up of male and female parts.

Make a hole in the appropriate position and then place the piece of material face down and position the male part of the eyelet on the top of the die and feed through the hole. Lay the female part of the eyelet on top, position the setter over it and strike several times with a steel hammer.

On a dodger, the eyelets should be spaced at around 150mm (6in) intervals and need to be big enough to get your lacing line through them. Size 4 or 12mm (½in) is a good size.

Below **Eyelet kits are relatively inexpensive to buy and contain everything you need to produce neat eyelets.**

INSERTING THE EYELETS

Place the canvas on a block of wood, and then twist the cutter firmly through the canvas to create a hole.

Place the male half of the eyelet on top of the die and underneath the canvas, so that it is poking through the hole.

Put the female half of the eyelet on top of the male half, and place the eyelet setter over the top.

Gently tap the eyelet setter with a steel hammer to push the female and male halves of the eyelet together, before giving it a good whack to make sure they are sealed tightly.

Lacing on the dodgers

To lace the dodgers in place, first tie each corner to the forward and aft stanchions, using a short piece of light line. Then, using a continuous length of line, lace the dodger onto the guard wire using a half hitch to hold it securely in place. Repeat with separate pieces of line along the other three sides.

Applying letters to the dodgers

Many boatowners choose to put their yacht's name or its sail number on the dodgers and, provided you have a piece of acrylic canvas of a contrasting colour, this is easy to do.

- First, measure the length of the dodger.
- Then, divide this measurement by the number of letters in the name or sail number, plus two more to allow for space at either end of the dodger.
- Using templates of the right size, cut the letters or numbers out of acrylic canvas and apply an adhesive tape or glue to the reverse side.
- Draw a chalk line along the dodger where you want the bottom of the letters or numbers to be aligned, before putting them on the canvas. You should then stand back to check that it looks okay prior to securing the characters in place.
- When sewing them permanently in place, use a 4mm (5/32in) zigzag stitch to sew along each edge. This will not only look smart, but will prevent the raw edges from fraying. The edges can also be heat-sealed before stitching using a flame to prevent fraying.

Above **Use half hitches to lace the dodger onto the guard wires.**

Left **Use a contrasting coloured canvas if you want to apply the boat's name or sail number to the dodger.**

Lee cloths

Simple and easy to make, lee cloths are a very useful piece of canvaswork to have on board. They can prevent your gear or crew ending up sprawled on the cabin sole, and possibly prevent a few bruises, too!

Once you have mastered dodgers, lee cloths will be very easy to make, as they are essentially the same. The only differences are that they have fewer eyelets and they need an additional piece of canvas attached to the bottom edge, which is then permanently fitted to the bunk tops, underneath the bunk cushion.

Measuring for lee cloths
Start by measuring the space. Most lee cloths do not run the entire length of a bunk, as you want to allow space for air to circulate around the occupier's head and feet, as well as to avoid any feelings of claustrophobia. Therefore, make the lee cloth a good 30cm (1ft) shorter at either end than the length of the bunk. The exception would be if the bunk is to be used by a small child whom you wish to contain, then it would be more appropriate to use a full-length lee cloth. Don't forget to add an extra 50mm (2in) to the length, however, for the hems.

The height of the lee cloth should be around 460mm (18in), but to this you need to add on extra material to account for the piece that will be attached to the bunk top and the height of the bunk cushion, as well as 100mm (4in) for the hem. On a standard-sized bunk, this would mean that the height of the cloth required is around 790mm (31in).

Making the lee cloth
Once you have decided how much material you require, next decide what type of cloth to use. Although lee cloths don't need to be as hard-wearing as canvaswork on deck, they do need to be made of a material that won't go mouldy, as they will spend most of their working life underneath a bunk cushion where ventilation may be poor. Acrylic canvas is therefore a preferred choice because of its resistance to mildew.

Below **Measure the length of the bunk. The lee cloth should be 60cm (2ft) shorter than the total length.**

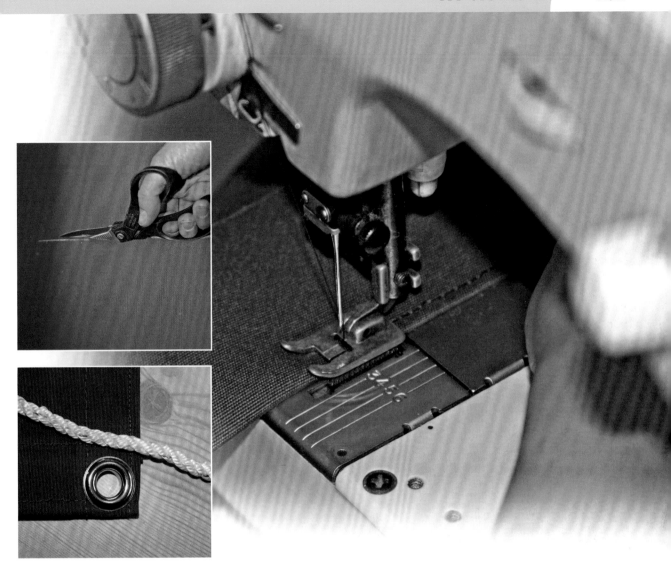

Top **Cut the canvas with a pair of sharp scissors or hot knife. Don't forget to add extra for the hem.**

Top right **Sew along the length of the hem, 6mm (¼in) away from the fold.**

Above **Insert an eyelet into the two top corners of the lee cloth to attach it to the deckhead.**

To make the lee cloth, proceed as follows:

☸ First, cut the canvas out to the required size, double checking that you've left enough extra for the hem.

☸ Hem the top and sides of the lee cloth with a double-rubbed hem. To do this, fold up 50mm (2in) along one edge, crease to create a solid fold and then sew along its length, 6mm (¼in) away from the fold.

☸ Next, fold 12mm (½in) of the raw edge of the canvas underneath and sew along its length, 6mm (¼in) from the new fold.

☸ Repeat along the two side edges.

☸ Put eyelets on the two top corners of the lee cloth (see page 84), to allow you to attach the lee cloth to the deckhead with a sturdy line.

Lee cloths 2

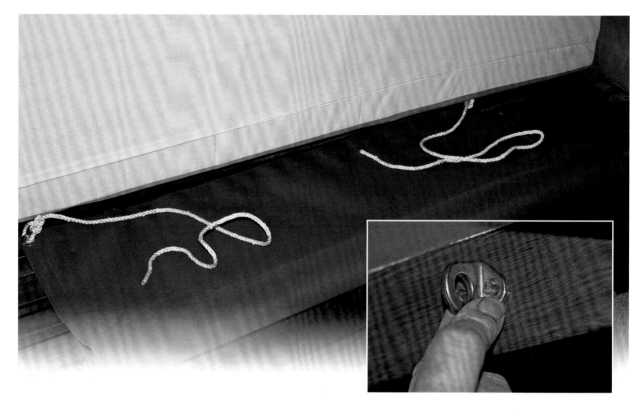

Attaching the lee cloth to the bunk

Once three sides of the lee cloth have been completed, and the eyelets put in, it is time to consider how it will be attached to the bunk. This is usually done by screwing the bottom section of the cloth directly onto the bunk top.

- ✪ Start by sewing a double-rubbed hem on the bottom edge of the lee cloth.
- ✪ It is a good idea to reinforce the area that is to be screwed down, and the easiest way to do this is to insert a strip of webbing into the pocket of the hem. Choose webbing that is slightly narrower than the width of the hem pocket, and once you have inserted it, run a line of stitching along its length to hold it in place.

Above **When you don't need the lee cloth it can be stowed underneath the bunk cushion.**

Inset **Once you have checked carefully for the correct position, fasten the eyebolt or pad eye to the appropriate beam or place on the deckhead.**

- ✪ Lift the bunk cushion and place the bottom edge of the lee cloth on the bunk top, so that the rest of it drapes over the bunk front and onto the floor.
- ✪ Then, place a 12mm (½in) wooden batten over the bottom length of the lee cloth and carefully drill and screw through them at 150mm (6in) intervals into the bunk top to hold the lee cloth in place.
- ✪ Once the bunk cushion has been replaced, the lee cloth will wrap neatly around its outer edge.

Above **Tie a length of rope to the eyelet using a bowline or round turn and two half hitches.**

Securing the top of the lee cloth

The top of the lee cloth should be secured using line attached from the eyelets to eyebolts or strap eyes on the deckhead or deck beams. Make sure the eyebolts are in an accessible place, which can be reached by the bunk's occupant without too much difficulty.

Attach the line to the lee cloth using a bowline or a round turn and two half hitches, and then run it through the eyebolt. The best knot for securing the lee cloth is the trucker's hitch, as this will allow you to tension it sufficiently to take the weight of someone or something leaning on it. If the line is too slack, there is a risk that the occupant will fall out.

When it's not in use, the lee cloth can be neatly folded away under the bunk cushion.

Below **The finished lee cloth will help prevent the bunk's contents from falling on the cabin sole when the boat heels over.**

TIP

Flexible webbing or line can be tricky to feed into a canvas hem pocket. An easy way to do this is to attach a large safety pin to one end of the webbing and then feed it into the hem pocket. By gently easing the safety pin along, and gathering the material as you go, you should be able to feed it through without too much difficulty.

Domestic

The ideal galley

There is no such thing as the 'perfect' galley, as every boat is something of a compromise, but some simple alterations to the galley may make a large difference to how effective this vital area can be, especially for long passages or when living aboard.

Most long-distance sailors will tell you that one of the biggest problems with a yacht's galley is the lack of storage and accessible work surface. Galley space is often at a premium, but there are some clever ways to optimise the areas available and give them multiple uses.

The galley

It's fairly easy to add a bit more functionality with fold-out work surfaces, more equipment and better use of the space available. Alternatively, you could modify the galley at a structural level and relocate ovens and fridges, or build in new cupboards. Keep in mind that you should be able to move between the galley and the cockpit easily, and move safely around the galley itself, too. You can also change the shape from a linear galley, for example, to an L-shaped or U-shaped one, which provides a good surface area and is also a safe place to wedge into.

The galley will quickly get hot and steamy when in use. Make sure that the area has some sort of extraction system for smells by opening ports or an overhead hatch (or all three). A window so the cook can see out is also highly desirable. At night, the area should be adequately lit.

Above **This 1970s' galley can be stripped out to emulate the galley below by using the engine box as a countertop and relocating the sink. Other alterations could include fitting a larger, gimballed stove with an oven and adding a stylish worktop.**

Below **Good use of counter space is evident on this Hallberg-Rassy 37. Note the removable top over the cooker, infills for the sink and a pull-out cutting board. There's even a speaker overhead to keep the chef entertained.**

Above **A U-shaped galley from a 20m (67ft) Discovery. The area is well lit with high fiddles, opening ports and plenty of work surfaces. There is a safety bar across the oven and an extractor fan above. A microwave oven allows for quick meals on the go.**

Left **When refitting a yacht, the galley can be built outside the project using a flat platform as a base and precise measurements, and then reassembled aboard when convenient, saving time.**

Sinks and taps

The sink should be wide and deep, and a double sink is preferable if space allows. Sinks are best located along the centreline, making drainage easier on either tack. A foot-operated sea water tap is a good idea for general washing and for boiling vegetables. A foot pump for the fresh water tap also prevents overuse. Watermakers and water filters are now regular additions to the water system.

Gimballed stove

Ideally, the stove should be gimballed or fitted with robust retaining clamps for deep pots. The more burners it has the better, and the oven should be big enough to cook for all the crew. Marine stoves should have latches to lock the door shut. The preferred fuel for voyagers is propane, as it burns hotter and freezes at a far lower temperature than butane, but diesel stoves are also popular. Fitting an electronic shut-off to the propane bottle is a

good safety measure. A safety bar across the front of the oven and a retaining strap for the chef (see page 96) are also wise additions.

Hardwearing countertops

Countertops should be made of a hardwearing surface that can withstand a hot pan. The development of honeycomb laminate has allowed the use of some attractive stone surfaces without a weight penalty. Extra space can be made with slide-out or swing-up tables, and the use of sink infills, with the reverse side holding a cutting board. Deep fiddles, removable for cleaning, will enhance the galley's functionality.

Efficient fridge-freezer

A good sized fridge-freezer is now standard equipment on larger cruising boats. Bear in mind that a top-loader loses counter space, but retains more cold air. The front loader is easier to use, but requires deep partitions inside to prevent

spillages when heeled. The fridge should be well insulated and able to operate for long periods, even with the boat out of the water.

Generous storage

The galley can be organised so that objects needed immediately are to hand, while less frequently used items, such as tins, can be located elsewhere. Ideally, absolutely everything should have a secure and dedicated space. Areas of 'dead' space can be harnessed with the use of sealed storage containers.

Good rubbish disposal

Often overlooked, a deep, sealable rubbish bin is a necessity. Bigger yachts frequently have a rubbish compactor. The back of a low-level locker door is sometimes used for a swing bin, with the lid keeping in any smells.

Gimballing the stove

In a seaway, cooking can become extremely difficult unless you have two essentials on your stove – a pair of gimbals, and a set of pot clamps. Both can be retrofitted, although gimballing may need some redesigning of the galley to allow the stove to swing freely.

A gimbal is simply an arrangement of pivots that allows an item to stay more or less level while the boat moves around beneath it. On small items, such as a steering compass or a traditional oil lamp, gimbals can be set in two planes, so the item can move freely in all directions. Some small single-burner stoves work this way. On larger cookers, the gimbals can usually only work in one plane, thus the stove is located so it can swing to port or starboard, rather than fore and aft, as a yacht will spend a lot of its time heeled when sailing.

Many marine stoves have gimbal lugs pre-installed on each side with the receptors supplied as accessories. A barrel-lock is needed to hold the stove steady when the gimballing isn't needed, and a flexible, armoured hose is a prerequisite for the gas supply.

Above **Small single-burner stoves that are fully gimballed are readily available, and are ideal for small cruisers. These also make good heavy weather stoves for larger boats with fixed cookers.**

Below **On cookers using bottled gas, a flexible armoured hose feeds in the fuel. There needs to be enough space behind the cooker for this hose to move freely.**

Below **A gimballed stove allows the cook to work safely in the galley with the yacht heeled when hard on the wind.**

If fitting a gimballed stove for the first time, allow it plenty of room to swing towards the hull. Some models are built with an angled back, to allow more rearwards movement, although this does restrict the size of the oven. Ideally, the stove should be able to swing back by 30 degrees, although some galleys have been designed to accept up to 45 degrees. This is achieved by giving the rear of the recess a suitable angle.

The lugs that support the gimbals are usually designed to prevent the cooker from jumping out, but can also be slid sideways to allow for cooker removal. On the casing there is also a lock that clamps the cooker in the upright position.

If you need gimbals, then you also need pot clamps. The most effective are made from square bar, as this keeps the clamps at right angles, and gives a better support for the locking screws.

Above **A barrel bolt is used to hold the cooker level. It has to be fairly substantial, as illustrated by this stainless steel version with a locking plate. The best position is at the front.**

Right **Square, rather than round, pot clamp rails give the best grip as they won't allow the clamps themselves to rotate up or down, and so lose purchase.**

Using a gimballed stove

Before using your gimballed stove choose a set of pots and pans that will fit comfortably. These must fit neatly over each burner, and be big enough to catch all the flame with none spilling up the sides. The handles need to be arranged so they won't snag on the sides of the work surface – or with other pots – as the stove swings. The clamps must also be able to grab the body of each pot firmly, but be quick and easy to release when needed.

If the boat rocks while cooking, there is a knack to cooking with the stove in motion. While the gimbals counteract the rocking and prevent items falling off, additional weight on the stove requires caution. If you are using one heavy pot, this will probably be at the front, where its

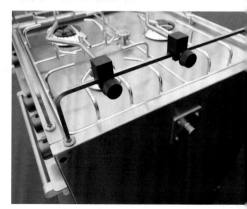

laden weight will slightly unbalance the stove. Having secured the loaded pot, watch the stove for a moment or two and see how it is sitting. Then, to compensate, fill a kettle with water and place it on one of the rearmost burners, adjusting the amount of water for an exact counter balance. This will make the stove sit more upright so it is easier to use, which is also important if you want an evenly baked result for anything in the oven. A safety clip stops the door swinging open.

TIP

Some yachtsmen fit a multiple position lock so that when the yacht is settled onto a tack the cooker can be locked off at the angle closest to the average heel on that tack. This keeps the cooking surface more or less level, with the pot clamps doing the rest of the work. It's very important, however, that the skipper warns the chef before going onto the other tack!

Galley straps

The last thing you want when cooking down below in rough weather is to lose your balance and be thrown across the boat. The fitting of simple galley straps can provide you with something to brace yourself against and keep you secure.

If your boat has a galley that extends along one side of the boat's length, it can be very difficult to keep your balance or find something to lean against when the boat is being thrown all over the place in choppy sea conditions. The solution to this problem is, however, very simple; as with the addition of one or more sets of galley straps you can provide yourself with some security.

Galley straps can be made from anything, but are essentially bands of webbing, canvas or rope that are attached via snap hooks to the galley's bulkheads or fronts, and which fit around the galley user's waist, providing them with something to brace themselves against. They can be adjustable in length to fit different crew members, easily movable so that they can be

TIP

Fit an adjuster to the galley strap, which allows it to become longer or shorter, depending on who is using it.

relocated to a different position in the galley, or part of a long strap that covers a larger section of the working area.

Below **A galley strap in use. In rough conditions galley straps can hold you in place and prevent you from losing your balance.**

Making galley straps

You can buy galley straps from most chandlers or online suppliers, but with a few materials, they are very easy to make yourself. All you need is a length of webbing or canvas, a couple of snap hooks, two or more pad eyes – the number will depend on how many locations you want the galley straps to be placed in – and a recessed adjuster, if you want to be able to shorten or lengthen the straps to fit other crew members.

The amount of time you spend in the galley will determine the width of the galley strap. For general-purpose use, 50mm (2in) heavy-duty polypropylene webbing will be sufficient, but if you intend to spend more time in the galley then a 200mm (8in) band of canvas – possibly even padded – will provide you with a bit more comfort.

To make a webbing galley strap:

☸ First, decide where you want your galley straps to be located, and then measure the length that will be required, using a piece of rope. If in doubt, make them longer than necessary. For example, for safety reasons, if the galley straps are located near a gas stove, you don't want to be held too close to a naked flame.

☸ Attach your snap hooks to either end of the webbing. If the attachment eye is of a smaller width than your webbing, then you will need to taper the webbing so that it passes cleanly through the eye without rucking up. Before cutting your webbing, make a paper template so that you know exactly how much you need to taper it. It is essential that you seal the edges of the webbing as soon as you cut them, as they

have a tendency to unravel before your eyes. Use a match or lighter to seal them.

☸ Once you have put on the snap hook, sew the two parts of the webbing together to form a secure attachment. If you are fitting an adjuster on the galley strap, put it on the webbing before attaching the second snap hook. You will also need a snap hook that is designed specifically for webbing – ie, with an eye the same width as the webbing – to allow the strap to be adjusted easily.

☸ Fit two or more pad eyes in suitable locations within the galley, either on bulkheads or galley fronts.

MAKE A GALLEY STRAP

You require only a few materials to make galley straps. Polypropylene webbing is a good material to use.

If the eye on the snap hook is of a smaller width than the webbing, you will need to taper the webbing to fit. Use a paper pattern before cutting the webbing.

After passing the webbing through the eye, stitch firmly and don't forget to seal the edges of the webbing once you have cut them. They will unravel quickly if you don't.

Attach pad eyes in several locations on the bulkheads or galley fronts for you to clip the snap hook onto.

TIP

Instead of using a match or lighter, a suitable tool to use for sealing edges is a powered fabric cutter and sealer hot knife tool, which is widely available.

Deck handholds and footholds

Adding more handholds and footholds to a deck can greatly improve safety for your crew, but they can also make the deck more functional, and even more stylish.

Just about every boat has a basic selection of handholds on deck, ranging from the pulpit and pushpit through to grab handles on the cabin top and beside the main hatch, but these aren't always enough. Sometimes they are too small, too low, or in entirely the wrong place. Similarly, the outside edge of the deck sometimes only has the slightest lip to stop the edge of a foot from slipping over the side.

Fortunately, it is very easy to bolster a boat's provision of handholds and footholds with some pre-made or DIY additions, and this is a great opportunity to add some

sculpted rails in strategic areas to facilitate everything from disembarkation to stowage. Here are some ideas that have proved their worth:

Main hatch

Handholds on each side of the companionway are often quite small, so an improvement is to make then much longer. Some designs take the handholds right down to the cockpit sole, and right up and over to run parallel with the sliding hatch. This forms a foot brace if stowing the mainsail at the boom, or while sitting on the cockpit coaming.

Mast base

If you work your halyards at the mast, then so called 'granny bars' are a popular addition. They form a static rail each side of the mast for you to brace yourself against when both hands are needed on the ropes. They can be modified to double as fender stowage or halyard attachment points, but need to be through-bolted to substantial backing plates.

Below **Tall stanchions, strategic handholds and a good toe rail are all ingredients for a safe deck to move around on.**

Right **So called 'granny bars' allow the crew to work the mast winches with both hands while fully braced. Note the fender stowage and padded backrest.**

Far left **Adding swimming pool-style handholds on the bathing platform also aids disembarkation into a dinghy. These ones are quite low, but tall ones work even better.**

Left **Putting a break into the guard wire with a gate will make boarding from amidships so much easier. Pre-made gate stanchions are readily available.**

Bathing platform

A great addition here is a handrail that sweeps up from the bathing ladder, rather like the ones you see in public swimming pools. They are easy to fit using ordinary stanchion bases. The rail can be pre-bent to suit your height, allowing not only easier bathing, but also far greater safety when climbing in or out of a pitching inflatable.

Guardrail embarkation point

Many production yachts have a continuous guardwire from bow to stern, requiring some athletic boarding. An easy cure is to add a pair of boarding posts amidships, where the hull will be nearest the pontoon. These create a gateway into the wire and also act as a handhold. Retrofit versions are readily available, and fit standard stanchion bases. They can be gated with a stainless steel chain or short sections of wire with captive hooks (pelican clips) for quick release.

Boom gallows

A boom gallows is a raised goalpost arrangement at the front of the cockpit designed to nest the boom. Made of stainless steel, it forms an ideal attachment point for horizontal rails to be taken forward before sweeping down to secure to the deck.

Sprayhood

The sprayhood (or dodger in the US) is another good place to add extra handholds, and will stop a crewman grabbing the canvas shape itself. They are often designed into the structure, but can be added with standard tube attachment fittings so they protrude clear of the structure, on top, underneath or to the side.

Toe rail

Your boat may already have a toe rail as part of the moulding, but this can be heightened by adding a capping rail in timber, or by bolting a length of attractive hardwood to the outside of the stanchions. Some owners raise their toe rails into solid bulwarks of about 100mm (4in) and fit scuppers to allow sea water to drain away. A tall bulwark helps with carrying external containers, as the bases are held firmly aboard when the decks are awash.

Right **Some serious offshore cruisers adapt the boom gallows as a fixed bracing point, and add rails that are at a good height and travel a long way forward.**

Fiddle rails

Fiddle rails stop items from sliding off work surfaces and tumbling to the floor in a seaway, but they aren't always fully effective. Redesigning your fiddle rails, or making them detachable, can greatly improve their functionality.

Whenever you have a flat surface that is liable to tilt there will be some sort of barrier around it to hold everything back from falling off the edge. These 'fiddle rails' are often very deep, and on many boats are fixed into place and shaped to double as a convenient handhold.

However, a deep fiddle can be a bit awkward when sitting at a dining table, as it forms a lip over which you have to reach to use your cutlery and makes an uncomfortable ridge when resting your forearms.

Detachable fiddles

Many owners fit a detachable fiddle rail to areas they want to be able to use unencumbered when the boat is relatively steady, but where a fiddle rail will be useful at sea. There are several ways to achieve this, the simplest being to set short lengths of copper pipe into the table with matching shanks made from cut-off screws, set into the fiddle itself. Other methods involve using a long bar of stainless steel, bent at each end to form a long loop, again to catch any larger items that roll across the surface.

Voyaging yachtsman Larry Pardy designed a system of fiddles that bolt into the edge of the table or work surface, with a captive nut in the woodwork. When you want to fit the edge on the fiddle, simply line up the holes with your hardwood fiddle and screw the slotted, countersunk bolt in.

Fixed fiddles

Increasingly popular on long-distance yachts are deep fiddles that are gently curved, and often with a groove on the inside to act as a fingerhold. These look as if they are

Below **Deep fiddles are a great bonus in a seaway, but some owners like to be able to detach them in harbour.**

Left **Laminated fiddles and grab handles are made using a series of thin strips of wood. The craftsman here is rolling epoxy onto new strips while another set is curing in the mould.**

made from a single piece of wood, but are in fact made up of several very thin veneers of the same timber laminated together. You will require a 'former' to lay the wood against, which will replicate the basic shape of the fiddle rail prior to cosmetic finishing. This former is usually made from MDF, plywood or chipboard, with a glossy inside edge for laying up against, so a release agent can be used.

The strips of wood are coated with epoxy to seal the grain, and then painted with thickened epoxy (except the outside of the outermost strips) before being inserted into the mould. A series of long sash clamps, and lots of them, are used to pull the thin strips tightly together, expelling some of the epoxy but making the wood appear as one solid mass. Once all the strips have been added, and the glue has cured, the solid shape is removed and then sanded and routed before being varnished and fitted.

Making fiddles this way means that the wood chosen can match the rest of the interior joinery exactly. Other fixed fiddle rails can be made from pre-cut lengths of decorated trim or polished metal set in posts to various classic designs.

If you decide that fixed fiddle rails are the best way forward, making sure there is a small gap at each corner will greatly help with cleaning, as dirt can be brushed there for easy removal.

Milled fiddles

Another fixed fiddle solution when rebuilding a galley is to have the work surfaces made from a milled material such as Corian or laminated granite. These are all bespoke items,

made to measure, so the supplier will usually be able to mill the material to leave a gently sculpted edge on one side, with the additional benefit of being an integral part of the structure. Many yacht builders specify this kind of worktop as standard as it merges easily into the interior design.

Below **A Corian work surface, with the subtle fiddles carved into the edge by a milling machine, makes an unobtrusive ridge that is easy to clean.**

Simple veneers

Applying a veneer, such as teak, to plywood is not a difficult job, but requires preparation of the plywood surface and correct adhesive for best results. It is a good idea to buy veneers from a specialist supplier. Although teak is the most expensive type of veneer, it is used for a traditional look.

The first step is to build whatever it is you are planning to veneer – in this case it is a table for the wheelhouse of a motorboat. A simple rectangular design motif is incorporated into all the veneered panels, which makes this a little more complicated; it could almost be called marquetry, but it's still very straightforward.

Below **The tabletop with its first coat of varnish, but basically finished.**

Laying the central motif

This teak veneer comes in 150mm (6in)-wide strips with machined edges, making it easy to butt up against a long edge. The first stage is to outline the position of the design motif on the ply panel. Then mark each piece of veneer and cut it to length using either scissors or a craft knife and straight edge, whichever you feel more comfortable with. It is a good idea to number each piece as you go along to ensure that you put it in the correct place. Once you have cut all the pieces, lay them in position to check they fit properly.

Apply adhesive to the ply within the marked area, followed by an application onto each of the cut veneers. For boat interiors, a thixotropic contact adhesive is recommended. This is a gel that provides a permanent bond when applied to a clean, abraded plywood surface and the veneer. Leave the surfaces to become touch dry for a few minutes, and then carefully place the first veneer into position, followed by each subsequent piece in turn. Use a roller to ensure the veneer is properly bedded down onto the adhesive. You can use a

fibreglass roller, but on larger areas a vinyl flooring roller is a better choice as it covers a bigger area more quickly.

Use a palm sander to both smooth the veneer surface as well as to force it more firmly into the adhesive. If there are any tiny gaps between the veneer pieces, the dust from the sander fills them and is forced into the adhesive. Now you can accurately trim the veneer using a straight edge and craft knife. After trimming, lift the excess veneer with a sharp chisel as the adhesive will not be fully cured for 24 hours.

The next stage involves using teak iron-on edging. Cut a 45-degree angle for the first corner. You can use vinyl trimming snips with built-in guides, but a protractor and craft knife are just as accurate. Carefully position the corner, and apply a domestic iron (set on a medium heat) to the end of the edging, pressing down to melt the adhesive and hold it in place. Remember to always follow the direction of grain.

Before gluing down the entire length, cut the second corner after carefully marking its position against the corner of the rectangle. You can now heat and fix the remaining length, followed by the other three sides. Once the finished central design is ready, you can begin to place, glue and position the rest of the panels.

Check the length of the first panel and mark the veneer before cutting it to length. Apply adhesive to the back of the veneer and to the face of the ply, and position the first piece making sure it fits along the edges before attaching and rolling it down.

LAYING THE VENEER

After marking out the design on the table, cut each piece of veneer to shape.

Apply adhesive to the marked area as well as to the back of each piece of veneer.

Once you have carefully placed the design motif into position, roll it down using any type of roller. A standard GRP laminating roller is being used here.

Once the rectangular section is ready the edge can be applied using iron-on edging. Begin by cutting the shape for the first corner.

With the iron set on medium heat, bond the entire length of the edging to the tabletop.

Cut the veneer piece to length and, after applying adhesive to both surfaces, lay the veneer into position around the design.

Simple veneers 2

Repeat for the rest of the panels, making sure that they are tightly butted together along the edges and rolled down onto the ply.

Turn the tabletop over and carefully trim any excess veneer from the edges of the table using a craft knife with a new blade to ensure it does not pull the veneer during the cutting process. Then sand the entire surface smooth to embed the veneer.

You also need to sand the edges of the veneered panel, taking care to keep them square with the front face. Sand the edges by hand to avoid the possibility of damaging the delicate edges of the main panel pieces. Apply iron-on edging all round the edge. Trim any excess edging from the underside and face side of the panel, taking extreme care when trimming the face side.

Varnishing and waxing

You can now apply the varnish to keep the finished surface clean. The varnish finish protects the veneer and the underlying adhesive, so make sure you properly coat the finished veneer with a high-quality varnish rather than just waxing or oiling the surface to complete the job.

If you want a waxed appearance, use a satin varnish and then apply wax over that. This can provide an attractive finish as well as long-term protection. Beeswax is ideal and will give a satin finish but needs to be well rubbed in when first applying it. Beeswax can reduce the appearance of surface scratches and will give a smooth surface.

LAYING THE VENEER 2

Turn over and trim any excess veneer from the edges of the tabletop using a new blade in the knife.

Apply iron-on edging along the table edge using a domestic iron, carefully trimming it all around after it has been glued on.

Take care trimming excess off the back but even more care trimming the front!

Sand the piece, taking care not to sand through the veneer. Hand sand the edges as this is where damage could be caused.

Other veneered surfaces

The possibilities with veneer are endless. Once you have practised the technique of veneering you could, for example, make up a compartment with a rounded corner (in this case made from four pieces of plastic wastepipe), disguised by veneer.

Apply the veneer in exactly the same way as shown with the tabletop, although take care when going round the corner to ensure that each piece of veneer follows the edge of the previous piece to provide tightly butted edges.

TIP

When using iron-on edging, smooth out the edging to avoid blistering. However, blisters may still form as the edging cools. These can later be ironed out or removed by flattening the piece with a heavy object.

When gluing the veneer in place, make sure that the grain of the veneer is running in the direction you want it to before you glue it to the plywood. If you don't, you might have veneer running in four or five different directions.

The whole interior of a cabin or wheelhouse can be veneered in teak, perhaps repeating the design motif, but on the surface of the veneered panels rather than flush, as on the table. The overall effect can be very upmarket at a minimal cost.

TIP

These techniques are only recommended for boat interiors and not for external parts of a boat, which are exposed to weather.

Right **Veneered panels, including the rectangular motif on the surface of the veneer and the finished rounded corner.**

Below **A neat idea for easy rounded corners. Cut a piece of plastic wastepipe lengthways into four quadrants and then use these for the corners.**

Charcoal heater

This is the easiest form of on-board heating to install – on many boats the job can be done in little more than a couple of hours. A charcoal heater will produce up to 1.5kW of heat and needs minimal servicing as it has no moving parts and does not require any electrical power.

Safe positioning

Start by identifying a safe location for the heater. Both the body and flue can get dangerously hot, so it should be positioned where someone won't accidentally fall against them in a rough sea, or inadvertently attempt to use the flue as a grab rail.

If possible, locate the unit as close to the floor as you can so some heat reaches your feet. This may not, however, be feasible on many small boats where the heater is usually bulkhead-mounted above bunk level. In this case, there should be at least 300mm (12in) of flue between the heater body and the deckhead.

Always follow the manufacturer's advice when fitting the heater – apparently similar models may have small but important differences that affect the amount of additional heat shielding that needs to be fitted.

Most recommend either a metal plate or ceramic tiles as a heat shield for the bulkhead behind the heater. In addition, there needs to be a further insulating barrier between this and the bulkhead, such as 25mm (1in) thick calcium silicate board, plus a further 10mm (3/8in) air gap.

Solid fuel heaters are fairly heavy, so bolt the unit securely through the bulkhead. In the UK, there is now a (voluntary) British Standard specification for installing solid fuel stoves, which should be consulted.

Right **Charcoal heaters are a traditional way of heating a boat. Today they can still be fitted as relatively inexpensive and self-contained units.**

Through-deck fitting

Although it can make the chimney reluctant to draw strongly, an advantage of the narrow diameter flue used for charcoal heaters (the outside diameter is typically 25mm/1in) is that heat travels relatively slowly up the flue. This has a double advantage in that there's less heat loss to the environment and the issue of heat-sealing between the deck fitting and the structure of the boat is less of a problem than for heaters with a wider flue.

Right **A charcoal heater can be the quickest and most cost-effective way to install heating on board.**

Different models of heater use different styles of through-deck fitting for the flue. At the point the flue passes through the deck, some have a second circular section of pipe outside the flue pipe that helps to shield the deck from the worst of the heat. Others, don't have this and need the flange that's screwed to the deck to be mounted on a heat-resistant pad of about 10mm (³⁄₈in) thickness. If the deck is cambered or curved, a pad that is shaped to match the profile of the deck will be essential, whatever the design of the through-deck fitting. You should use heat-resistant sealant on all the joints.

SAFETY TIP

Although a well-installed charcoal heater is a safe option because it expels combustion gases through a chimney, carbon monoxide poisoning is a possibility with any kind of open-flame heater. A carbon monoxide (CO) alarm is therefore an important safety precaution and should be installed and tested regularly.

Above **On deck the chimney must be properly sealed against water ingress.**

Above **The deck fitting should allow for a gap between the chimney and the boat's structure to allow heat to dissipate. The deck seal does not allow water to penetrate down below.**

Hot air diesel heating

There is a variety of choice of heating systems on board, from solid fuel heaters to gas and diesel heaters and each system has its own advantages. A more complex system of central heating uses hot air provided by a diesel heater, which requires an exhaust outlet. The heat generated runs through ducts, to several locations in the boat.

While hot air heating is very effective, it is also the most complex type of heating to install, although still well within the scope of the DIY boatowner. Marine kits have improved greatly over the years, making the system as easy as possible to fit. The kits supply everything down to the cable and pipe clips, as well as the screws for attaching them.

Below **Cable wiring looms being run through the ducting to the heater control position.**

Exhaust installation

Having selected the installation position for the heater, the first job is to install the exhaust outlet, beginning by marking its position on the inside of the hull.

Next drill a small pilot hole through the hull to indicate the position of the fitting on the outside. Using a bevel set to the angle of the exhaust fitting, enlarge the pilot hole set to the angle indicated by the bevel. Using a hole saw, make a hole to suit the size of the exhaust fitting,

allowing for tolerance. Using the bevel to double check the angle, complete the hole. Check the fitting to make sure the flange of the exhaust fitting sits flush to the hull, and mark the holes for the securing bolts onto the masking tape before drilling them in place.

Apply silicone sealant to both the flange of the exhaust fitting and the hull to ensure the joint is watertight. Place the exhaust fitting in position. Tighten the bolts and wipe off any excess silicone with a paper towel.

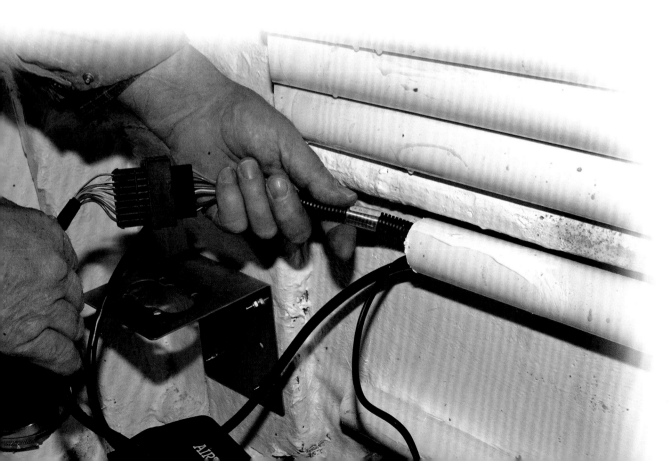

INSTALLING THE EXHAUST

As the exhaust fitting is set at an angle, use a bevel to set the drill at the corresponding angle.

Drill the hole for the exhaust fitting at the correct angle.

Tighten the bolts then wipe away any excess silicone with paper towels before it cures.

Heater and wiring loom

The next step is to install the heater, which may require a wooden base to be bonded to the hull for the mounting bracket to bolt onto. Thread the nuts and bolts through the base prior to bonding it to the hull and protect the threads with masking tape. Now bolt the bracket onto the pad ready for the subsequent installation of the heater.

The next task is to pass the cable wiring loom through the boat. If you have ducting running along the inside of the hull this is ideal, but most boats will not be equipped with such luxuries, so you will have to find the best way through and then protect the cables with cable trunking (plastic protection). Once the cables appear at the control position, pull them through ready for connecting to the heater control on the main panel.

Cut an aperture in the main panel so the plug on the end of the control loom can be passed through, followed by the cable. This will enable you to connect the plug on the cable from the control to the socket on the loom. Then clip the cable into place.

Run the 12-volt power cable through the bilge where you can clip it out of harm's way. Terminate the cables with crimp terminals and plug them onto the two fused connections. You can now place the heater unit onto the mounting bracket, tighten the nuts onto the fixing studs and connect the loom plugs and sockets.

Below **The heater is bolted onto the bracket and the wiring looms connected.**

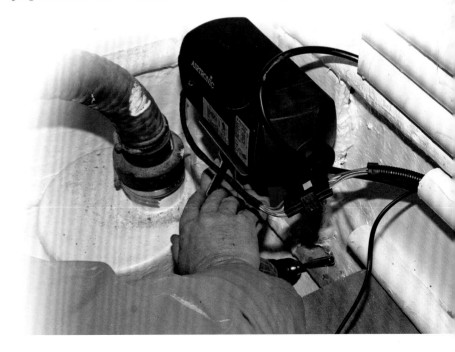

Hot air diesel heating 2

Hot air ducting

The hot air outlets are to be installed into the wheelhouse in this case. Using a hole saw that is slightly oversized for the outlet fittings, cut the two outlet holes in the front of the bunk at each end to spread the flow of air. Cut two pieces of ducting to length, then clip each of them to an outlet fitting and pass each one through its hole in the front of the bunk. Then screw each outlet into position. Attach both outlets to a 'Y' connector beneath the bunk, allowing warm air to flow to each outlet simultaneously. Run the trunking along the side of the hull up to the heater unit along a pre-planned route, and clip it to the heater unit. The pre-planned route makes it a much easier task. Without one, running the trunking can be the most arduous part of the job.

Fuel system and pump installation

The fuel pump comes with a rubber-mounting bracket that pushes over the pump body and holds the pump firmly in place, while also cutting down on vibration. The fuel tank fitting is one of those clever items that can be installed from outside the tank and will come with a set of instructions. The cutaway on the flange of the pick-up pipe allows this to slip through the hole in the tank and the instructions should indicate how the fitting is installed.

Screw a simple bracket to two of the hull stringers (attachment points) as a base for mounting the pump and, once the pump is in position (with the cable connector on the upside of the pump), you can connect the plug on the loom. You must run the pipework from the tank to the pump and on to the heater in an upwards direction to

Below **One of the heater outlets together with trunking being installed into the front of the bunk.**

Right **Pump fitted and pipework connected.**

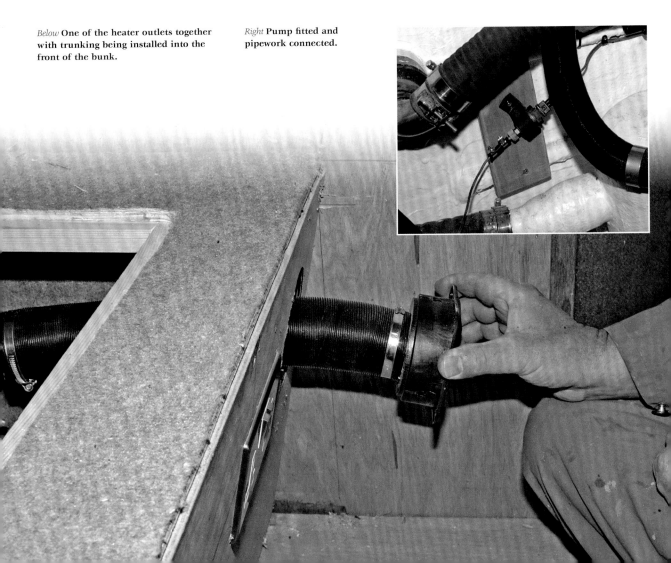

ensure that air bubbles cannot become trapped anywhere in the pipe-run. This means carefully choosing the position of the pump to ensure there is a smooth rise to the piping.

You can now connect the piping to the heater unit using one of the short lengths of hose and clips supplied, and also onto the pump. At the tank end, you would generally use a compression fitting (a threaded plumbing connector), assembling it in the normal way, taking care not to overtighten it and distort the olive (a brass or copper seal around the pipe that makes a leak-free fitting).

Ducting insulation

It is important to insulate the ducting so as to prevent heat being lost through its walls. You can use various types of insulation, but it is best to use purpose-made duct/pipe lagging purchased on a roll. Wrap the insulation around the ducting so there are no gaps anywhere, then cut a length of polythene and wrap that around the insulation, making sure that it does not touch the ducting because it gets hot. Finally, secure the polythene with duct tape. Press the start button and stay warm!

Above top **Tightening the compression fitting from the diesel tank to the pump pipework.**

Above **The completed heating system, with insulated trunking running neatly along the inside of the hull.**

Inset **Finally, testing the system to see that it works!**

SAFETY TIP

Keep all systems in good order and repair, with regular visual checks. Ensure the boat is well ventilated in case of leaks. Carbon monoxide (CO) is without smell or taste so it can go undetected. Whatever type of diesel heater you install, always fit a CO alarm in case something goes wrong (see page 107).

Diesel cooker

Although liquid petroleum gas (LPG) is safe and convenient when used properly, some boatowners worry about having a gas system on board. If your boat runs on diesel, you can use the boat's fuel supply for cooking. One advantage of diesel is that it is readily available around the world.

There are various forms of diesel cooker, from the drip-feed types that operate in a similar way to the old-fashioned 'Primus' stove, to the latest ceramic hob types, which look similar to a modern electric hob.

You first need to remove the old gas oven and hob and think about modifying the galley to suit your new equipment. The amount of work required to do this, however, will depend upon the old equipment and how it was installed. Check how well your new installation fits into your galley space. You will need a direct fuel feed to the cooker from the fuel tank and will have to insert exhaust outlets above the waterline.

Installing the exhausts

Exhausts can be run a maximum of approximately 4m (13ft) from the cooker, and it is important to keep the outlets as far above the waterline as possible. A substantial curve in the pipe ('swan neck') is also needed to prevent water coming into the system. For this installation, the exhaust had to run from the galley into the wheelhouse to achieve a height above the waterline. The exhaust runs through holes cut in the half bulkheads from the cooker to the outlet positions and through holes cut in the hull.

Below **This diesel cooker replaced the old gas oven and hob and is now ready for some heavy duty cooking.**

If you need to cut holes in the hull, use a bead of waterproof sealant on both sides of the cork gasket to ensure a watertight seal on the exhaust outlets when bolted in. Wipe off any excess sealant with paper towels and methylated spirit.

Installing the fuel feeds

The oven and hob need their own dedicated fuel supply direct from the diesel tank, whether it is the main engine fuel tank or a small auxiliary tank. In this installation, the feed is from the main tank. The fuel piping specified is a 3mm (1⁄8in)-diameter copper tubing and one run is sufficient to feed both the oven and the hob, with a tee at the galley end to allow both units to be connected. The maximum run for fuel piping is 8m (26ft), unless the system is gravity fed (downward pipes).

If the tanks are mounted higher than the oven or hob, you should fit a solenoid valve at the tank end to make sure fuel cannot run into the units when not being used. The valve switches on automatically with the hob or oven so there is no need for any additional switches. In this installation, the tops of the tanks were higher than the galley so the solenoid valve was installed into this system.

Right **Place the new hob in position to ensure it will sit on the edges without any additional filling in. This hob will have a brushed stainless steel cover to fill the space taken up by the old hob.**

EXHAUST INSTALLATION

You may need to cut holes in the partition to allow the exhausts to be run through to the exhaust outlet positions.

Drill holes in the hull for the exhaust outlets, with the internal ply sheath cut open to allow room for the 'swan necks'.

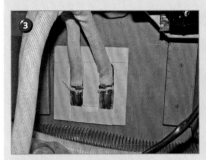
Connect the exhaust pipework, covered in a sheath of heat-resistant insulation.

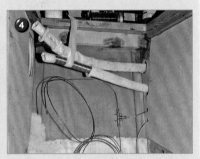
The exhaust piping for hob and oven ready for connection to the appliances. The fuel feed from the solenoid valve on the tank runs into a tee piece.

Diesel cooker 2

Run the fuel piping through to the galley end and connect it using compression fittings at the tee. At the same time, also run through the cable controlling the solenoid valve. At the tank end, mount a new fuel pick-up pipe into the top of the tank incorporating the solenoid valve and optional fine filter, and connect the piping. Use clips to support both the fuel piping and exhaust throughout their length.

Below **The solenoid valve mounted on the engine service tank.**

Below bottom **The compartment lined with heat-insulation board. The oven-mounting bracket can also be seen.**

Below right **The front clamp is fitted onto the oven to complete its installation.**

Preparing the heat-resistant housing for the oven

Because of the heat generated by the oven you need to insulate the housing with fire-resistant board. This is available from builders' merchants and is generally used for insulation around wood burning stoves and ranges. When the hob is mounted above the oven the heat from the oven must be prevented from warming the underside of the hob, otherwise the built-in overheat protection will switch the hob off.

The first job is to build in a shelf for the oven to sit on and then paint it prior to fitting the oven. A ventilation opening in the shelf also assists airflow. Measure the position for the cooker rear mount and screw the mount in place. Place the rear feet of the oven into the mount.

Power cables and solenoid

The size of cable required will depend on the length of the run – for example 4mm ($5/32$in) has been used for a maximum run of 4m (13ft). The cables are run from the hob and oven housing through to the fuse board ready for connecting. The hob and oven are prewired separately with plugs and sockets to allow easy connection and disconnection.

As both the hob and oven operate the fuel cut-off solenoid (a sensor that switches off the fuel if there is a leak), the solenoid requires a relay switch in the circuit to allow them to operate independently. This can be mounted in any position to allow convenient connection of the solenoid operating feeds. The relay control current from the hob and

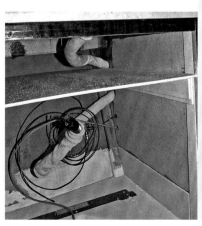

oven is via a prewired plug. (The solenoid power supply can be fed from either the hob or the oven, whichever is more convenient.)

Installing the oven

The controls for the oven and hob are mounted remotely in any chosen position. Before putting the oven and hob into place the control connections are plugged into their appropriate sockets. For this installation the controls are mounted on the front of the galley above the oven. The simple brushed stainless steel panel was made up by a local engineering company.

With the oven standing in place the first connection to be made is the power lead. Next fit the exhaust and securely tighten the hose clip. The fuel piping can then be connected. With the oven set up, slide the fireboard, which divides the hobs from the oven, into place. The final job on the oven is to fit the front clamp, which locates onto the front feet.

Installing the hob

The hob is secured with brackets bolted onto each side with further bolts screwed up under the worktop. Once the hob is in position, the corners are marked so that self-adhesive rubber seal strips can be fitted and the hob mounting brackets fitted and tightened followed by the exhaust and fuel connections. Finally, the control panel connections are plugged in and the panel is screwed into position. Care is needed not to catch the wiring between the cabinet and the panel during the final fitting.

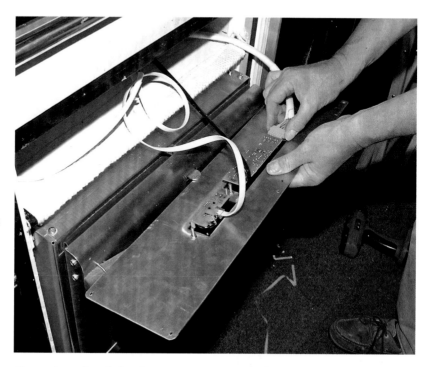

Above top **Apart from fitting the stainless steel cover, the hob installation is almost complete.**

Above **Oven and hob controls connected into the loom before fitting the front panel.**

Fridge and cool box

Both a fridge and a cool box will keep food and drinks fresh, but which one to choose may depend on space and budget. Perhaps you want to replace an older fridge, while modifying the area where it is to be fitted. This is quite a similar job to fitting a fridge into a locker for the first time. The cool box is an alternative cooler when galley space is short.

While the design of a fridge and its components has improved greatly in recent years, the amount of electricity it uses still concerns many owners. You will need to include a dedicated battery with its own split charging system to avoid putting additional strain on the main battery banks. If you want maximum storage space, you should consider a model with an external compressor (the motor and pump). This means the equipment layout must be decided on before starting the work, including the runs for the pipework and cables. If overall space on board is tight, it may be better to opt for an inbuilt compressor.

Fridge and compressor installation

The equipment used in this installation consists of the fridge unit itself (Vitrifrigo), the compressor, a 70Ah battery and a DC-DC charger (which could equally well be a voltage sensitive relay) for providing a split charge feed.

TIP

A 15-amp fuse is required in the main positive feed to the fridge. As the fridge runs from its own battery, a dedicated single fuse holder is fitted onto the fuse board adjacent to the new isolating switch.

Below **The new fridge fits perfectly into its modified space.**

INSTALLING A FRIDGE

The main parts of the installation: fridge unit, compressor, battery, DC-DC charger (to charge one DC battery from another).

The fridge compartment prepared and ready to accept the new fridge.

Pipework is run through the boat to the compressor.

Connecting the compressor pipework to the compressor itself.

Dedicated fridge battery mounted next to the main batteries.

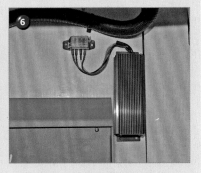

The DC-DC charger mounted and ready to connect.

To make sure the new fridge will fit, carefully measure the installation space. You will need various ventilation holes in the mounting area to allow the fridge to operate properly. Before you install the fridge, connect any electrical feeds. Once positioned and secured, cut holes through the locker bulkheads for the compressor pipework to run to the compressor mounted nearby. Next, connect the pipework from the fridge to the corresponding connections on the compressor before tightening it.

As you tighten each coupling, you will hear a slight hiss of gas as the stop valve opens before the coupling is fully tightened. This helps to blow out any remaining dirt in the coupling. Finally, fit the fridge into place.

Split charge system

The split charge feed ensures the fridge can't ever run down the main battery banks. To include a split charge system you need to assemble a battery box, supported on an engine compartment stiffener and bolted to the side of the main battery box. The split charge module is a self-contained unit that connects between the main battery bank and fridge battery, and begins charging when the main batteries are receiving enough charge to raise the voltage level so it can cut in.

Fridge and cool box 2

Cool box installation

If there is no room in the galley for a fridge then a cool box makes a viable alternative. For this installation, we bolted a large ice chest onto the top deck and fitted it with a supercool unit.

The simplest way to cool the box is to use a thermoelectric cooler unit. These small, self-contained, fully electronic coolers depend on the Peltier effect for their cooling operation. In simple terms this means that when an electric current is passed through the junction of two dissimilar conductors, it will either heat or cool the point of contact between them. Using this basic principle, very efficient cooling units have been produced requiring no gases or moving parts other than two long-life fans.

As with any fridge or freezer, the key to good performance is the thickness of the insulation, and the larger the capacity of the box, the thicker the insulation should be.

Installing the unit

The first step when fitting the unit is to mark the cut-out on the side of the box as near to the top as possible. Then, cut out the hole carefully, ensuring the jigsaw blade is kept square to the side of the box.

Depending on the thickness of the box, you may need to make an angled cut (chamfer) of 45 degrees to allow an easy airflow through the hotside cooling fins on the outside. It is sensible to seal the raw edge of the insulation using a flexible marine adhesive, once the cutaway is completed. Check the fit of the cooler before sealing.

Left **A large ice chest is used as the basis for the cool box.**

Left **The supercool unit along with a control panel, gasket and electrics.**

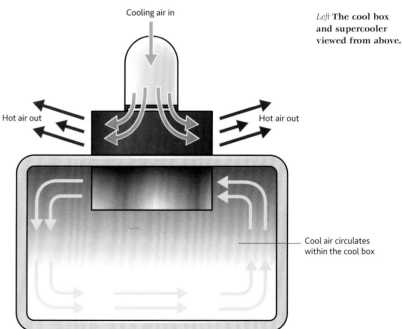

Left **The cool box and supercooler viewed from above.**

Cooling air in

Hot air out

Hot air out

Cool air circulates within the cool box

Install the unit from inside the box and secure it with four screws. The soft rubber gasket on the back of the cooler ensures a good seal between the box and the cooler unit. (If the inner skin is too thin to accept screws, you can use nuts and bolts instead, but be careful not to crush the skins together). From the outside, you can see the cutaways to allow a proper flow of air.

Unit protection

Although an installation may not require additional external cooling, it must be protected from the elements. To provide a flow of cool air, the warm side hose coupling is used to allow an intake hose to be fitted. Tumble dryer hose from a local DIY store can be used for this. The hose not only lets cool air in, but it also prevents warm air being recirculated into the unit.

The protective cover for the unit should enable hot air to escape, for example a stainless steel louvre vent on each side. The cool air intake hose protrudes through the bottom, providing a protected flow of cool air in with no possibility of recycling hot air.

Keeping cool

For the installation to operate well, warm air needs to disperse from the hot side of the cooler. The hot side requires a free flow of air, and where the unit is built into an enclosed locker, cooling air must be provided to expel warm air. This may require an additional small fan to move air through the locker, although a well-ventilated locker with large vents top and bottom should provide enough natural airflow. The only sure way is to try it and then decide whether fan cooling is needed.

To keep the unit working at peak efficiency, keep the airflow pathways clean and unobstructed, free from dust. Computer fans are cheap and quiet in operation and are often all that is required for an air-circulation boost.

INSTALLING THE COOLER UNIT

The cut-out in the cool box for mounting the cooler unit.

The cut-out edges are sealed with a flexible polyurethane sealant.

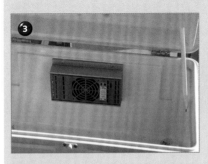

The self-contained supercool unit is installed from inside the box. In effect, it is a heat pump that transfers heat from one side of the unit to the other.

The chamfered edges of the outside of the cut-out, allowing a full flow of air over the cooling fins. The cool air-in hose prevents hot air from the outer fins entering the box.

TIP

Keep in mind that the most important elements of keeping the fridge cool are the amount of insulation and the condition of the seal on the door or lid. A top-opening lid helps to keep the cool air within a fridge, although a front-opening door with shelves inside may be quicker to use and less cool air will be lost from the inside.

Air conditioning

Basking under a hot sun, the temperature inside a boat can rapidly rise, especially if it has a lot of windows. However, air-conditioning units are now so compact that even the smallest of cruisers can fit one.

In today's market, there is a wide choice of compact air-conditioning units that can be fitted to craft as small as 8m (26ft) making venturing into the hottest cruising areas not just comfortable, but positively enjoyable too.

Most marine air-conditioning units use sea water as a heat sink (heat exchanger), and the cooling process not only lowers the temperature, but also strips a lot of the moisture out of the air too, reducing the humidity and preventing mildew and the growth of mould.

While portable battery-operated units are available, most cruising boats fit a more powerful self-contained unit. All the major components are attached to one basic chassis, which can be installed under a bunk or settee, or in a locker. Usually, one unit is required for each cabin, but to save cost or space the air can be ducted into two or more cabins if necessary.

To choose the right unit, you need to know the British Thermal Units (BTUs) required to cool the cabin space. Used in different countries, one thermal unit is equivalent to around 1,055 joules. There are several different formulas for calculating BTUs, but one, used by Dometic, a US marine company is as follows:

Divide your boat up into three basic load areas:

1 Below decks: Where the cabin slopes in towards the keel and there are very few windows.
2 Mid-deck: Areas above the waterline where there are a few shaded windows.

3 Upper deck: Areas with large glass windows and direct sunlight.

✪ Measure each cabin and living space to give you the total floor area in square metres for the deck. Use the 'mid-deck' only for smaller boats.

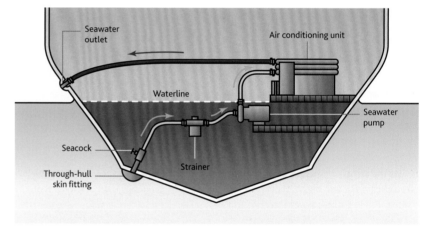

Above **A diagram showing the through-hull skin fitting for the inlet sea water below the waterline which is connected to the seacock, strainer and sea water pump.**

The sea water outlet through-hull skin fitting is for draining sea water and condensation and is sited between 100–200mm (4–8in) above the waterline.

Right **A typical fixed air conditioning unit in place, suitable for a larger vessel. These units need a solid base, AC power (DC units use a built-in inverter) and good drainage.**

Left **The outlet grills should be placed as high as possible in the cabin. Aiming the cold air at the deckhead will help to displace the warm air and aid convection. The average distance travelled of a forced cold air draught is 2–3m (8–10ft).**

Below left **The temperature control panel is usually very neat, and can be set positioned conveniently in the cabin.**

- Decide which type of climate you will be cruising in, either temperate (air temperature maximum 27°C/80°F) or tropical (air temperature exceeds 27°C/80°F).
- Determine the right 'factor' to apply. Typical factors for a temperate environment would be: 60 (below decks) 90 (mid-deck) 120 (above deck). Tropical factors are 80, 120 and 150 respectively.
- Multiply the factor by the floor area in square metres to find the BTU, then add 10–15 per cent to the total, but no more.
- The final calculation will be: Square metres x Factor = xBTUs. xBTUs x 10% = Y xBTUs + Y = total BTUs.

Having totalled the BTUs required, choose the unit with the best size to match. If between models, then go for the bigger size.

Tips for fitting a basic unit
- Ensure that your generator can meet the high surge current needed when the air-con units first starts up (although modern AC units are becoming less demanding than they were).
- Air intakes should be straight back to the unit through a grill design that won't drop the pressure. Treated air should pass through a filter to stop dust clogging up the fins of the heat exchanger.

- Always ensure that the air intakes are only drawing air from inside the boat for recirculation, avoiding bilge air and engine fumes. It takes several passes over the chilled pipes to drop the air to the required temperature so the unit must be protected from receiving any hot air from directly outside.
- Keep the galley and heads compartment slightly depressurised with an extractor fan. This will help to prevent odours from being recirculated.
- The air-conditioning unit must be in direct communication with the room it is treating. If the unit is in one cabin, but treating another, a closed door between the two could cause problems with the return, unless there is a void such as a vented locker common to both cabins.

While DIY fitting is possible, professional installers will have experience of most problems you are likely to encounter, so the fitting of a reliable unit by a professional team should be very straightforward.

LED interior lighting

Over the past few years improvements in LED (light emitting diode) lighting technology, accompanied by a rapid and continued fall in price, has propelled this form of lighting from its niche position on exclusive yachts towards the mainstream.

The advantages of LED interior lighting compared to more traditional lamps include a minimal power drain (typically a 75–85 per cent saving) and improved bulb life. The power saving also means that heat output is reduced, which may be an important consideration for boats kept in hot countries.

Drawbacks are now mainly related to the upfront cost, because bulbs cost several times the price of a conventional bulb. However, that can be set against their longer lifespan, and reduced battery drain, which will prolong the life of the vessel's batteries. A more serious drawback is a small possibility of interference with other electrical equipment. This is rare, but for peace of mind it's worth the extra cost to buy from a reputable marine brand or outlet, where you know the units will have been used on many boats without problems.

Below **Improvements in LED lighting over the years have meant that LEDs now produce warm, diffuse interior lighting.**

Swapping bulbs

LED bulbs are available for almost all common light fittings produced for marine use over the past few decades, therefore it's possible to make an easy change to LED lighting without having to replace any fittings. In many cases, brighter LED bulbs are available than would have been feasible to fit in the original units.

However, it may also make sense to replace the entire unit with one designed from the outset for LEDs. These are likely to be more slimline and compact, as well as a more modern style, which can give a significant lift to the appearance of the inside of a boat that is no longer in the first flush of youth.

Warm white vs cool white

When powerful LEDs first became available for lighting, they tended to be criticised for producing a very cool and clinical blueish light. While they still found favour thanks largely to the reduced power requirements, cool white LEDs aren't conducive to creating the mellow and relaxed ambience that many boatowners seek when on board in the evening.

However, warm white bulbs, a more recent development, solved this issue and cast light very similar to that of traditional incandescent bulbs. Other colours of bulbs are also available, including red, which is ideal for use at night when under way, as it has minimal detrimental effect on night vision.

Top and above **Light is projected from all directions with warm white LED bulbs, which are direct replacements for older marine light fittings.**

TIP

LED emergency lighting

In the event of a failure of the boat's main electrical system, it's worth having a backup system of lighting on board. This can be achieved very easily with LED units. There are many small lamps sold with self-adhesive backings that can simply be stuck to a bulkhead, with a label reminding crew that they are for emergency use.

Below **When you replace your marine light fittings with an LED light, you can upgrade the existing housing to a more modern style if you wish.**

iPod

The MP3 player has revolutionised music on the move, and the iPod (the Apple version of the MP3 player) has matured into the ideal source of music for use on boats. No matter how old your current on-board stereo system is, you can always find a cheap gadget that will let you connect to your iPod.

An important advantage of using an iPod on board is that it removes the problem of CD skip in rough conditions, to which the iPod is immune. The one small drawback with this sort of player is that music can only be transferred to the iPod via a computer. However, nowadays the majority of people regularly use computers on board, so this should not be too much of a problem.

iPod options

Many boats are still equipped with cassette decks and these will play iPod music perfectly well. All that is needed is a good quality cassette adapter. Plug it into the cassette slot, press play on the cassette deck and enjoy hours of non-stop music.

Modern car stereos are designed with the iPod in mind and most now have a USB input that allows the iPod to be controlled and charged from the radio while showing track details on the display. Once the appropriate iPod holder is mounted, plug in and enjoy the music!

An alternative, much cheaper option is an adapter such as the Dension ice-Link, which is particularly suitable for boat use as it connects to the radio via the antenna socket. It is therefore compatible with all car radio stereos, no matter how old, and although it uses a modulated signal, it is totally legal as the signal is via cable rather than airborne.

Left **An iPod can be easily connected to your stereo system.**

Below **A simple cassette adapter for playing the iPod through a cassette stereo.**

More sophisticated options

The easiest gadgets for playing the iPod through the stereo need no installation at all. Simply plug in these dedicated wireless short-range FM transmitters into the base of the iPod, select a frequency on both the transmitter and the stereo, and the music is then transmitted from the iPod to the stereo.

Specific marine stereos with built-in iPod docks are now available and are particularly popular with owners of big RIBs as, being waterproof, they are designed for open cockpit installation. One model from Fusion allows iPod control from the radio and shows music details from the iPod on the display. Being a dedicated marine stereo Fusion offers several accessories to enhance sound quality such as standalone woofers and tweeters.

For owners of larger luxury vessels wanting something rather more sophisticated than a built-in stereo, they may opt for something like the brilliant Bose Acoustic Wave stereo with iPod dock. The Apple iPod dock is a simple method of connecting the iPod to stereos with standard input jack sockets, whether it is top of the range Bose or something more modest. This dock also comes with a small white remote control, which provides iPod control from the comfort of your helm seat.

Above left **A modern stereo with iPod input.**

Top **The Dension adapter plugs into the aerial socket, allowing the iPod to play through any stereo, no matter how old it is.**

Above **Fusion marine stereo with built-in iPod dock.**

Right **Top-of-the-range Bose stereo with iPod dock and remote control.**

Domestic tips

Here are a few ideas from various yachts and motorboats designed to improve the on-board comfort factor, and make full use of stowage space below. Some are manufacturer fitted, while others have been developed by experienced owners.

Rustproof gas stowage

Placing the gas bottle on a section of self-draining plastic swimming pool mat protects the bottom of the bottle from salt water corrosion and stops those ugly rust streaks.

Slide-out cool box

To avoid losing worktop space to access a top-loading freezer, why not install a well-insulated DC-powered cool box that simply slides out on rails? It can be retrofitted to most vessels and is easier to fit than a fixed fridge or freezer.

Hidden screen

If you enjoy watching TV in the saloon, but don't want the screen permanently on display, then why not hide it? One option is to hide it behind a picture – the picture simply lifts up and locks to reveal the screen, which can then swing out at any articulation.

Below left **Keeping your gas bottle clean and dry will prevent salt water corrosion and rust stains. Note also the useful tool pocket on the inside of the door.**

Bottom left **The TV screen is hidden behind a nautical picture when not in use. The picture is swung open and the screen can be manoeuvred out as required.**

Below **This top-loading pullout cool box from Hallberg-Rassy slides out from the side of the unit. It replaces a fitted unit, so saving worktop space.**

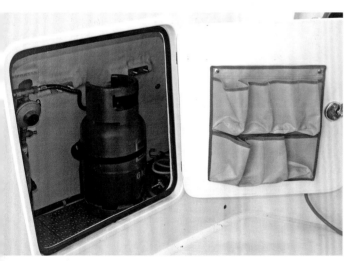

Foldaway workshop

It's handy to have an accessible work surface for general on-board jobs. One idea is to create an arrangement that hides a folding workshop or hobby area. A supporting strut is kept in the cabinet and is simply wedged down the side of the chair, allowing the work surface to fold out onto it. A full set of useful tools is kept in the cabinet for easy access.

Bottle wedge

To stop bottles rattling when the yacht is under way, you could use a set of removable dividers in rich varnished mahogany to keep them apart. Lift them out for access.

Cup stowage

Plastic glasses don't chink in bumpy weather, and by upending them on a rail a simple spring slip can keep them pushed together.

Above **When working on the boat a folding workshop is a useful space saver. This compact worktop is opened up in the saloon area, strengthened and held in position by a wooden support.**

OTHER TIPS

An ordinary wooden knife rack can be a useful item on board, especially if it is screwed discreetly to the wooden bulkhead. This means you can keep a set of knives handy, but very safely secured in a seaway. Some owners source a rack in a similar shade of wood to the rest of the galley.

Below left **Wedging bottles by using dividers is a secure way of carrying them on board.**

Below right **Keep plastic drinking glasses safely together by upending them in a rack.**

General mechanics

Mechanical skills

Using the correct techniques for each job will reduce the time the task takes to complete, minimise the risk of unnecessary damage to your boat, and significantly cut down the possibility of injury.

A good quality spanner should fit a nut or bolt head to perfection, allowing the maximum force to be used without the tool slipping off. When a tool slips, it rounds the corners of the nut, making its removal even harder. Adjustable spanners and wrenches are often expensive, and are rarely a perfect fit. They should, therefore, only be used for applications where little tightness is required – if at all.

Despite the initial appeal of these multipurpose tools, in most cases the money is better invested in a proper set of spanners and sockets. Even then, a spanner should be gripped with an open hand, so that if it does slip your knuckles will be spared injury.

The same principle applies to screwdrivers – if these don't fit the screw head exactly, there's a risk of slippage and the screw head being damaged. After low-grade tools, this is perhaps the biggest mistake made. It's wrong to think of the correct screwdriver as simply being one that's small enough to get into the slot; the screwdriver and slot should be an exact match.

Below **Don't skimp on tools. Good quality tools, of the right size for each job, will earn their initial cost many times over.**

Above **Lateral thinking can work wonders. Here, detergent is used to ease the installation of a water pump impeller.**

Far left **Avoid damaging your knuckles by holding spanners and other tools with an open grip.**

Left **As with spanners and sockets, screwdrivers should be a precise fit in the head of the screw.**

Stubborn fastenings

We've all experienced nuts and bolts that won't come apart. In the marine environment, this can be exacerbated by corrosion and a build-up of salt crystals. The first step is to dissolve any encrusted salt with warm water, allow the item to dry, and then treat it with penetrating oil. This may free the fastening enough to allow it to move, but if not, providing there are no plastic, rubber or other components that would be adversely affected, heat can be used to help free the fastening.

This technique works on the principle that heating the nut with a blowtorch will cause it to expand faster than the bolt, therefore relinquishing some of its grip. Patience may be required at this stage – if the nut moves only a fraction, allow it to cool, and then repeat the process. Once you know it will move, you can be confident that it will come apart eventually. It's important to apply heat as evenly as possible around a casting, as uneven heating may cause it to crack.

An impact driver can also help at this stage. The traditional mechanical type works by turning a screwdriver bit a few degrees when hit with a hammer. The hammer blow helps to ensure that the bit remains in contact with the head of the screw, while simultaneously turning the bit. This principle has been incorporated into a device of a similar shape to an electric drill, which speeds up the process by repeating it several times a second.

Manual water pumps

If you already have a pressurised water system, this could at first sight appear to be a retrograde step. However, there are many advantages to having a manually pumped option.

The biggest attraction of adding a manual backup is improved reliability, as the boat can continue to be operated with relatively little disruption if the electric water pump fails or if the vessel completely loses electrical power. By contrast, if you are entirely reliant on electrical systems to get water out of the tanks, any failure will at best curtail your plans until the necessary parts have been sourced and the system repaired. At worst, an electrical failure on a long passage could leave you without sufficient accessible water.

Reduced water consumption

If you use water on board as freely as you do at home, then your water consumption will be high. This applies whether you're rinsing the dishes, cleaning your teeth or filling the kettle. It has been estimated that a boat with manually pumped water will typically use half to two-thirds of the consumption of one that uses pressurised systems. If your boat's pressurised water capacity is borderline adequate for your current usage, then adding a manual pump could be a simple solution that won't require the weight, space or time that's needed to fit additional tanks.

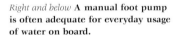

Right and below **A manual foot pump is often adequate for everyday usage of water on board.**

Saving gas and battery power

With pressurised water it's difficult to tell precisely how much water you put into the kettle, for example. However, with a manual pump you can count exactly the number of pumps needed per mug of tea, so the kettle boils faster and over time you can save on the amount of gas used. This may not matter for weekend cruisers, but it can be a factor for boats cruising in remote areas or for long periods of time.

Even the most frugal of electrical water pumps draws around four amps. Although it tends not to be used for a great deal of time, it is still possible for the pump to be using a considerable proportion of your battery charge.

How many pumps?

A single manual pump, usually located at the galley, is quick and easy to fit. You can also install additional pumps in the heads, although longer runs of extra pipework are needed. The best pump is usually the powerful double action foot pump – lower capacity hand pumps can be counter-productive as they are much more time-consuming to use, making the electric pump more appealing.

POSITIONS FOR PUMPS

This pump, which fits neatly into the locker below the sink, has a foot pump positioned for regular use.

This system is out of the way when not needed, but ready for immediate use in the event of a problem with the electric water pump system.

Locating the pump

The easiest way to install a single manual pump is to tee it into the existing water system, in parallel with the electric pump. Simply connect a pipe to the run between the tank and the electric pump, take this to the manual pump, and then insert a pipe from the output of the manual pump to the existing pipe run between the electric pump and the outlets.

This is ideal as a simple backup and works well as an additional galley pump. If manually pumped water is also wanted in each of the heads compartments, then a further pipe feed can be run from the water tank to each pump. No extra taps are needed – the manual pump will work perfectly well with those for a pressurised water system, provided the electric pump is turned off.

Left **Placement of an additional manual fresh-water pump in a system.**

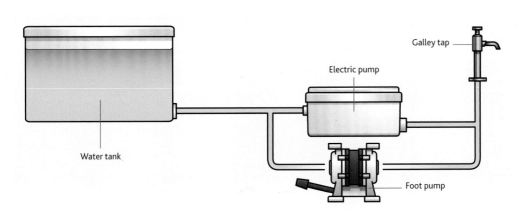

Galley tap

Electric pump

Water tank

Foot pump

Pressurised water

Pressurised water systems have been around for many years, but one of the most popular misconceptions is that the pressure switch built into the system actually affects the water pressure at the tap. In fact, the pressure switch turns on the pump when the tap is opened and off when the tap is closed.

The only way to increase the water pressure within a pressurised system is to fit a larger capacity pump to provide a greater flow of water. Although the water pressure at the pump is no higher, the restriction at the tap or showerhead provides higher pressure as the flow of water is restrained.

When there is pressure on the switch the electrical contacts are open and current cannot pass to operate the pump. Pressure within the system is created when the taps are all closed but the pump is still running. The pump will continue to run until pressure has reached the cut-out point of the switch (20 pound-force per square inch/psi in

the UK). Once this pressure setting is reached, the switch is operated by water pressure pushing against the rubber cover, which forces the switch to the open position and stops the pump. A non-return valve is fitted within the system to maintain the pressure, which keeps the pump switched off.

The most basic of cold water-only pressurised water systems includes the pressure switch in the pump, examples of which are the very robust and reliable Jabsco 3600 series pumps. An accumulator tank can be added to this system to give the smooth flow of water expected when a tap is turned on.

Above **A modern small bladder-type accumulator tank. The tank is pumped up with air, which pressurises the water.**

Below **A basic cold water system includes the pressure switch in the pump. Equipment such as fuses and strainers have been omitted for clarity.**

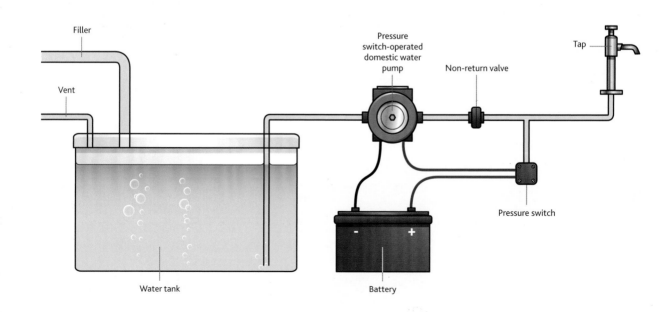

Types of tank

There are two types of accumulator tank. The most simple type comprises a small cylinder mounted vertically, which traps an air pocket in the top half of the cylinder as water fills from the bottom. A more sophisticated model incorporates an internal pressurised air bladder (rubber diaphragm) against which water pressure builds up. This type can be mounted in any orientation.

Connecting to the system

Both types of tank connect into the system between the non-return valve and the tap, and their purpose is to accumulate a pressurised air pocket within the cylinder.

The air pocket prevents the pump from rapidly switching on and off (cycling), which happens in systems using powerful pumps without an accumulator tank. As the pump runs, pressure builds up faster than the escaping water, which causes the pressure switch to operate and turn the pump off. This creates an immediate drop in pressure, which allows the pump to switch on again. This on/off cycle continues with the water pulsating out of the tap instead of running in a smooth flow.

With the accumulator tank in the system, the pressure fluctuation is smoothed out by the air in the cylinder compressing and decompressing faster than the pressure can build up to operate the switch, thus providing a smooth flow of water.

Right **A modern pump in a system with bladder-type accumulator tank, isolating valve and coarse water strainer to the left of the valve.**

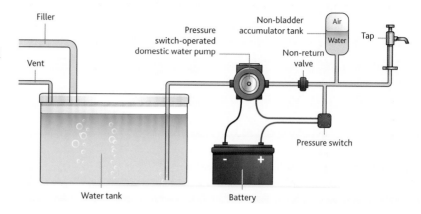

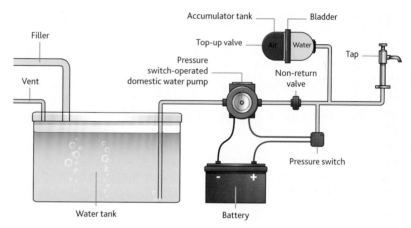

Top **A small, vertically mounted cylinder traps an air pocket in the top half of the cylinder as water fills from the bottom.**

Above **The more sophisticated model has an internal pressurised air bladder against which water pressure builds up.**

Hot water

Today most boatowners require both hot and cold water aboard. A calorifier is often the method chosen for heating water and it makes use of the heat generated by running the engine. This means there is no reason not to enjoy free hot water while under way, or from the built-in immersion element while connected to shore power.

A calorifier is similar in appearance to the standard household domestic indirect cylinder and works in the same way. A coil of copper tube inside the cylinder is connected to the engine cooling water system.

Water at engine running temperature is fed into the upper end of the coil. It passes down through the coil and is cooled during the process of heating the water in the cylinder. It is then returned to the engine where it is again heated and passed through the calorifier tube. A full cylinder of hot water will be available after about 30 minutes of running the engine from cold!

While calorifiers are generally run from fresh water (heat exchanger) cooled engines, they can also be run from raw water (direct) cooled engines. The heat of the water will be less than that from a fresh-water cooled system as the normal engine running temperature is around 50°C (122°F) for raw water-cooled-engines compared to 80°C (176°F) for fresh-water-cooled engines.

The high temperature of the fresh-water engines means that a much smaller calorifier can be fitted as the amount of hot water required for any particular use is lower. More cold water is mixed with it at the basin or shower to bring it to a usable temperature. Hot water from a raw water-cooled engine is already at a usable temperature, but still quite hot enough for a nice comfortable shower and general washing-up on board.

A pressure relief valve is an essential fitting on the calorifier and is set above the working pressure of the system, otherwise it would constantly be opening and preventing the pump pressure switch from stopping the pump.

Even better is a combined temperature and pressure relief valve, which will open in the event of excess temperature as well as over-pressure. This vents the system before the water reaches boiling point.

Right **A typical large calorifier ready for fitting.**

Below **Although a luxury, it is becoming increasingly commonplace to have hot water on board a smaller boat.**

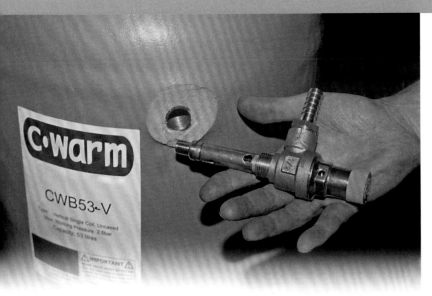

Dual power

A marine grade double-insulated immersion element to allow the water to be heated when connected to shore power is generally a standard fitting. Cheap domestic elements will work, but are likely to cause earthing problems with marina electrical supplies. Similarly, using lower wattage units will avoid overpowering the electrical systems in many marinas.

Below **A basic cold water system incorporating an accumulator tank, making the installation of an expansion tank unnecessary.**

If shore power is being installed for the first time, a standard domestic consumer unit will do the job perfectly as long as it is inside and well protected from the elements. Select a unit with room for using circuit breakers as well as for a residual current device to protect against current leakage. A shore power isolating switch should also be fitted as a safety measure. The mains system should only be installed by a qualified or suitably experienced person.

Above left **A combined pressure and temperature relief valve offers the greatest safety.**

Above top right **A marine-grade immersion element being installed into a calorifier.**

Above right **A shore power isolating switch should be fitted to allow shore power to be cut off without the need to pull out the plug.**

Expansion tank

An expansion tank needs to be included within the system to allow for expansion of the water within the cylinder as it heats up. Without this, the pressure relief valve would again be constantly opening, causing the pump to run. However, systems that include an accumulator tank (see page 134) do not require an additional expansion tank as the accumulator tank will happily perform both tasks.

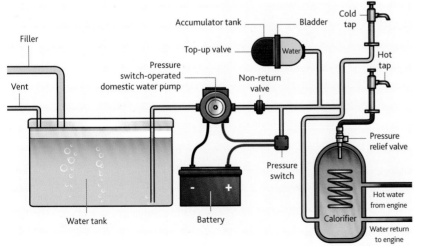

Shower

An on-board shower is a must for many people; however, it can be difficult to see how to install one on some older boats that were not originally designed to have one fitted.

Above **Don't imagine that if your boat doesn't have a sumptuous heads compartment like this one that it will be impossible to fit a shower.**

Left **This area ahead of the main bulkhead on a former racing yacht is easy to adapt to take a shower.**

Beyond the mechanics of supplying the water, and draining it afterwards, the biggest hurdle with fitting a shower in many older boats is in creating an appropriate wet area. The majority of modern vessels have the benefit of a heads compartment with a wipe-clean fibreglass moulding similar to those designed to also be used as a shower.

It's by no means impossible to create something equivalent on older craft, using heavy waterproof curtains and/or doors to contain both spray and steam. Although most heads compartments already have some form of external ventilation, an additional opening port or small overhead hatch makes a big difference to the amount of condensation that can escape.

Draining the sump

This can also be a challenge for any boat that was not designed at the outset with a shower in mind. It may be possible to simply drill holes in the bottom soleboards of the compartment, sealing the newly exposed edges of timber with epoxy, to allow the water to drain into the bilge. Although this type of system can work well, it can also be time-consuming to keep clean.

If you're lucky, the drain area will be contained within a single set of the structural frames, which will allow the water to be drained by a pump. If the drain area spans more than one set of frames, be wary of drilling holes through these to allow water to drain to the lowest point, unless you are sure that you can seal

Left **A heavy, waterproof curtain used to separate a full-width heads/shower area from the forecabin.**

the edges of the holes effectively against water ingress and that you are not compromising the structure.

Most boats with factory-fitted showers tend to have electric sump pumps, but this is not the only, or even the best, solution for every boat. They are relatively expensive, require a certain amount of vertical space (which may reduce headroom) and installation is more time-consuming, as the wiring needs to be run from elsewhere.

It's therefore worth considering installing a manual pump – the type of foot-operated pump that is more frequently used for fresh water systems is ideal. This can enable a shower to be fitted to a boat whose water tanks may otherwise be too small to make it a viable proposition. Whatever the type of pump used, a filter is essential to prevent the pump being blocked by debris such as hair.

Temperature control

For a boat only used in hot climates, it may not even be necessary to have a hot water supply. The possibility of having frequent short cold showers can be very refreshing. However, most boatowners prefer to have access to hot water (see p136).

The easiest way to adjust the temperature of the water at the showerhead is with a mixer tap connected to the shower hose, both of which items are readily available from chandlers.

A more complex arrangement is a domestic style shower temperature control. Whichever option you choose, fitting an anti-scald valve is a sensible precaution and makes it easier to adjust the water temperature to a comfortable level.

Below left **A shower drain operated by a manual pump is cheaper, fits in a smaller bilge space and saves water. A pipe can simply be led to the lowest part of the bilge, providing there's a filter fitted before the pipe reaches the pump.**

Below right **A mixer tap with shower attachment is the easiest way to control the temperature of the shower water. It can double as the tap for the basin.**

Electrically operated heads

You may wish to upgrade the heads from a manual to an electrically operated one, which is easy to work and has a sleek, contemporary appearance. You will need to add electrics – wiring, fuses and control panel or switch, depending on the make and type of heads you choose to have. The installation shown here uses a fresh-water supply to the heads.

TIP

If a sea water system is installed to supply the heads, you should insert a raw water strainer on the incoming water supply to remove any debris.

When installing a new heads, it may be worth renewing all the pipework, especially if it's more than about six years old. You could take the opportunity to install low-odour waste hose, which will keep the surroundings fresher. Although you may wish to start from scratch and renew everything, this is not necessary for most installations.

Before deciding on the model of heads, it's a good idea to get some feedback about various makes and models of electric heads, including gauging the sound levels of the mechanism. Some of the early models were noisy, making them a nuisance at night, but today's modern heads can be very quiet indeed.

Do also check the height of the heads and seat before ordering the heads as some are designed for floor mounting and others for plinth mounting, so make sure you buy the correct version for your boat.

Replacing the heads

If the job is being performed while afloat, first close the seacocks. Disconnect the old heads and lift it out of the compartment for disposal. When installing the new heads, tip it forward to enable you to connect the hoses before running them beneath the plinth and into the adjacent locker where the seacocks are situated.

Below **The finished toilet within the heads compartment.**

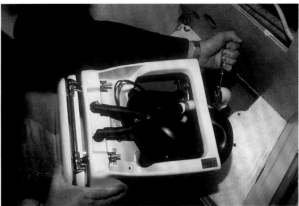

Above left **Removing the old heads after disconnecting the pipework (and closing the seacocks).**

Above right **Connect all the pipework and make certain that all hose clips are tight.**

Most modern heads are supplied with a wiring loom as well as plugs and sockets for ease of connection. Once you have cut the power cables to length, attach the cables with loom socket plugs, which can then be plugged into the loom sockets. Fit the heads operating switch panel in a suitable position next to the heads. You should plug all the cables into the main wiring heads loom.

You can use either fresh or sea water for flushing. Using fresh water from the domestic supply can make the compartment smell fresher when left unused, but the fresh water domestic tanks must be kept topped up. A further step would be to fit a sea-water supply feed to the sea water inlet to preserve fresh water in the case of shortage.

To ensure there is no cross contamination between the heads and the fresh water supply, an electric non-return valve should be fitted to the installation in the fresh water feed to the heads, installed using standard domestic compression fittings. The rest of the pipework is connected, including anti-syphon vents at the top of each of the pipes to stop backfeed occurring.

Above left **A cable wiring loom is generally supplied, but power connections will usually need to be made up to suit the boat's electrical system.**

Left **The control panel needs to be conveniently placed for ease of use.**

Right **The completed pipework. Note the non-return valve (between the small white plastic pipe and the brass drain-off cock) for the fresh water flush. The sea water inlet (bottom left) could be used as the feed for a sea water alternative to fresh water.**

Bilge pump and alarms

In an on-board emergency, such as a flooded hull, a bilge pump may be the only thing to keep the boat afloat while repairs are made. It is worth making sure that your boat has adequate bilge pumps (electrical and mechanical) that can cope if such a situation occurs. The number of pumps depends largely on the layout of the bilge.

If the whole bilge is connected, then one large capacity submersible pump should be enough, along with a manual backup, if you so wish. If the bilge is compartmentalised, you will need a smaller submersible pump in each compartment.

On bigger vessels you can install a large-capacity impeller pump, which, when combined with a simple valved manifold, allows you to select any compartment you wish to pump out. You can also use this system with the manual pump using the same manifold, so that you can manually pump out a compartment by opening a couple of valves. This is a good way of using one powerful pump to service several different compartments. However, it is a labour-intensive system to install on a small vessel.

Sensors and switches

Electric bilge pumps are more commonly found on board smaller vessels, often fitted with a sensor called a float switch. A float switch operates the pump automatically when the water level rises in the bilge to a certain level. Float switches have a poor reputation for long-term reliability, but if you test them regularly they won't present too many problems. It is also possible to purchase solid-state sensors with no moving parts, which are normally more reliable than float switches over the longer term. These are often fitted with an alarm to alert you if any problems arise.

> **TIP**
>
> A manual pump can be a useful addition on a yacht or motorboat in case the electricity fails. A manual pump is inexpensive and takes up little space in a locker, so is a worthwhile piece of kit in the event of minor flooding.

Below left **A modern submersible pump with built-in level sensor.**

Below right **A high-capacity manual pump and manifold for selecting different areas for pumping.**

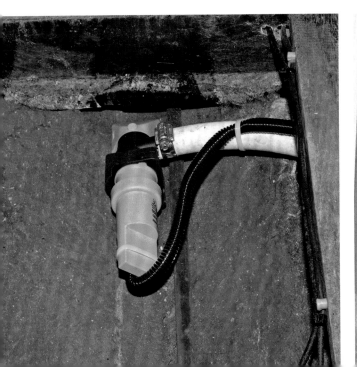

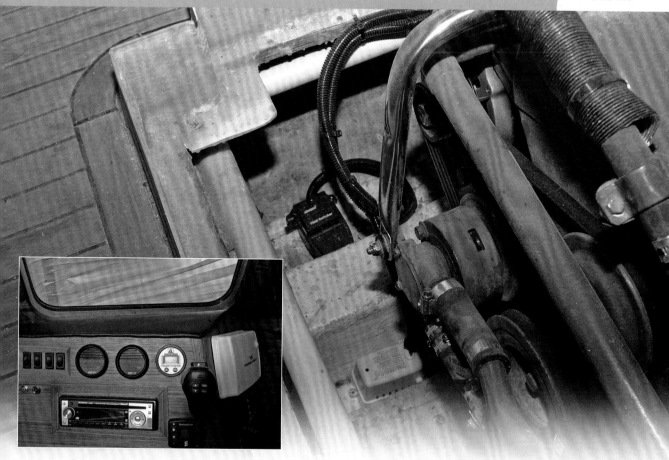

Dedicated switch panels are available to allow you to select either manual or automatic pump operation, which makes wiring of the system straightforward.

Unattended pumps

Having an effective pumping system is fine when you are on board but what happens when the boat is unattended for long periods? The answer is to have the automatic pumps on a dedicated circuit that bypasses the main isolating switches so that they are powered at all times.

A further refinement to this system monitors all bilge pump activity while the boat is unattended and retains this in its memory. When you come back to the boat, you will be able to see at a glance

Above **Float switches located in different parts of the bilge (pumps are installed under the engine).**

Above inset **A pair of bilge water alarms (top centre), mounted on the auxiliary instrument panel.**

whether the pumps have been running, which could indicate serious potential problems that can be dealt with before any damage is done by flooding.

Wiring for these bilge monitors is straightforward as they only require a lead from each float switch/level sensor, as well as their own power supply, to enable them to monitor every pump.

Above **A typical bilge pump monitor. When the boat is unattended the monitor records the pump activations for up to eight different bilge pumps. All activity is recorded in the monitor's memory for when the boatowner wants to check it.**

Engine-driven bilge pump

A bilge pump that is driven by running the main engine doesn't rely on the power of the boat's batteries to function, nor does it require any manual pumping. This makes it an ideal type of bilge pump to have in an emergency. As long as the engine is going, large quantities of water will be removed from the boat.

Engine-driven bilge pumps are fitted with an internal clutch so that when the pump is not required the pulley on the pump will freewheel, using only a negligible amount of engine power. Clutches can be manually lever operated or electrically operated. If the pump is being fitted for use in an emergency, then it is probably better to have a manual lever clutch pump rather than an electrical clutch, removing the need for electrical power to make it work. However, if the pump is electrically operated, it can often be controlled remotely, usually from the helm.

An engine-driven bilge pump contains an impeller that operates from the pump shaft. The pump works in an identical way to an engine-cooling pump. It is powerful and self-priming (meaning it can start pumping without bilge water coming through). One drawback, however, is that it cannot run without water for more than about 20 seconds before the impeller starts to suffer damage, so it is vital that the clutch cannot inadvertently be engaged when the pump is not required.

TIP

Never leave the engine-driven bilge pump running dry because the rubber impeller will get hot through friction and wear out. When you have finished pumping water, always turn the lever back to the idle position.

Installation

Installing an engine-driven bilge pump is not difficult, but is more complex when no provision has been made in the original engine design. The first thing that is required is an additional pulley to drive the pump pulley. Many engines have additional pulleys already fitted for other uses that can be utilised. If no extra pulleys are fitted, it may be possible to extend the belt on the alternator and run the pump off the same pulley.

Below **Offering up the pump to ensure the belt does not snag on anything prior to fitting. When the pump is in idle position the fan belt is slack. When the clutch lever is engaged, the fan belt is tightened, therefore operating the pump.**

Brass operating clutch lever

Bilge water pipes connection points (each end)

Housing for the impeller

Pulley block mechanism

Above **A typical lever-operated clutch pump, which is driven by a belt from the crankshaft pulley.**

It is essential to get the geometry correct to ensure that there is sufficient belt surface on the pulley. You will need to make a mounting bracket for the pump to be fixed to the engine, which may require some rudimentary arc welding. You could ask someone in the boatyard to do this, or local engineers should be able to make up a bracket for you.

When designing the bracket, it is vital to ensure that the pulleys on the pump and the engine are in perfect alignment, otherwise the belt will wear very quickly. If the holes for the mounting bolts are slotted, this will provide the necessary movement for belt tightening. It may be a tight fit to get the pump mounted on the engine.

The manifold

The manual bilge pump section (see page 142) outlines how to use a manifold to allow the manual pumping of different compartments of the bilge. This same manifold can be used for both pumps, therefore providing the ultimate bilge pumping arrangement, as any pump can pump out any area of the bilge. It is not difficult to fabricate a manifold using valves and fittings

readily available from a local hydraulics supplier, as with the correct fittings everything will screw together.

When assembling any bilge pump arrangement it is essential to use only spiral-reinforced hose; otherwise the piping will collapse under suction from the pump and prevent the pump working. It is also good practice to fit two hose clips on all pump pipework to ensure an airtight seal on the pump of the engine hose pump.

Above **Offering up the pump to ensure the belt does not snag on anything prior to fitting. When the pump is not required the clutch is disengaged and the pump pulley freewheels without driving the pump.**

Below **The ultimate pump and manifold arrangement, allowing any part of the bilge to be pumped out by any pump. Here the aft cabin is being pumped out. The skin fitting for removing the bilge water through the hull is above the waterline.**

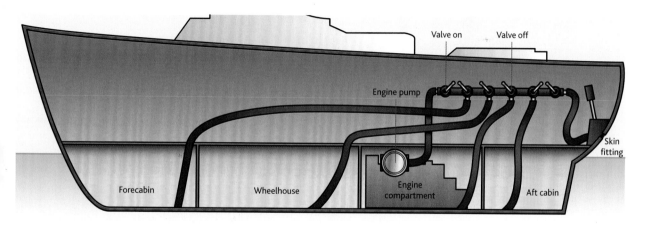

Watermaker

Having a watermaker on board not only allows a cruising yacht to be totally self-sufficient by carrying its very own 'well', it also guarantees the water quality. Although the hardware is complex and requires regular cleaning and maintenance, it also brings some unexpected benefits.

Sea water normally has a salinity of 35g of dissolved salts per kilogram of water, so it can cause harm – and even death – if consumed in significant quantities. This is because its salt concentration upsets the delicate osmotic balance of the cells in the human gut. However, sea water can still be used for cooking some types of vegetable and fish on board, which helps to extend a boat's fresh water supply, so a yacht's galley will often have a salt water tap over the sink.

To remove the salt from water (and a host of other contaminants), watermakers work on a process called reverse osmosis (RO). Sea water is sucked on board, passed through a series of pre-filters, and then pumped at high pressure (often around 800psi) through a microscopically porous membrane. This membrane is so fine that only the tiny H_2O molecules can pass through. Almost everything else, including dissolved elements of sodium, chlorine, calcium, sulphates and potassium along with a legion of bacteria, are all stopped by the membrane and flushed away as waste. The end result is very pure water, which is available at the touch of a button. Advances in technology have turned watermakers into a reliable piece of kit, with models ranging from simple hand pump survival units producing a mouthful every ten minutes to large, built-in devices capable of creating large quantities of water in a day.

Right **Being able to make almost unlimited fresh water from the surrounding sea greatly enhances a yacht's self-sufficiency.**

Above **The heart of the system. A cylindrical membrane filters water at a molecular level so only pure water remains. This one produces over 900 litres (200 gallons) a day.**

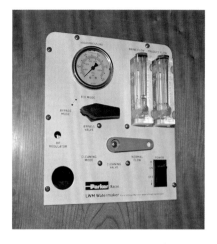

Watermakers, however, remain expensive and demand a lot of electrical or mechanical power. They also require regular use and a diligent maintenance programme. In return they offer complete freedom in terms of a yacht's potable water supply. For many, this self-sufficiency is priceless.

Reasons for fitting a watermaker

- **Reduces weight:** Water weighs 1kg per litre (10lb per gallon), so by making your own water on board there is no need to fit extra large tanks, or carry heavy jerrycans filled from the quayside tap. Smaller tanks mean a lighter and faster boat.
- **Provides good quality water:** Potable water in some parts of the world can be suspect at best. The watermaker produces only pure water, with additional UV safeguards against any viruses small enough to beat the membrane.
- **Extends range:** Not being reliant on finding shore supplies or catching rain means the possibilities for exploration

are endless. As a precaution, containers to cover the longest leg away from shore supplies should be carried just in case the watermaker fails.
- **Saves money:** In some popular areas, such as the Caribbean, water is very expensive and can make a big dent in the cruising budget. In more remote areas, where only bottled water may be safe to drink, it still has to be sourced, paid for and carried.
- **High demand:** If you have a young family the demand for fresh water may be higher than average. A watermaker means you can run a washing machine, flush the heads with fresh water, have regular showers, and even wash down the anchor chain.
- **Emergency water:** If your tanks become contaminated, or a seam splits, the watermaker can keep the crew hydrated until repairs can be made. Small hand-powered units can also be included in a liferaft grab bag.

Above left **Water intake and pre-filters. A low-pressure pump draws in sea water and pushes it through a series of increasingly fine filters.**

Above right **The controller, tucked away in the aft cabin of this yacht, allows the system to be monitored with 'at-a-glance' sight gauges for product and waste flow.**

Below **The force behind reverse osmosis comes from the high-pressure pump assembly. This one has an energy recovery unit to increase electrical efficiency.**

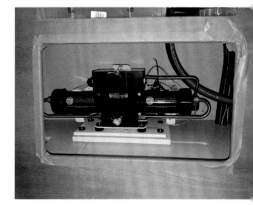

Watermaker 2

Choice of watermaker

The choice of commercially available watermakers is huge and they benefit from regular advances in technology. Watermakers can generally be divided into three main types: engine driven, AC powered and hand pumped. The hand-pumped versions are normally found in liferaft grab bags.

Some units are self-contained within an open frame or enclosed cabinet, but tend to be found on larger yachts. Others are modular, allowing the various components to be spread out around a yacht. Each set-up will consist of three main elements; the sea water intake and pre-filters, the high-pressure pump, and the cylindrical membrane assembly with its three connections – one for intake and flushing, one for product and one for brine waste.

The engine-driven versions can also usually be run off the domestic batteries. Some yachts are set up so that a series of solar panels supply enough energy to power the watermaker in hotter climates. Most use an 'energy recovery' system for improved efficiency, but rapidly lose performance when the batteries fall below a certain level.

The engine-driven types rely on a high-pressure pump powered by a belt from the engine. However, this depends on there being enough room in the engine bay for the pump assembly to be effectively connected. Watermaking usually coincides with routine battery charging, so an engine-driven system has many advantages.

The AC system versions rely on power from a separate generator set to produce the mains power required. These are usually the most efficient and productive watermakers and are found on larger yachts and charter vessels.

Choosing the right unit

A watermaker is not only a big investment in terms of cash; it will also need a great deal of ongoing maintenance, and a regular supply of pre-filters. It will also be vulnerable to poor sea water quality and oil-based pollution found in some harbours. However, if treated well, the watermaker should produce fresh water for up to five years, meaning the system will more than pay for itself in convenience and savings when cruising in areas limited by availability or poor water quality.

The first choice to make will be capacity. How much water do you want to make, and how much spare electrical power do you have available? The higher the capacity of a watermaker, the greater its cost and complexity and its power demands. The biggest decision will be how much water you need to make on a regular basis, and how

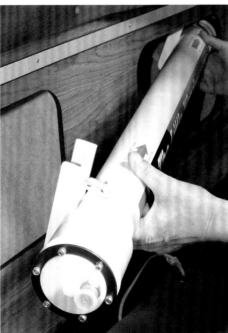

Far left **The various modules can be placed out of the way in lockers. Here, the main unit is being installed near the galley. Before completion make sure everything can be easily accessed.**

Left **Finding space for the lengthy membrane tube can also prove a challenge, especially as it has to remain accessible.**

much electrical capacity you can spare. It's also a good idea to choose a proven make with a good distribution network to make the purchase of spares and consumables easier.

Undertaking the installation

Having decided on the right unit, the modular design of the smaller units will allow the hardware to be spread out, and many yachtsmen choose to undertake the installation themselves so they can fully understand the system, and position it for the best access for servicing.

The key considerations are:

- Filters will need to be changed often, so will need quick and easy accessibility.
- Some of the equipment will be noisy, so consider where it can be placed so as not to interfere with sleep.
- The waste brine should be discharged overboard above the waterline, making it easy to assess its quality.
- The intake should be very deep, to avoid air being sucked into the system, and on the opposite side to the toilet discharge.
- Watermakers left unused for a while will need to be 'pickled' with acid and alkaline cleaners and run for a while before they can be used again.
- Diverter valves should be in place to allow the system to be flushed through, and for the product to be tested before being put into the tanks. Some systems will do this automatically.

- As an additional virus killer, some sailors add a clear section of pipe from the product take-off that is irradiated with an extra UV light.
- With a good supply of fresh water available, it can be used more freely. Some yachtsmen have dedicated tanks for the heads or outdoor showers, and keep a separate tank purely for drinking water, sometimes mixed with mineral water.

Above **The sea water inlet needs to be as deep as possible to avoid flow interruptions, and on the opposite side from any waste discharges.**

Below **The low-pressure intake pump has been housed in front of the engine. An engine-driven high-pressure pump would need to be belt-connected, which can sometimes prove tricky.**

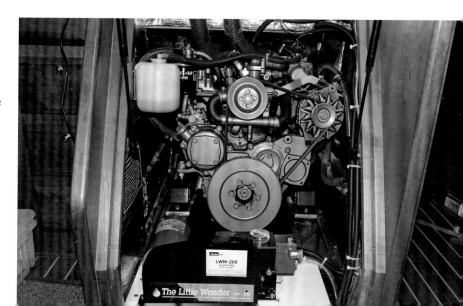

Ventilation

The importance of good on board ventilation is something that should not be underestimated. Without adequate ventilation, boats can soon become damp, musty and unpleasant, and in the case of wooden boats, poor ventilation can compromise their longevity.

If there is one thing that will improve both the condition of your boat and life on board, it is proper ventilation. With no airflow down below, a boat will quickly become damp and musty inside. It doesn't take much for condensation to form on the inside of GRP and metal hulls, and this can encourage mould to grow as well as speed up corrosion of metal fittings, fastenings and electrics.

On wooden boats, damp conditions will encourage rot and, unless ventilation is carefully assessed and monitored, this will affect the condition of your boat, perhaps later leading to very costly repairs.

How can you tell if your boat is poorly ventilated?

The simplest way is to ask yourself, 'Is there a smell on board?' If the moment you step down below you smell mustiness or stuffiness, then your boat is probably poorly ventilated. Look for visual clues, too. Condensation on the cabin sides or portholes, black mould on the deckhead or in lockers and damp bunk cushions and upholstery are all signs of poor ventilation. Good air circulation is not something that generally happens naturally, so unless you do something about it, the conditions will only get worse and the number of problems is likely to increase.

Right **Boats can be dry and sweet smelling if air circulation is good and interiors, lockers and compartments are not sealed tight without any ventilation.**

Below **Black mould in lockers or on deckheads is a good indicator that your boat is suffering from poor ventilation.**

Common mistakes made

One of the biggest mistakes made when it comes to ventilation is that the flow of air through the boat is not taken into consideration. It is all very well installing ventilators at either end of the boat, but if they are not set up properly so that the air circulates through the boat, then they will do the opposite to what they are supposed to do.

For ventilation to work properly, air has to be sucked into the boat at one end and then extracted at the other. This might sound simple, but quite often airflow doesn't do what you would expect it to do. If a cowl ventilator, for example, is not orientated in the right direction, then it may suck in air when you want it to extract it and consequently you might have a situation when you have two ventilators that are both sucking in air, therefore increasing the amount of dampness/condensation on board as there is nowhere for the air to escape.

CABIN VENTILATION

Angled louvres allow the air to flow into a space, but not the rain.

An alternative to a louvre door is a louvre grill plate.

Hit and miss vents can be opened and closed as required.

Leaving hatches or portholes slightly ajar is a simple way to improve ventilation.

Types of cabin ventilation

Not all ventilators have to be deck-mounted. Other ways to encourage good airflow through your boat include:

- **Louvre doors:** Angled louvres in part of the cabin door will allow air to flow into the boat. Alternatively, decorative patterns can be drilled into washboards or bulkheads.
- **Door vents:** Louvre grills can be fitted to washboards or lockers. These can't be closed, so are a good choice for areas where permanent ventilation is required. Due to the angle of the louvres, they will not let rainwater inside.

- **Hit and miss vents:** These can be opened or closed as required and fitted to washboards or locker fronts.
- **Open hatches and portholes:** The simplest form of ventilation is to leave hatches or portholes slightly ajar. This may not always be practical at sea, but if you are leaving a boat on a mooring or in a marina berth, provided the hatches are not open to the prevailing winds, then it will encourage some ventilation. Windscoops, which fit over open hatches, are a good idea in tropical climates as these improve airflow (see page 76).

Ventilation down below

Slats instead of solid bunk tops can help airflow in lockers and prevent bunk cushions from getting damp. Gratings at the bottom of lockers can also help, as can holes in bunk fronts or locker doors. The bilges should be ventilated, too, particularly on wooden boats – either with holes in the floorboards or with electric extractor ventilators.

If you leave your boat for some time, lift bunk cushions, leave locker doors open and lift floorboards to encourage air to circulate.

Ventilation 2

Engine ventilation

Good ventilation in the engine compartment is crucial. Not only do engines need an adequate and steady supply of fresh air in order to work properly, but without sufficient ventilation, noxious and potentially dangerous gases can quickly build up. All engine compartments should be vented to the outside with clam shell vents. These are often fitted to transoms or hull sides and are used to vent engine rooms or fuel tanks. Extractor fans can also be used for the same purpose.

How you set up your ventilation and promote good air circulation through the boat is often a case of trial and error, but you can help it to work using a variety of different ventilators on deck.

Types of on-deck ventilators

The location of ventilators is extremely important, not only in terms of promoting good air circulation, but in deciding what type of vent you are going to fit.

For ventilators that are fitted on coachroofs or hatches, low-profile versions or cowls with large apertures can be suitable, but they should not be fitted to fore- or sidedecks or anywhere where the likelihood of being flooded by water is high. Instead, if fitting ventilators to the deck, choose tall types, such as mushroom vents on towers, which have a seal so that water cannot flood them if hit by a breaking wave.

Above **Engine room or fuel tank vents can be installed on a boat's transom.**

Below **A typical arrangement for ventilation on a yacht. The arrows show the direction of air flow in and out of the boat.**

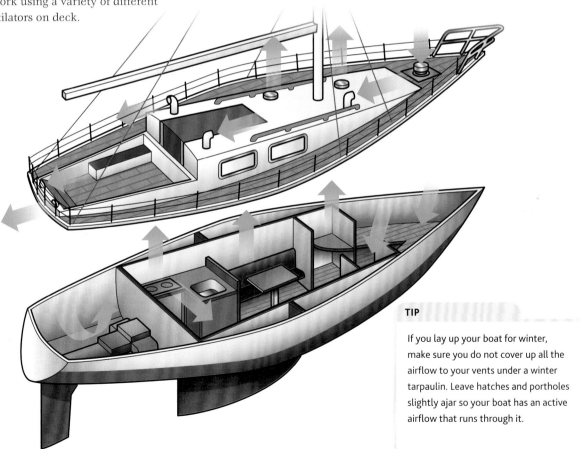

TIP

If you lay up your boat for winter, make sure you do not cover up all the airflow to your vents under a winter tarpaulin. Leave hatches and portholes slightly ajar so your boat has an active airflow that runs through it.

There are numerous types of ventilators for sale, which all have advantages and disadvantages.

- ⚙ **Cowls:** These are one of the most common ventilators and come in a range of shapes and sizes. Generally made of metal or a flexible PVC, cowls can be rotated to encourage the best airflow, or in a marina can be twisted away from the prevailing winds. Many are of a venturi-type, so will encourage the extraction of air from within the boat, creating good air circulation if they are matched with another ventilator that sucks air into the boat. They can often be fitted with cover plates so the holes can be plugged if you are at sea in bad weather.

- ⚙ **Dorade vents:** Named after the famous yacht *Dorade*, to which they were first fitted, the Dorade vent is a cowl-type ventilator that is mounted on a box (also see page 30). Integral water drains and a protective upstand within the box prevent water from entering the boat, while allowing good airflow.

- ⚙ **Mushroom vents:** A popular choice for use on deck, the height of these can be altered, with the top cap being mounted on an adjustable screw so that it can be wound up or down to open or close them. Modern versions are fitted with mosquito screens.

- ⚙ **Low-profile static vents:** Another common choice on modern yachts, these vents can either be permanently open, or adjustable so they can be closed. However, they are only suitable for coachroofs or areas that are not liable to flooding.

TYPES OF ON-DECK VENTS

Cowl vents will encourage air circulation through the boat, but should be fitted in places that are not liable to flooding, otherwise water will end up down below.

Dorade-type vents are cowls that sit on boxes. The boxes are designed to prevent water from flooding the vents and going down below.

Mushroom vents are ideal for deck use as they will not get flooded. This one has an integral decklight.

One of the most popular forms of ventilator, these static vents often have integral fans so they will work all the time.

Many can be fitted with electric or solar-powered extraction ventilators to improve airflow. Be sure to buy one that can be switched on and off, though, as vents that include solar-rechargeable batteries to run the fans at night can be very noisy!

TIP

Use a hygrometer to measure the level of relative humidity in your boat. If you still have problems with mould, use a dehumidifier to keep the relative humidity down.

Gas alarm

The dangers of gas on board are well known to boatowners. Liquid Petroleum Gas (LPG), which is stored in a gas bottle, is a potential explosion hazard, and leakages from any part of the gas system will cause gas to accumulate on board.

If the boat has any sort of gas installation – cooking, heating or in some cases even lighting – then it is essential to have a gas alarm fitted. This may be required for insurance purposes, but it is far more important that your life and that of your crew are not placed in danger. LPG, in the form of either butane or propane, is heavier than

Below **A control unit is normally mounted in the galley area.**

Inset below right **Gas alarm control unit, with alarm lights and warning sound.**

air, and therefore in the enclosed environment of a boat's hull has nowhere to escape in the event of a leak, filling the boat with explosive quantities. Thankfully gas explosions on boats are rare, but they still happen and a gas alarm is the first line of defence against such a disaster.

Fitting a gas alarm

It is easy to fit a gas alarm. Ideally you should mount the control unit, which houses the alarm lights and warning alarm, near the gas

appliances, as a constant reminder of the dangers involved. The alarm may have several sensors with different circuits. You should mount one of these sensors as low in the bilge as you can, in order for it to detect any small leakages as soon as possible, although be aware that sensors do not tolerate getting wet and will occasionally fail in a wet bilge. It is advisable to mount another sensor beneath the galley equipment – cooker, hob or fridge (if gas powered) – to give an early warning of serious leakage.

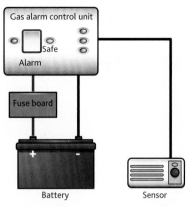

Far left **The sensor is ideally placed at the lowest point in the bilge, where gas may accumulate.**

Left **Wiring the gas alarm is straightforward, as this typical diagram shows. The sensor has its own leads that connect into the control unit.**

Wiring is quite simple, with the sensors having their own leads that connect into the control unit and with power supplied from a low amp fuse (or circuit breaker), according to each unit's own particular installation instructions.

Even if your model incorporates an on-off switch, it is a good idea to keep it switched on so the device comes on as soon as the main battery-isolating switch is operated. It will usually take about a minute for the unit to set itself up, at which point the 'safe' light will illuminate, indicating that all is well. In the event of the unit detecting a leak, a warning light will come on and the buzzer will sound until the leak is cured or the unit is switched off.

Carbon monoxide detector

In a poorly ventilated environment, using any gas-burning appliance will cause levels of carbon monoxide to rise, sometimes to levels where they may become dangerous due to a lack of oxygen. Carbon monoxide (CO) is odourless and therefore undetectable to the human nose. So another important alarm to fit is a carbon monoxide detector. Carbon monoxide alarms generally have integral sensors and should be mounted on the cabin bulkhead. As most are battery operated, it is a simple procedure to take it out of the box, fit the batteries and mount it onto the bulkhead.

Below **A typical domestic carbon monoxide alarm is inexpensive and takes minutes to fit.**

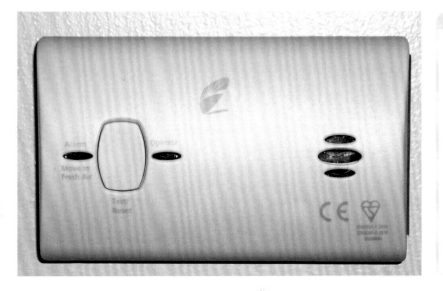

SAFETY TIPS

✿ Install a gas and a carbon monoxide detection system.

✿ Turn on the gas bottle and supply valves only when you are using an appliance. Make sure you turn it off when you have finished.

✿ Regularly hand pump bilges to remove low-lying vapours.

✿ Keep the cabin well ventilated to avoid a build-up of poisonous gases.

✿ If you detect gas in the cabin, air the cabin completely and scoop out the gas with buckets (gas is heavier than air).

Generator

Generators are becoming common on even quite small boats, allowing complete electrical freedom from AC shore power. High draw items such as air conditioning units, dive bottle compressors and other luxuries can now be run at anchor, although the completely silent marine generator is still some way off.

Compact and reliable, marine generator sets have also become increasingly affordable in a highly competitive market. Some generators are fully portable, and can be run on deck for powering hand tools or a small watermaker, or for just topping up flattened batteries. If you want more power, then an installed generator set is a good investment, especially if it can run off the same fuel as the yacht's main engine. Great advances have been made in efficiency and noise reduction in recent years.

The first decision when deciding on a generator is whether you need a full AC system, supplying mains-quality alternating current, or a DC system, which is designed to simply top up the batteries. Many yachtsmen don't want to run a full AC generator when moored in a peaceful location, instead opting to have a powerful battery bank with an inverter of the equivalent output of a mains generator. A smaller and cheaper DC generator can be used to charge the batteries when under way, allowing the crew to enjoy a quiet night at anchor running all their AC domestic appliances from the inverter.

How much power?

The first consideration is to calculate how much mains (AC) power you will require on board, so you need to compile an 'energy shopping list'. Bear in mind that some types of electrical equipment such as fridges or air conditioners have a high start-up load, known as the 'loaded requirement.' Other items, such as televisions, have a resistive load, which is constant throughout the operation.

Each piece of mains-powered equipment should have a label that gives its peak load requirements, and by adding these together you will reach a figure for the total demand. It is unlikely that every mains appliance will be running at peak load simultaneously, so estimate what is most likely to be on at the same time, calculate the peak load demands, and then add a 10 per cent margin. This will give you the ideal size of generator set for your boat.

Another point is to decide for how long you want to run an AC generator at any one time, as in a peaceful anchorage even the quietest generator can still radiate its muffled noise and exhaust far and wide, as well as disturb the sleep of those on board. Good power management can mean that the generator is only needed for short periods, and by sizing the set to the yacht's requirements, it need not be too big, complex or expensive.

Right **Having a generator on board means you don't have to ration the power, or worry about how long you can keep the lights burning.**

Types of generator

Petrol-powered portable: Enclosed in a neat plastic carry case, the portable generator usually uses a quiet, constant speed four-stroke motor with full electronic power management. The smallest sets are the size of airline-approved carry-on bags, delivering between 600 watts and 2kW depending on the model. Some will have a dedicated 12-volt DC outlet for battery charging while also powering another mains device.

Enclosed diesel: This type is designed for small to mid-range yachts, and is supplied as an engine in its own enclosed housing to minimise noise and vibration. The compact case means it can be mounted almost anywhere suitable on board and can run off the yacht's own fuel supply. Additional exhaust mufflers help to keep noise to a minimum.

Main Genset: Designed for use in larger engine rooms where there is already substantial soundproofing and good ventilation, these larger sets are intended for more or less constant operation when the yacht is crewed, especially on charter yachts where air conditioning and fully equipped galleys are central to the yacht's functioning.

Hybrid: A hybrid is a generator attached to the back of the yacht's main engine, which simplifies the installation enormously. It can also be used as an engine starter and auxiliary propulsion system.

Diesel-electric: This is where the generator is the heart of the boat, where every system, from the cooker to the propulsion, is entirely electric. Large cruise ships use this system, but now compact solutions are being trialled for smaller craft. The generator becomes a multipurpose power station with

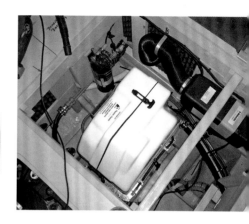

Above left **The simplest way to carry mains power aboard is with a quiet running portable four-stroke generator like this example from Honda. Some have built-in 12V battery chargers.**

Above right **Popular with small- to mid-range cruisers and motorboats is a self-contained unit such as this DC generator from Fischer Panda. It is enclosed in a sound-deadening shell.**

a variable speed motor for the best use of fuel, plus built-in inverters and battery chargers that sense the energy demands, and adjust the current flow accordingly.

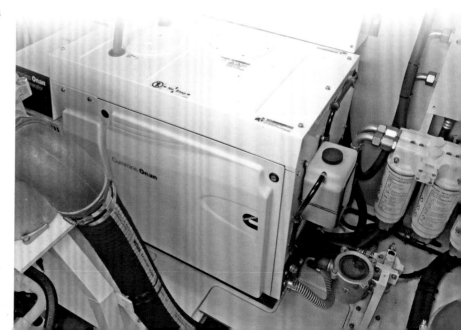

Right **Larger vessels will carry a stand-alone generator in the engine room, where there is already the provision for fuel feeds, ventilation and soundproofing. Note the array of fuel filters.**

Generator 2

Installing a generator

Having chosen a generator of a suitable capacity, the next task is to install it into the boat and configure the power takeoffs. A professional generator installer will need about 3–4 days for a complete job, although a competent DIY enthusiast could also tackle the task after some careful planning.

To start with, the boat will need to be out of the water for the skin fittings to be drilled and fitted. For most generators of up to about 30kVA (kilovolt amps), an 18-mm (¾-in) skin fitting is needed for the cooling intake, and you'll need a 25-mm (1-in) outlet for the underwater exhaust discharge.

You'll also need to find a suitable location for an enclosed system. On some motorboats, there will be space in the engine compartment or the adjacent lazarette, but on smaller sailing yachts you may need to find an empty locker instead. Remember that a Genset must be able to draw in air for combustion and sea water for cooling, while also being able to discharge the exhaust as unobtrusively as possible. You need to also consider whether the set will interfere with other mechanical or electrical systems.

Before fitting the generator, it's best to run in all the services needed first, such as air ducts, cooling hoses, starter battery cable, AC cable and fuel lines as it may be more difficult once the set is in place. The service side of the generator – the filters, dip stick and so on – should be easily accessible for routine checks, so ensure this is outward facing.

Above **The generator should be mounted on a firm base that cannot vibrate, but in an area that can be vented and has access to fuel pipes and cooling water.**

Below **When installing the generator set, make sure it is orientated in such a way that you can reach the key service points, such as dip sticks, air filters and drive belts.**

Left **It is a good idea to have the service items such as fuel filters in the most accessible place, such as their own dedicated locker nearby.**

Noise issues often occur if the set hasn't been properly mounted. Sometimes, the flat base supporting the set becomes a diaphragm, and transmits vibrations into the structure of the boat. The manufacturer will provide guidelines about the correct way to site the product so the noise-absorbing mountings can work at their best.

Check how the generator's own starter battery will be recharged. If the generator doesn't have its own charging output, you'll need to run a charge cable from the main battery charger, or install an independent battery charger drawing off the generator's output. Alternatively, you can use the boat's own battery banks as a starting source. Usually,

motorboats (where engines run all the time when underway) will tap the genset starter into the engine batteries, and a yacht will use the domestic ones.

Portable generator sets will have their own integral fuel tank, but fixed generator sets usually draw off the boat's own fuel supply. On larger boats the generator may well have its own tank, but fitted with changeover valves so it can draw from any of the other fuel tanks on board.

The shore power changeover switch and generator start and control panel are usually mounted by the navigation station, where the circuit breakers are often located as well. Main sockets that were powered from the shore power can now also supply AC output from the generator.

The generator in use

Finally, do have some consideration for your neighbours if using a generator at night. There is nothing worse than lying close to a yacht with a badly installed genset popping and gurgling incessantly, especially if the exhaust keeps rolling clear of the water. A properly sized and installed generator can be used judiciously with very little impact, while providing a whole range of mains-powered comforts on board.

Left **A completed installation in a 16m (54ft) yacht. The generator is sharing the systems supplying the engine room, and is fully accessible for servicing.**

Fuel capacity

If you want to increase your usable fuel capacity but have no room for any additional large tanks on your boat, the 'full-use' fuel system may be a viable alternative, depending on your existing tank layout.

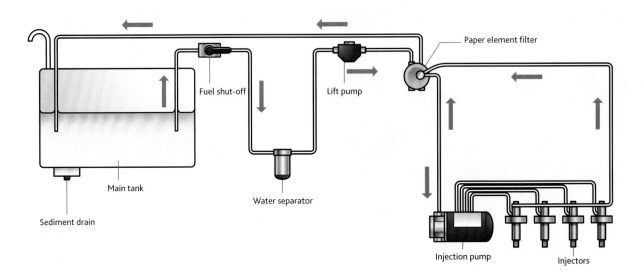

Paper element filter

Fuel shut-off

Lift pump

Main tank

Water separator

Sediment drain

Injection pump

Injectors

The standard tank layout has the fuel feed for each engine taken through the top of the tank, via a tube extending down to a point a small distance above the bottom. This leaves room for sediment to settle so as not to be drawn into the fuel line. There may be a small sediment sump below the feed pipe with a drain cock or plug below, enabling the tank to be drained regularly.

The drawback with this system is that no matter how well the tank is baffled to prevent excess fuel movement, once the fuel level drops below about 20 per cent of the tank's capacity, it is impossible to prevent air entering the feed pipe during rough weather due to the fuel slopping violently around within the tank. This means that a fuel tank with a 1,000-litre (220-gallon) capacity will always have about 200 litres (44 gallons) of fuel that cannot be reliably used.

Above **A standard fuel tank layout, with fuel being drawn from the top of the main tank.**

Below **A typical service tank with fuel take-offs and air vent on the central inspection hatch, plus a large drain valve on the front.**

Improvements

The 'full-use' tank system has proved to have many advantages over conventional systems, although it is rarely installed by builders. The fuel feed to the engine (and other equipment such as diesel heating) is taken from the top of a small service tank with a capacity of about 5 litres (1 gallon). This is situated below the level of the main tanks. The fuel feeds are often incorporated into a small inspection hatch on the top of the service tank so that the interior of the tank can be inspected for corrosion at three-yearly intervals.

Ideally, the bottom of the service tank is shaped into a 'V' form, with a slope towards the front where a gate valve is fitted. Fuel is gravity fed into the service tank via a large bore tube from the main tanks. A gate valve is fitted at the union between the balance pipe and the main tanks to allow the service tank to be isolated from the main tanks for cleaning and draining purposes.

Another outlet on the top of the service tank acts as a permanent air bleed back to the main tank, preventing the service tank from becoming air locked after draining or air finding its way in from the main tanks during rough weather.

With this system, it is possible to run the tanks down to the last 30 litres (6½ gallons) or so with no fear of air entering the fuel feeds due to fuel slop within the main tanks. For the (total) 1,000-litre (200-gallon) main tanks this represents a figure of 3 per cent unusable fuel against the 20 per cent of the conventional system.

Draining the service tank simply involves closing the gate valve on the main tank, removing the stop plug in the end of the service tank

gate valve and placing a large bucket beneath the outlet. You then open the gate valve fully and drain the contents of the service tank into the bucket. As this happens most of the sediment and any water are flushed out into the bucket.

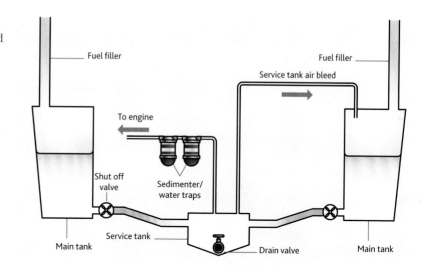

Above **The 'full-use' fuel system, with a small service tank below the level of the main tanks from which the fuel is drawn.**

Below **Draining is simply a matter of removing the stop plug and opening the valve to drain the tank into a bucket.**

Tank level gauge

When you're out on the water with the engine running, it's helpful to know how much fuel you have left without having to look inside the tank. A sender attached to the fuel tank will transmit a signal through a wire to the appropriate gauge, mounted on the instrument panel.

Other types of tank that can also benefit from having a level gauge fitted are the water tank and a waste tank. In a fuel tank, the sender is a float, which rises and falls with the level within the tank. While each type of tank requires a different type of sender, fitting a sender is similar for all three types of tank.

Gauge and sender compatibility

The most important point to bear in mind when fitting an electrically operated tank level gauge is that the gauge and sender must be calibrated to each other or the readings will never be correct. Senders and gauges from different manufacturers will not operate together.

There are also two standards for sender resistance: European and American, and again they will not operate together. A fuel sender supplies the gauge with a resistance (measured in ohms), which the gauge then displays on a dial.

A European resistance fuel sender will have an output of around 10 ohms on empty. As the fuel level rises, so will the level of ohms. A US resistance fuel sender will have an output of around 240 ohms and the resistance will decrease as the fuel level increases. This difference is why you need to match the resistance of the gauge and sender – or the gauge will give the opposite of its proper reading. So to avoid problems, buy the gauge and the matching sender at the same time.

Left **Fuelling up in harbour. The fuel sender transmits a signal to the gauge, indicating the level of fuel in the tank.**

Below **A float-type fuel sender attached to a gauge with temporary wiring to allow it to be checked for accuracy.**

Types of gauge

While fuel gauges generally use a simple float arm to measure the level, water gauges today often use a float that slides up and down a stainless steel dip tube, with the electronics sealed within the tube, to avoid any long-term corrosion. This type of dip tube can be used on fuel systems, too.

Waste tank gauges also use a system sealed within a tube and no float. This system relies on the liquid to provide the contact to allow the level to be monitored and, with no moving parts, avoids the problem of any waste matter stopping a float from sliding up and down.

Installation and electrics

Installation is broadly the same for most types of sender. The float-type fuel tank sender has a recess in the mounting flange that allows it to be passed into the tank to allow fitting from the outside, but alternatively, you could install the sender into the inspection hatch (similar to a window) positioned on the top of the tank.

Wiring for all types of level gauge is straightforward, although you should always consult the diagram provided with the gauge and sender to ensure there are no differences.

Left **A water tank sender with sealed electronics, which will also work in fuel tanks.**

Left **A solid state waste tank sender with no moving parts, plus gauge.**

Left **A stainless steel inspection hatch with fuel filler and vent spigots, plus the hole for installing the fuel gauge sender.**

Below **The electrical circuit for the fuel sender and gauge.**

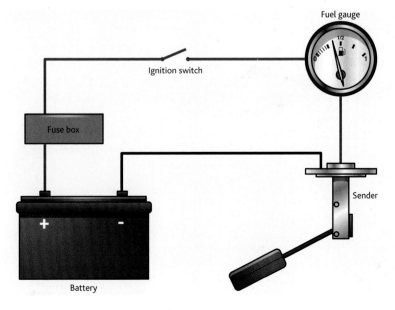

Fuel gauge

Ignition switch

Fuse box

Sender

Battery

SAFETY TIP

Be extremely careful if you are working on a petrol tank that has had fuel in it as the vapours are highly volatile.

Windlass

An electric anchor windlass can be a vital improvement on a boat that does not have one factory fitted. Installing an electric windlass is not a difficult job, although it does need to be mounted on a strong base if it is to operate safely.

The modern anchor windlass is a very compact but powerful mechanism. Today's anchor windlass is a fraction of the size of its predecessors, yet has as much, if not more power and a generally higher operating speed. An electric windlass may have a horizontal or vertical axis. Vertical windlasses or capstans are usually compact due to the motor being mounted below deck, and offer a very low profile compared with the more traditional horizontal type where everything is contained within the windlass body above the deck.

There is very little difference in the installation process for vertical and horizontal windlasses as the electrical connections, including the main circuit breaker, reversing contactor and the wiring, are all identical.

It is generally not advisable to fit a dedicated battery for the windlass as this complicates the charging system for all the other batteries and still requires heavy charging cables to be run through the boat. As long as power cables specified for the length of run are used, the system will operate perfectly.

A windlass kit

Windlass kits are available to purchase and will be the best method of installing a new windlass anchor yourself. Typically this includes the windlass, a manual operating spanner, the chain feed ring, which protects the sides of the hole where the chain passes into the chain locker, the windlass operating switch, the mounting gasket and the steel backing plate that fits below the deck, as well as a set of instructions.

Left **The Lewmar V700 windlass is a sleek flush-mounted design with a stainless steel housing. With a vertical axis, the motor is hidden down below.**

TIP

It is essential to only use calibrated chain of the correct size on a windlass, otherwise the chain will jump and slip off the gypsy (wheels that allow the chain to engage).

Mounting the windlass

Position the cutting and mounting template on the deck. If the deck is not perfectly flat, you will need a mounting pad to take up the curvature where the windlass is to be fitted. There must also be a sufficient drop inside the chain locker to allow the weight of the chain to draw it off the gypsy when hauling in. A minimum of 300mm (12in) drop is required.

Use hole saws to cut the motor and chain access holes next to the holes for the mounting studs, which are drilled. Ensure that the mounting studs are snuggled up tight on the windlass, and then fit the mounting gasket. Apply polyurethane sealant to the deck around the cut-out and place the windlass into position ready for tightening down.

Electrical connections

It is important to use the correct size of cable for the length of run to avoid voltage drop and reduced performance. The cable run is the total length of the positive and negative cables when added together. Follow any wiring diagram supplied with your windlass kit.

The electrical panel is a simple piece of ply, with the circuit breaker and contactor screwed to the front and connections made at the back. Use heavy-duty crimp terminals for the cable terminations, and connect and tighten the in and out feeds to the circuit breaker. The connections to the contactor consist of heavy-duty crimps for the main power supply and standard terminals for the operating current. Use suitable cross-section cable for the power cable run. Connect the windlass switch using crimp terminals and set it into the main instrument panel.

FITTING THE WINDLASS

The basic windlass kit, excluding the reversing contactor (a type of switching device) and main circuit breaker.

Using the template supplied for cutting the access holes and drilling for the fixing bolts.

After sealing the edges of the holes with polyurethane sealant, place the windlass into position.

Connecting the circuit breaker and contactor.

Connecting the operating cables to the contactor with heavy-duty crimp terminals.

The operating switch mounted on the side of the main instrument panel.

Chain counter

A chain (or rode) counter is used for measuring the amount of chain running when it is out of sight of the helm. This gadget is able to 'count' the amount of chain being hauled or veered around the gypsy (the wheels that allow the chain to engage), and this is displayed on a gauge. Some chain counters are more straightforward to install than others, as not all windlasses are equipped to work easily with a rode counter.

You should be able to fit chain counters to any make and type of windlass, but each installation will vary depending on the style of windlass. The sender consists of a sensor and a magnet. Each time the magnet passes the sensor it 'knows' that the gypsy has made one turn, which equates to a certain amount of chain being hauled or veered. The display on the gauge can be adjusted to suit the circumference of the gypsy and therefore the amount of chain moved with each revolution.

The first step is to decide the position of the sensor. It will need to be protected from physical damage, while also being close enough to the gypsy to sense the magnet passing close to its face.

A suitable position is also needed for mounting the magnet within the gypsy. If there are no appropriate external mounting positions for the sensor, it should be mounted somewhere inside. To fit a chain counter, you can purchase chain or rode counter sets, which normally include a gauge, sensor, sensor holders and two magnets of different sizes.

Dismantling the windlass
The first job is to take the windlass apart. Remove the clutch nut, chain stripper and clutch insert from the

Below **The chain counter kit with gauge, sensor, magnets and brackets.**

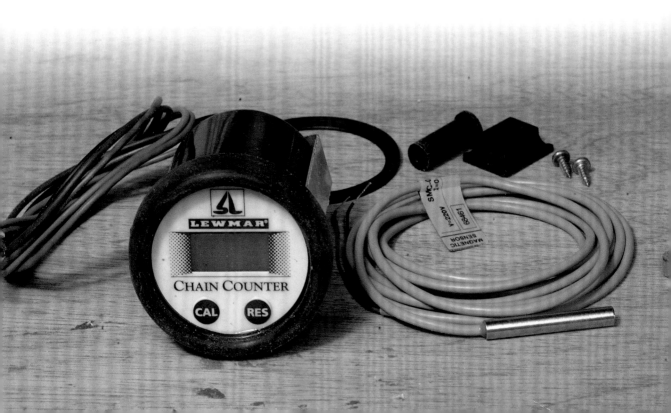

drive shaft of the windlass. Also remove the two drive pins that are found between the clutch insert and drive shaft, followed by the chain control arm and gypsy. Turn the windlass over and remove the six cover screws before lifting off the side cover.

Planning the sensor position

Lift out the various drive gears to make room to examine the interior to find the best mounting point for the sensor. The most suitable position for this particular unit is below the gypsy, which means the sensor has to be mounted at an angle to clear the large drive gear. It is important to ensure there is sufficient thickness on the gypsy to accommodate the magnet – perhaps behind one of the chain 'teeth'.

Fitting the magnet in the gypsy

Use a centre punch to mark the position of the hole for the magnet on the side of the gypsy. Drill the hole with an 8mm (⁵⁄₁₆in) bit or whatever size corresponds to the size of the magnet, taking extreme care to ensure the drill only goes far enough in to accommodate the magnet, with an additional 1mm (³⁄₆₄in) for sealing with epoxy.

Clean the hole with methylated spirit and a paper towel prior to sealing in the magnet with epoxy. Fill the hole with epoxy before inserting the magnet, which is placed into the hole and pushed down gently so that the adhesive squeezes up around it. This ensures the hole is completely filled, with no empty voids remaining to weaken the chain 'tooth'. Place a final drop on top and clean off the residue.

FITTING THE SENSOR AND MAGNET

Unscrew the clutch nut, chain stripper and clutch insert from the drive shaft. The method will vary depending on the make of windlass but is generally an easy task.

Unbolt the case securing machine screws. Once again, this will vary between makes but the securing screws or bolts are generally fairly straightforward to locate.

This shows the position chosen for the chain sensor on this windlass. Find a position that is protected from the elements and from physical damage.

Install the magnet into the gypsy by mounting one through the chain gripping teeth. This allows enough depth for the hole to be drilled without passing right through.

The magnet can be seen sitting in place in the drilled hole. Pour epoxy into the hole. This forces some of the epoxy out but ensures that the hole is filled.

The magnet is totally sealed into place. The epoxy that surrounds the magnet ensures that maximum strength is returned to the area where the hole was drilled.

Chain counter 2

Installing the sensor

The next step is to install the sensor so that the magnet passes over its face on every revolution. You need to accurately measure from the centre of the gypsy to the centre of the magnet, and transfer the measurement to the body of the windlass. After marking and centre-punching, place the drill bit in the correct position for drilling (in this case the hole has to be drilled at an angle). Check the position of the sensor to ensure it won't foul the gears inside or protrude too far.

To mount the sensor, create a simple 1mm (³⁄₆₄in)-thick stainless steel bracket in the vice and drill it to accept the mounting clamp that was supplied with the kit. Drill a countersunk hole in the base of the windlass body for mounting the sensor holder. Clean the inside of the hole for the sensor face with methylated spirit and paper towel, ready for installing the sensor on its mount and bolting it into place. Make any final adjustments to the sensor on its mount and tighten the bolts. Use epoxy to seal the sensor into the body inside and out.

The sensor cable

Run the sensor cable out of the bottom of the windlass body through the same aperture as the motor cables. It is a good idea to apply polyurethane sealant onto the sensor cable to bond it to the windlass base and prevent any possibility of it moving and getting snagged in the gears. Once the sealant has cured make sure that the cables can't come anywhere near the gearing before finally closing the case.

THE SENSOR INSTALLATION

Drill a hole to install the sensor. This hole is drilled at an angle, so begin with a small drill bit and gradually increase the bit size until the hole is the required diameter.

Bolt the sensor into place on its bracket, ensuring that it lines up correctly with the drilled hole and finally tighten the securing nuts and bolts.

Seal the sensor into place with epoxy. Ensure that the hole is completely filled to prevent water entering the casing and also ensure the sensor is protected.

Pass the sensor through the same hole as the motor cables (if there is enough space). Push silicone sealant into the hole around the cables to make the seal.

Refit the case onto a bed of polyurethane sealant. This model of windlass has no gasket and just relies on the sealant. Other models may be sealed by a gasket instead.

The finished job with the sensor and magnet protected behind the gypsy. The new chain counter can now have a final test to ensure everything is in position.

Reassembly

Grease the gears and reassemble them before closing up the case with a bead of sealant around the edge (as there is no gasket for this joint). Place the side cover over the main shaft located on the two alignment pegs and press down onto the casing. Apply thread-locking fluid (an adhesive) to the threads of the Allen head machine screws, and insert them into their places in the casing.

Tighten them a little at a time, until all are secure and sealant has squeezed out all around the joint.

Reassemble the gypsy, stripper, clutch insert and nut in the reverse order to their removal. The reassembled windlass looks no different now it is complete, apart from the additional sensor wire.

Finally, fit the gauge close to the windlass operating switch in any convenient position.

> **TIP**
>
> Calibrate the chain counter before use to ensure that it is reading accurately. You can set whatever measurement system you wish (such as feet or metres) via the settings on the gauge.

Below **The final positioning of the gauge for the chain counter (also see** *inset***).**

Wheel steering

Fitting a wheel steering pedestal in a yacht's cockpit to replace a tiller arrangement can greatly improve the enjoyment of sailing, and also form a platform for tables, drinks holders and instrument mounts.

Production yachts under about 9m (30ft) are often supplied with tiller steering, but most can be converted to wheel steering with relative ease. While a tiller can give great feedback from the rudder, it also has to be directly connected to the rudderstock so the helmsman is limited in where he can sit while retaining a good view forward. Tiller extensions can help, but a wheel is more straightforward to use, and if correctly set up has very little weight on it, so youngsters or those new to sailing can enjoy steering the boat intuitively under supervision.

Because it is indirectly connected to the rudder, the pedestal supporting the wheel can be located further forward than a tiller, and thus becomes the focal point of the cockpit. The pedestal also becomes a support for a social table, as well as for the throttle controls, keeping them right by the helmsman. Navigation instruments, engine gauges and important switches such as the anchor remote control and navigation lights, can all be mounted easily to hand, rather than scattered around the cockpit.

Wheel steering particularly lends itself to small motorboats and RIBs, usually requiring just a single Teleflex cable. This allows the wheel, or a 'jockey' console, to be placed well forward in the boat. This centres the helmsman and greatly improves overall trim, resulting in better performance under way.

On some boats that have been converted to wheel steering, the rudderstock can retain its ability to take a tiller, so this gives an emergency steering option, and also allows windvane self-steering to be attached more easily. To steer by a wheel, the rudderstock needs to be fitted with a quadrant, which is usually a quarter section of a large pulley wheel to take the steering wires, or with an arm that can accept the terminal fitting of a pushrod.

However your boat is designed, most manufacturers will have a solution for converting from tiller to wheel.

Left **Wheel steering will create a focal point in the cockpit, and make handling a boat more intuitive for less experienced yachtsmen.**

Below **Even quite small yachts such as this 23ft (7m) one can benefit from a conversion to wheel steering. This pedestal has been modified to carry a small instrument panel that can easily be monitored by the helmsman.**

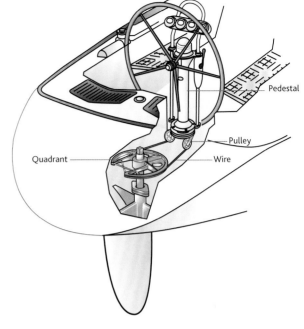

Pedestal

Pulley

Quadrant

Wire

Above **This Halmatic motorboat has an emergency tiller arrangement where the tiller bar drops into a slot in the rudder stock. Many yachts with wheel steering have a similar arrangement.**

Types of tiller to wheel conversion

When deciding whether your boat can be converted from a tiller to a wheel without compromising the looks or functionality of the cockpit, you need to take into account how the rudder is designed and supported. This will tell you how feasible each type is for the design of your vessel:

Teleflex cable: Ideal for RIBs and small motorboats, this very simple system uses a single push-pull cable within a fixed outer sleeve. The inner cable simply pushes or pulls the outboard or tiller arm to port or starboard.

Cable and wire: Another relatively simple system, with the benefit of allowing for complicated twists and turns within the hull. The wheel has a chain attached to geared sprockets within the pedestal body, the lower one of which is attached to a drum. Two steel wires are wrapped around the drum, each being led to the rudder quadrant by a system of pulleys.

Rack and pinion: Similar in operation to a vehicle's steering system, the wheel operates a rack and pinion that connects to the rudder via solid metal bars. Rugged and robust, with direct feedback, the only downside is that the bars have to run in straight lines.

Servo assisted: This is essentially a power-steering version of the rack and pinion, where a motor within the drive chain takes the weight off the wheel by providing additional thrust.

Hydraulic: A hydraulic pump on the wheel boss operates a hydraulic ram connected directly to the rudderstock. These systems can be very powerful, but also don't give much feedback, and can suffer a little creeping in the pump, so they aren't so good for wind-powered self- steering systems that connect to the wheel by control lines.

The rudderstock may need adapting with the fitting of a steering quadrant, or a connection point for a lever arm. It will also need rudder stops to prevent the rudder

Above **This simple wheel conversion shows the fitting of wires to a quadrant. More complex and powerful systems are available that use car-style rack and pinions, hydraulics and even servos for power assistance.**

exceeding 30 degrees each side of the centre. Attaching an autopilot is very straightforward. Some steering set-ups, such as the hydraulic and servo assisted, have the pilot operating on its own independent system. Others are physically connected to the wheel instead.

TIP

A nice finishing touch is to wrap the wheel with a leather trim, which is kind on the hands and provides a good grip in the wet. Some wheels, such as a model from Lewmar, can actually fold inwards when not in use to give more room in the cockpit, while others are easily detachable.

Bow thruster

It doesn't take much of a breeze to make berthing a boat a little tricky, but a correctly sized bow thruster will provide enough lateral thrust to take the drama out of manoeuvres.

A bow thruster is simply a propeller set below the waterline and usually in a tunnel, although some can retract up into the hull via a hatch while others can be mounted in an external pod. The propeller is set at right angles to the keel and coupled to an electric or hydraulic motor. By running the motor forward, or in reverse, a powerful jet of water is pushed out to either port or starboard, driving the bow in the opposite direction.

Below **A bow thruster will allow a much greater degree of control, especially when reversing or when short-handed. This singlehander is moving the yacht's bow into the wind to clear the pontoon.**

Bow thrusters are now very common, and many are fitted as standard on some new yachts and motorboats. For cruising vessels over 12m (40ft) they are almost obligatory in today's crowded marinas. Even quite small craft greatly benefit from having that extra bit of control at the bow, especially long-keeled boats that have to reverse into a tight berth. Bow thrusters are also hugely useful for large, heavy yachts that may be lightly crewed, allowing a couple to handle the boat without ever leaving the deck.

The use of remote control enables a singlehander to keep the boat held against a windward dock while the mooring lines are released.

For many skippers, it's like having a crewman on the foredeck with a handy boathook.

Owners who have retrofitted a bow thruster often say how much more relaxed their cruising has become, and how they can now visit quite restricted waterways and harbours that would have deterred them in the past. The fact that their boat can be spun within its own length, accurately steered in reverse and, with an interplay between rudder, prop and bow thruster, even moved bodily sideways, affords them much greater control at close quarters.

TIP

As the boat must be out of the water, fitting a bow thruster is best done during the routine winter haul-out, which will avoid the cost of additional cranage.

Left **A twin propulsion unit like this Norwegian one is typically suitable for larger boats (13–18m/42–60ft).**

Below left **The tunnel for a bow thruster below the waterline. The propulsion unit has one or two propellers that assist in manoeuvring the vessel without having to use forward motion.**

Bow thrusters are readily available on the retrofit market, and are usually sold as a kit. Competent DIY enthusiasts should be able to fit one fairly easily, provided they have knowledge of electrics, as the current used by the motor is quite high, and the circuit involves solenoids and breakers. Specialist fitters will be happy to fit one for you – or simply do the tricky bits – and will usually have experience of boats similar to your own.

Before fitting a bow thruster, you have to decide how much power you want. Most manufacturers will offer a guide to this in their promotional material, but it's not just the length of the boat that matters, it's also its profile. This is because the biggest effect is the surface area the wind will strike, known as the windage factor. Most manufacturers recommend a bow thruster that can overcome a 25-knot wind directly on the beam of your particular vessel. The underwater profile will also determine how effective a bow thruster will be. A shallow forefoot will prove quite skittish, but a deep bow will have more resistance. Each manufacturer will have a bow thruster model to suit your craft's

size, shape and windage factor perfectly, and some even offer a few simple formulas to make the right choice. If caught between models, it pays to go up a size so you have some power in reserve.

Some bow thrusters will have a single propeller, while others will have two on the same hub, which makes the thrust more even in both directions. When choosing a thruster, look how much maintenance it will need and how easy it is to get to the anodes for periodic replacement.

Installing a tunnel unit

A bow thruster can be fitted to virtually any hull type, so steel, aluminium, GRP or even ferro-cement will present no problems.

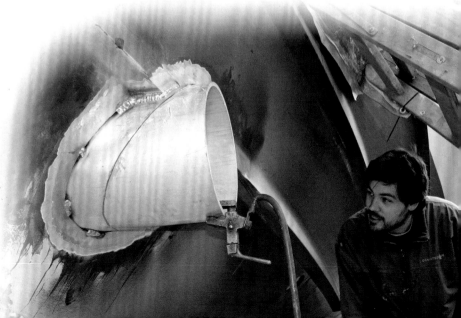

Right **Bow thruster tunnels come in a range of materials and diameters to match a yacht's hull, such as this example going into a steel motorboat.**

Bow thruster 2

FITTING THE TUNNEL

1 Measure and make small holes for the centre of the cut-out on each side of the hull. Pass a rod through with a rotating arm and a scribe attached, set to the outer diameter of the tube to draw the cut-out.

2 Cut the hull to the marks. Remove the waste and abrade back. Gouge back any exposed foam core and then seal the foam with strips of wetted rovings and fibreglass paste.

3 Insert the fibreglass tube and check for size and fit. Carefully mark the protruding ends before removing the tube again and cutting the ends to fit the shape of the hull.

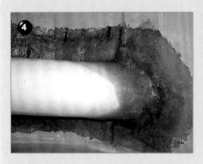

4 Fibreglass the tube into place, ensuring a completely watertight seal, especially on the hard-to-reach underside of the tunnel. Paint the fibreglass with topcoat for a clean bilge area.

5 Sculpt an eyebrow over the protrusion of the tunnel, although some boats opt for a flush opening. Apply thickened fibreglass paste and shape while still wet. Abrade back when cured.

6 Apply three layers of gel coat laid 'wet on wet'. The fibreglass matt deflector eyebrow at the mouth of the tunnel helps to prevent air being sucked in the tunnel.

The key factor, however, is the positioning. The tunnel should be as far forward and as deep as possible. However, even though you may be able to identify the ideal position from the outside, it's the interior structure that is the decider. This is why specialists always make their first location marks on the inside of the bow to ensure the tunnel is clear of any bulkheads or other internal obstructions.

Ensuring a good fit

A successful installation requires accurate measurements, so the twin props can be optimally positioned within the tunnel for equal thrust in both directions. Each thruster unit is already matched to a specific tunnel diameter so the prop sits centrally with an even gap all round. For cruising yachts, tunnel diameters typically range from 140mm (5½in) through to 300mm (11³⁄₁₆in) and are also supplied in various lengths.

After measuring, cut a hole through the hull, following the ellipse left by the scribe – the outside diameter of the tube. A sabre saw is best for use on GRP. This part is often left to professionals, although a DIY enthusiast can tackle the job with the right tools. Err towards a slight over-cut, as any gaps can always be filled later. Insert the tube and mark where it needs trimming before removing it again to make the cut with a fine-tooth metal saw.

To prevent the risk of water absorption in a foam sandwich exposed by the cut-out, it's important to scoop back the exposed foam and seal it with fibreglass rovings and paste before the trimmed tunnel goes back in. If fitting an external deflector or 'eyebrow', which can help water flow, thoroughly abrade the hull around the tube where the deflector will be sculpted to aid adhesion. Where the tunnel is very near the waterline, sometimes a horizontal 'eyelid' is added to prevent air being sucked in when the bow thruster is working.

The next job is to fit the bow thruster unit itself, using a template applied to the outside of the tunnel within the boat to show where the bolt holes will go. The template should indicate how much offset to allow so the propeller will sit directly above the keel (single prop gear legs). The whole unit can be installed at an angle, fore or aft, so it can fit under the floorboards or in a forward locker. The gear leg assembly, which holds the propeller, is detachable. After the watertight gasket is covered in sealant, the gear leg is inserted up through the tunnel for connection to an inner bracket, which will also support the motor.

With the motor positioned correctly you can consider the cables and provision for the bow thruster's battery. Most installations feature a traction battery very close to the

motor itself, and charged by thinner wires from the engine alternator. Check the cables running from the battery to the motor for length, allowing a bit extra for flexing before cutting them to size and adding the terminals. Shrink wrap the crimps. Add the control box to the circuit along with a high-amperage fuse.

Control of the bow thruster can be accessed by push-buttons on the deck, or a joystick or buttons by the helm. Hard-wired or wireless remotes are also available, and controls can be repeated between helm stations.

FITTING THE MOTOR

①

Attach the motor to its mounting and place against the tunnel. If space is tight, the motor can be set at an angle or laid almost flat with a support. Mark the securing holes and drill them into the tunnel body.

②

Fit a watertight gasket where the leg enters the tunnel, coat with sealant, feed the gear leg into the pre-drilled hole and bolt it into place. Fit the propeller and anode to the hub, with the motor attached inside the boat.

Right **Consider where the battery will go. It is best to have the battery box as close as possible to the thruster unit to save on heavy-duty cable runs. This battery bank, which also powers the electric windlass, is charged by thinner cables from the engine alternator.**

Stern thruster

Even twin-engined boats can benefit from having a thruster at the stern, and when used in tandem with a bow thruster, a boat can be docked in the most trying of conditions. Fitting a stern thruster is usually less complex than installing the tunnel version on the bow.

Stern thrusters are often found on very large yachts, or on motorboats above 15m (49ft) in length, mainly to help overcome the additional windage these larger vessels attract.

A propeller is mounted at 90 degrees to the yacht's keel, and is run backwards or forwards to push the stern to port or starboard. Just as with bow thrusters, there are several types available. The stern is usually too wide for a conventional tunnel across the yacht, so the most common alternative, particularly

on vessels with a flat transom, is to attach an external tunnel unit to the underwater section of the stern, as central and as deep as possible.

On stern-drive boats, the drive legs sometimes interfere with the thrust, as the unit has to sit between them, so the tunnel has 'eyebrows' to deflect the thrust downwards for the best effect. This also helps if the hull is quite shallow. The motor can be mounted inboard, or is sometimes contained within the external unit itself.

On large sailing yachts, retractable thrusters are a good solution. Although more expensive and complex than exterior tunnel units, they have the added advantage of being able to gain some depth when deployed, so can be used at the extreme ends of the hull. This is very useful on shallow-draught sailing yachts, especially at the bow.

Two other types of stern thruster are available. One is an external pod, a scaled-down version of the tunnel thruster and streamlined to stay

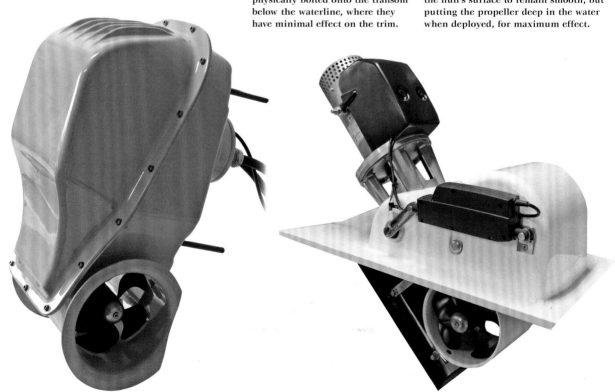

Left **Stern thrusters on motorboats are commonly independent units physically bolted onto the transom below the waterline, where they have minimal effect on the trim.**

Below **A larger sailing yacht may use a retractable thruster for the stern, allowing the hull's surface to remain smooth, but putting the propeller deep in the water when deployed, for maximum effect.**

permanently attached to the underside of the hull. This type is easy to fit as it only requires two small holes through the bilge. A water-powered thruster uses jets of water directed to port or starboard through nozzles in the hull. This system allows one centrifugal pump to power jets in the bow and stern at the same time, and requires very little surgery to the hull itself. It is a very quiet system, unlike the notoriously noisy tunnel thrusters.

Choosing a stern thruster

When fitting a stern thruster, you have to ensure that it will be effective, and manufacturers will advise on which of their models will pack the right amount of torque for your vessel's profile, while also taking the amount of windage into account. A paper template will be supplied with the kit to ensure the various bolt and wiring holes are correctly aligned.

Stern thrusters are often found on vessels that already have a bow thruster, so dual controls can

Below **An 'Exturn' pod thruster under the keel of a yacht. This type of stern thruster is very easy to fit as it only requires two relatively small holes through the hull.**

FITTING A STERN THRUSTER

First use a template to accurately cut the bolt holes and aperture in the transom for the inner gearbox bracket. On this model, the motor is inboard.

Get one person to lift the unit into position so another person can feed the bolts into place. Use sealant around the flange to ensure there is no leakage.

be used to allow the skipper to manoeuvre using both thrusters in tandem. Safety cut-outs on electric thrusters prevent the overheating of the motors with extended use, but hydraulic thrusters can be used indefinitely (although they do rob the main engine of some revs).

A stern thruster is likely to be used less than its bow-mounted equivalent, but it will come into

its own on a windward dock, or when you need precision to move the boat sideways, or even in a complete circle.

Left **External thrusters can be mounted at both the bow and the stern. This graphic shows the 'Exturn' model fulfilling both roles.**

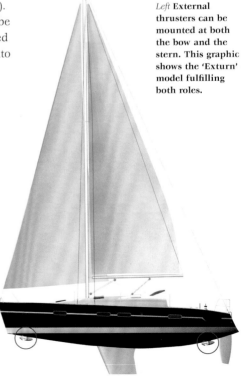

Trim tabs

Trim tabs, which are fitted to the transom of a motorboat, can improve ride comfort, safety and fuel economy significantly. They are relatively straightforward to replace, or fit from scratch.

Trim tabs help keep motorboats at an optimum fore and aft pitch to maximise speed and fuel economy. A different setting is needed when operating the boat at different speeds, and for different loads being carried – for example, when the number of people on board varies. One of the most popular upgrades therefore is to replace trim tabs that can't be adjusted by the helmsman with models that have electric or hydraulic actuators.

Aside from changing worn-out units, other reasons for replacing trim tabs include fitting a more powerful model, or upgrading to hydraulic systems. These tend to have fewer problems relating to water ingress in the electrical components and are therefore inherently more reliable.

Size and position

Most trim tabs are 23cm (9in) long, and, as a general rule, stay in proportion to the length of the boat. However, 31cm (12in) long trim tabs may be appropriate for semi-displacement boats and other relatively slow vessels with a cruising speed of under 14 knots. Boats with limited transom space, such as those with multiple outboard motors or outdrives, can also be fitted with a 31-cm (12-in) model. They should be located just above the bottom of the transom, and 25–100mm (1–4in) inboard of the edge of the chine.

Many trim tabs are held in place with self-tapping screws, rather than being bolted through the transom. To ensure the screws have maximum grip, it's vital to confirm the correct size of pilot drill is used for making the screw hole. A marine adhesive sealant should be inserted into

Below **Trim tabs can increase speed and reduce fuel consumption. Upgrading is a popular and worthwhile modification.**

FITTING THE TRIM TABS

1. Position the tabs 10cm (4in) in from the chine and mark the position of the screw holes.

2. Bed the tabs on sealant and screw the fastenings into pre-drilled pilot holes.

3. Attach the actuator strut base to the tab, then drill holes for the transom mount.

4. Connect up the hydraulic hose or wiring, as appropriate, before…

5. …finally fitting the top of the strut, bedding it on marine sealant.

6. With this system the actuating motor can be placed in a dry place below deck.

the screw holes, as well as around the edge of the fitting. Avoid the temptation to overtighten the screws, though, or you will squeeze all the sealant out.

Electric and hydraulic trim tabs

Electric trim tabs have powerful motors that draw a large electrical current, albeit for only short lengths of time, so they should be wired with large diameter cables to minimise power losses between the battery, switchgear and motor.

Electric models have the actuator within the piston, so to prevent damage from water ingress, it's important to ensure a good seal

between this and the transom. Hydraulic models, however, have their electrics remote from the piston, so they can be fitted somewhere where they won't get wet. The key to installing the hydraulic element is to make certain everything remains meticulously clean – the smallest amount of dust or grit will rapidly accelerate wear on pistons and seals.

Right **A newly installed trim tab. The base of the tab should be located above the bottom of the hull.**

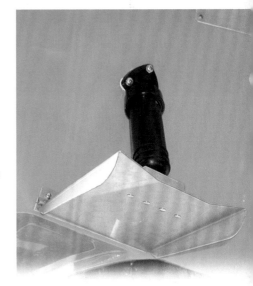

General mechanics tips

Many yachts are destined for long-distance voyaging, so need systems that are easy to maintain in remote areas of the world. Here are some ideas that will help keep your mechanical systems running smoothly, particularly when it comes to preventative maintenance.

Ready for an oil change?

Changing the oil should be a regular service job on a long cruise and greatly enhances engine longevity, but it can be awkward to assemble the various components needed, plus the oil change itself can be messy. If you have everything in place in the engine area – the electric pump, dipstick extractor tube and drain tube – they can all be ready for a quick oil change.

Essential tools

Keeping tools in a toolbox can lead to corrosion, and could require digging in a locker in an emergency to find the right one. An engine room bulkhead toolbox could be the start of a dedicated tool collection. Owners can add to the basic factory-supplied selection with their own favourites over time.

Fuel junctions

On yachts that have several fuel tanks, it is important to be able to close off each tank and allow each motor to draw from another in case some contaminated fuel is picked up, or the diesel bug affects one of the tanks. This may create a complicated junction, but if each lever is clearly marked this allows the engine or generator to draw off any of the separate tanks, and also divert the return to a tank that is uncontaminated.

Below **This Hallberg-Rassy has everything already in position for when an oil change is needed.**

Bottom left **The owner of this Nordhavn is able to close off fuel tanks by referring to the clearly marked junctions.**

Below **A bulkhead toolbox safely stores tools and prevents them going rusty, which can sometimes happen when they are left in a traditional toolbox. Note the torch.**

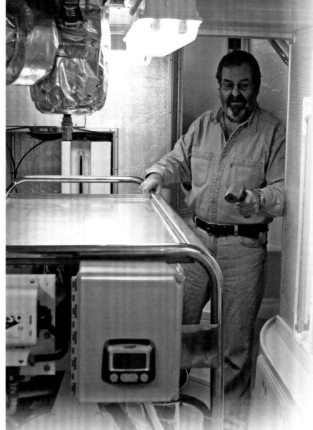

OTHER TIPS

Tools required for more specialist tasks can also be kept in the engine compartment in their own brackets, so they can't get lost or confused with general tools. Many motorboats also keep the fuel filters and the tools required to change them in a very accessible place right by the inspection hatch.

Top **All of the tanks in this motor yacht have glass sight gauges, carefully set up and protected between steel cheeks to avoid accidental damage.**

Above left **Sensitive alarms tell the owner when the temperature rises above the pre-set optimum level.**

Above **A laser probe can be used as part of routine temperature checks.**

Fuel gauges

Fuel tank gauges vary in reliability, but an infallible check is a site gauge, where the liquid level is indicated on a clear tube. They are most useful in motorboats where they are carefully calibrated and protected. Fuel usage is also monitored accurately. Equally important is the flow of liquids, which can be seen with arrow indicators. This will greatly assist any mechanic abroad who may need to work on the system.

Temperature alarm

Most engine-configured overheat alarms only operate when the water temperature is close to boiling, by which time damage from a cooling blockage may have already occurred.

Available now are adjustable temperature alarms that are easy to fit, and can be set to just a few degrees above the engine's maximum operating temperature. They sound an alarm the moment the pre-set threshold is crossed. Sensitive electrical probes can be taped against the surface of any component that may get hot early, such as impeller cases.

Spot temperature handset

Another immediate check is to use a laser probe in the engine compartment. The battery-powered handset reads a spot temperature, so it can be aimed at the most susceptible parts of the engine or generator cooling system. It only takes a few seconds to check every cooling component in the engine area, and can be done as a routine check every hour or so on passage. This is particularly useful on hard-to-reach components.

Electrical

6

Electrical skills

To many boatowners, marine electrics are something of a black art, but the fundamentals of fault-finding and repairs are governed by only a few basic principles.

Multimeters are the key tool used for diagnosing electrical problems – the resistance settings of a meter can be used to check the integrity of electrical equipment, from fuses and bulbs to complex items such as water pumps and heaters.

Battery state

The simplest way to check the state of charge of the batteries is by using a meter to test the battery's voltage – digital models are ideal for this, as they give a resolution better than 0.1 volts. It can take several hours for the voltage of a battery bank to stabilise after charging, or using

power, so the longer you can wait before taking voltage readings the better. However, most of the change in voltage occurs in the first 30 minutes.

When fully charged, a battery with a nominal 12 volts will, in theory, provide 13.2 volts, although 12.9 volts is a more realistic maximum. When this figure has reduced to 12.2 volts, only 50 per cent of the battery's capacity is remaining, and it should be recharged to maintain its lifespan. At 11.9 volts the battery will be around 90 per cent discharged. Some larger boats have a 24-volt electrical system, in which case the values above should be doubled.

Using a voltmeter can lead to a false sense of security with batteries that are near the end of their life,

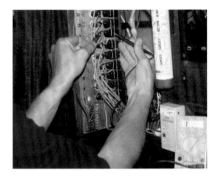

Above **A digital multimeter is a key diagnostic tool used in electrical repairs.**

because the meter won't show whether the battery's capacity to accept charge has declined dramatically. However, if navigation lights are turned on during the test, a change in the reading will give an indication of the battery's condition. Ideally, only a small voltage drop will be noticed for a battery that's in good condition. If a large voltage drop is experienced – ie, over 0.3 volts – then the battery is suspect.

Below **Using a digital multimeter to check the voltage of a battery. At 12.21 volts, this one is holding about half of its full charge.**

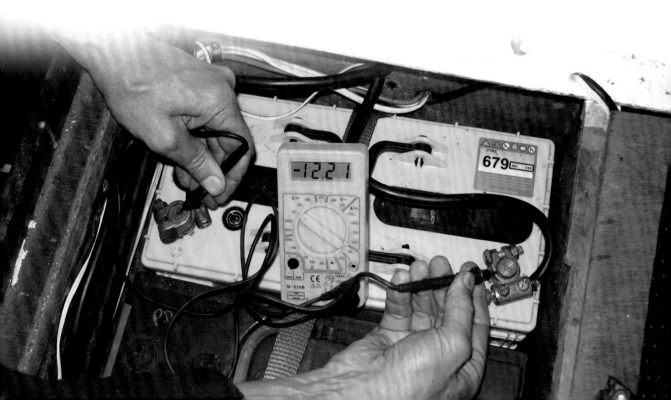

INSTALLING A DECK GLAND

Loosen the top ring and drill a hole a little smaller than each wire through the rubber part of the gland using a sharp drill bit.

Pull the wires through the rubber part of the seal. Soapy water can be used for lubrication if necessary.

A watertight seal is created when the top part of the gland is screwed down tightly, compressing the rubber.

Wiring diameter

When electricity passes along a wire, some energy is lost as heat. The smaller the wire for a given current, the greater the heat. To minimise energy loss in a long cable run, use a wire one or two sizes larger than the recommended minimum, especially for high-load items such as anchor windlasses and bowthrusters.

The dangers of using wires that are too small cannot be overemphasised: a wire that becomes too hot will catch fire. If fuses rather than circuit breakers are used to protect circuits and equipment, it's important to use the correct-sized fuse for each circuit. To work this out, find out what each device or circuit draws, and then select a fuse that is the next size up.

If you know the voltage of your boat's electrical system and the power rating of the device in watts, simply divide the number of watts by volts to get the current the device will draw.

For example, an interior lighting circuit with eight 10-watt bulbs will draw 80 watts, so:

$$\text{Current drawn} = \frac{80}{12} = 6.67\text{A}$$

Therefore, an 8A fuse is needed.

If a fuse blows repeatedly, don't be tempted to replace it with a larger size – fuses are designed to protect wiring from overheating. Instead, identify the fault and rectify it.

Waterproofing

Although most boats' 12-volt and 24-volt DC electrical systems don't present the dangers inherent in mains voltage systems, water ingress can cause damage. Any cable passing through the deck should therefore be led through a deck gland to ensure water is kept out of the wiring.

Never leave the waterproofing of connections to chance – join the cables within a waterproof junction box or use waterproof wire connectors. Standard electrical connections should not be used, as they will not keep the water out.

Right **Water ingress is a common problem. Corroded contacts should be cleaned with fine emery paper.**

Radar

Although in reality it is probably one of the least used pieces of equipment on board, for many boatowners radar is very close to the top of the equipment wish list. You'll certainly be grateful for it when unexpected fog rolls in or you have to enter a strange harbour late at night.

Radar is straightforward for the competent DIY boatowner to install. The kit consists of two main items, the radome (or scanner) and the screen, which are connected by a multi-core cable.

The radome needs to be mounted as high as possible; on a sailing yacht this is likely to be two-thirds of the way up the mast and on a motor cruiser this will be either on a mast or the wheelhouse roof. It should be accessible but clear of other large objects and the compass.

Fitting the radome

Before you can install the radome, you must prepare it by fitting the rubber drain tube into the aperture. Once fitted, you can trim it to length from underneath to suit the height of the radome on the mounting spacers. The 10-mm (3/8-in) nylon spacers are supplied for mounting the radome on a flat surface, which keeps the water drain tube clear of the surface. If it is to be fitted on a stand-off mast bracket, there is no need for the spacers.

Above **Once only the province of commercial vessels and large yachts, radars are now commonplace on smaller boats.**

You would generally run the cable from the display to the radome, rather than the other way around, as the connections on the radome end are much less bulky. These usually come encased in a heat shrink cover, making them as small and compact as possible, to ease passage through the vessel's trunking.

TIP

Before deciding where to fit the radome, check the length of your cable. This is supplied in a pre-cut length, and you want to avoid having to lengthen it if at all possible.

Running the cable is always going to be the most troublesome part of the installation, and there is no easy answer to getting cables behind bulkheads and through trunking.

An electrician's 'mouse' (these are lightweight fibreglass rods that clip together) can be a real help. But you can use other items to pass cables behind bulkheads – for example, the long plastic handle of a feather duster works well!

Once you have carried the radome up to the mast and bolted it securely in place, you can prepare the scanner end cabling for connecting by carefully cutting the heat shrink cover off the end and separating the cable ends from the in-line connector. You then remove the waterproof gland cap and sealing ring from the scanner and slip them over the end of the cable.

Once you have removed the radome cover, pass the cables through the gland, and plug the in-line connector into its socket. You then need to fit the four power cables into the connector block. After completing the connections, refit the inner cable cover and tighten the gland on the outside to prevent water entering through the cable aperture. Finally, refit the radome cover; the scanner installation is now complete.

INSTALLING A RADOME

The rubber drain tube needs to be fitted into the aperture.

The heat shrink-protected cable end makes it easier to thread the wires through.

The cable end is prepared for connecting to the radome by removing the heat shrink cover and separating the ends.

The connector plug and cable connections are joined up to the scanner.

Once the connections are completed, the cable cover can be fitted.

The radome can now be fitted and the scanner installation completed.

Trim angles

Before fitting the radome, it is important to decide whether it will need 'shimming' to adjust its angle, or whether it can be installed horizontally. This depends on the normal running trim of the vessel and is more relevant to motorboats. If the boat tends to run with a pronounced bows-up trim, the radome can be mounted on a wedge with a slight forward-down attitude, so that it is in the horizontal plane at cruising speed.

Radar 2

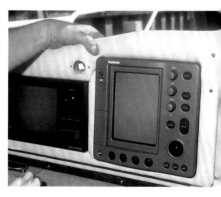

Where to fit the display

The ease or otherwise of fitting the radar display depends on whether the installation is to replace an old unit or whether it is being fitted for the first time. You may prefer to build all the instruments into the console rather than having them mounted on brackets. However, for many installations this will not be possible, so the first step is to find a suitable mounting position.

On sailing vessels the display is often mounted at the chart table down below, and on motor vessels at the helm. There are no set rules for the position so it is up to you to decide, depending on your own preferences and working practices.

Daylight-viewable colour LCD (liquid-crystal) displays are lightweight and their compact design makes them easier to fit into small spaces. However, there are still many CRT (cathode ray tube) displays on the second-hand market offering good performance.

Installing the display

In this upgrade, an old stand-alone system is replaced with a 180-mm (7-in) Raymarine display to interface with the rest of the integrated navigation system, which includes autopilot, GPS, chartplotter, speed/distance log, depth and electronic compass.

If you are replacing an old system, first remove the old monitor and position the mounting bracket to carry the new display. To have everything flush-mounted, you will need to align the new unit with the front of the instrument panel.

You may need to make minor modifications to the fascia panel if your display is a slightly different size. Fit the display onto the bracket and hand tighten the mounting nuts alongside. If you need to fill any space between the new radar and other instruments, cut a piece of ply to shape and cover with vinyl to match the rest of the instrument panel. Press this into position to fill the gap and provide a neat finish between the two instruments.

Above left **The display position with the old radar display still set into the console.**

Above right **Once the old mounting bracket has been removed, the new one is fitted in its place.**

Above **A small trim piece can fill the gap between the instruments if the new display is a slightly different size and shape from the old one. Once done, the display looks like an original fitting.**

Connecting the cables

The next job is to prepare the monitor end of the cable that had previously been run through the boat to the display. The three power cables are red (positive), black (negative) and unsheathed (drain). The latter is for connecting to an RF (radio frequency) ground system. Most small cruisers have no RF ground system, so this is connected to the battery negative supply. Use crimp terminals to make up the connection ends for the positive, negative and drain wires – a male spade for the positive wire, and a female spade for the negative – as this avoids any confusion when later disconnecting and reconnecting.

At the other end of the cable is a moulded plug that can be directly connected to the display. The power feed must come from the vessel's fuse or circuit breaker board, preferably a dedicated circuit, and be protected by an appropriately rated fuse or circuit breaker.

Plug the power cable into the back of the display, alongside the cable from the radome. The cables and plugs are totally different so there is no room for confusion. Once you have double-checked all the connections, you can switch on and test the unit.

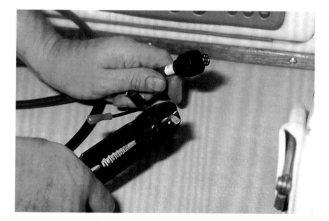

Left A crimping tool and terminals are the best way to achieve a reliable connection.

Left Connecting the cables to the display is simple as the plugs are totally different and cannot be confused.

Below Finally, switch on the radar and test.

Navtex/AIS

Navtex (Navigational Telex) has been around for many years and provides navigational, meteorological and safety information for vessels at sea, operating worldwide. AIS (Automatic Identification System) is a tracking system for identifying and locating other vessels. While Navtex and AIS both offer different types of information, they are equally useful. They are also straightforward to fit on board.

Navtex

Navtex brings on board up-to-date buoyage changes, navigational warnings, weather forecasts and gale warnings, and stores them in its memory until they can be viewed. This means that weather forecasts are no longer missed and can be viewed at any convenient time.

Similarly, buoyage changes and navigational warnings can be checked before setting off, which is particularly useful if charts are not fully up to date, with many people nowadays relying on just their chartplotters.

Navtex is broadcast from various stations in different locations around the world and the units are easily programmed to receive broadcasts only for the area you intend to cruise. This avoids receiving information for areas that are not relevant. Navtex is one of the simplest pieces of kit to install, needing only a power supply and a lead from the display to a short aerial to install on the pushpit, gantry or coachroof.

Above **The Navtex aerial picks up transmissions from a distance of 500 miles or further, and these are broadcast on 518kHz frequency worldwide. The aerial (seen on the left) is normally mounted outside a vessel but can also receive transmissions when located inside.**

Below **A Navtex display (seen at the top in the middle). The Navtex provides maritime safety information and weather warnings in coastal areas every four hours, and immediately sends out urgent messages.**

AIS

While Navtex is an information-recording medium, AIS is a real-time information display, providing the course and speed of commercial vessels around you as well as the type of ship and its destination. AIS is mandatory on commercial ships and automatically transmits data in a continuous stream that alters as the ship changes course or speed. From this data, it is possible to ensure that the vessel is not on a collision course with you or to see if it is necessary to take early evading action.

You can fit stand-alone AIS systems, or more conveniently install an AIS 'engine' into your chartplotter so that everything is displayed in the same place. A standard VHF aerial is fine for receiving signals, or you can use a much smaller dedicated aerial, if preferred. It is also possible to have the same aerial for VHF and AIS with the use of a splitter (a device that divides signals).

INSTALLING AIS

The AIS unit is installed in any convenient dry location and the cables are plugged in.

The cable is next plugged into the socket on the plotter.

A typical kit for upgrading a chartplotter consists of the AIS unit itself as well as connection cables and instruction. Mount the unit in any convenient dry, protected area and plug in the cable. Plug the other end of the cable into the socket on the plotter, and once you have connected the aerial cable the system is ready to go. With some earlier plotters it may be necessary to upgrade the software to allow it to work with an external AIS engine.

Check the plotter manufacturer's website for details of whether an upgrade is necessary and, if so, how to do it.

Once the AIS unit is switched on, the plotter will usually display a note to say that AIS is active and the transmissions from surrounding ships will be displayed. To see the full data of any ship, place the cursor over the ship's symbol and press enter on the plotter. Data will then be displayed.

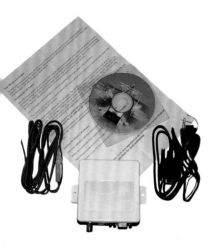

Above **A typical AIS 'engine' installation kit for the chartplotter.**

Right **AIS data is seen towards the top left of the plotter screen.**

Inboard autopilot

The autopilot is one of the most useful pieces of equipment on board, and once you have fitted one you will wonder how you ever managed without it.

The benefits of an autopilot outweigh those of just about every other piece of gear on board that is not directly related to safety. An autopilot removes the chore of steering a compass course for long periods of time, while greatly increasing precision when it comes to keeping to a course. It also gives you a chance to concentrate on the navigation and watchkeeping, without the need to constantly monitor the wheel.

Navigational accuracy will often improve, too, as there is more time for taking fixes or updating the chart position from the GPS.

Autopilots generally come as complete kits. As part of the vessel's steering, it is essential that all components of the pilot are properly installed. This is especially important for the steering actuator (the device that moves the rudder), as the forces involved in steering a boat, particularly in rough weather, can be considerable. If the actuator is not securely mounted, it may break away under feedback from the rudder.

However, where the system is installed on a vessel with hydraulic steering, the actuator is the steering ram. Steering power is then supplied by the hydraulic reversing pump, which is fitted as part of the autopilot installation.

On the other hand, where the actuator is a mechanical push-pull device, this must be installed as solidly as the steering mechanism itself. Although this installation uses a hydraulic pump, most autopilots will also operate linear or rotary mechanical actuators.

Equally important for the operation of the autopilot is the use of the correct electrical cable sizes, which are dependent on the length of the cable runs. Under-sized cable will cause a voltage drop, resulting in loss of steering performance as well as the danger of overheating the cables. So as long as you follow the installation instructions closely, you should achieve an installation equal to a professional standard.

Right **The finished installation of the inboard drive unit. Although this installation uses a hydraulic pump, other units operate linear or rotary mechanical actuators. Once fitted, all that should be seen is the control unit.**

The parts of the autopilot

The installation can be divided into three distinct sections: a) the hydraulic pump (or other type of actuator), pipework and fittings; b) the electrical system together with the control panel and rudder feedback sensor; c) the fluxgate compass and final calibration.

As with all boat improvements, finishing off the installation can take as long as the installation itself.

Hiding the wiring and making up trim panels can be very time-consuming, but they make all the difference between an adequate and a first class job. This is where the DIY owner will often spend more time than the professional installer to complete the cosmetic work and therefore finish up with a really impressive installation.

Above left **The rudder feedback sensor is mounted parallel with the tiller arm, and the link arm is parallel with the rudder crossbar.**

Above right **The non-return valve sits neatly on the shelf at the same height as the pump, where it is bolted down and connected into the systems.**

Right **Hydraulic reversing pump (or other type of actuator), dual non-return valve, rudder feedback sensor, control panel, hydraulic hose, hose fittings and electrical cables.**

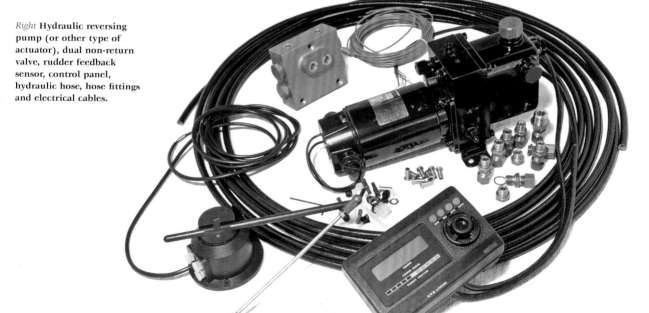

Inboard autopilot 2

Positioning the system

The first step is to plan the location of the various parts of the system, starting with the hydraulic pump and the dual non-return valve. You need to install these close to the steering ram where they are not exposed to water leaks, but in a position that avoids causing airlocks in the pipe runs.

The dual non-return valve is required on steering systems where the helm pump has no in-built non-return valve. Without the valve, the wheel rather than the rudder would turn. Where hydraulic steering is used with non-return valves built into the manual helm pumps, the dual non-return valve is not required.

The other piece of equipment you should install near to the rudders is the rudder feedback sensor, which tells the autopilot exactly how much rudder is being utilised so that it can automatically apply helm control to accommodate varying wind and sea conditions. The rudder indicator is mechanically connected by a rod and operates directly from the steering assembly. Its mounting base must be in line with the steering so that the correct geometry can be achieved.

Once you have finalised the position of the hydraulic pump and dual non-return valve, you should drain the original steering pipework of oil and disconnect it to allow the new equipment to be piped into the system.

The position of the fluxgate compass (an electromagnetic device) is very important as this will ultimately decide how accurately the autopilot steers a compass course. It needs to be away from sources of magnetism and large lumps of ferrous metal (particularly the engine). For best performance, it should also be mounted as low in the boat as possible to minimise

Right **An ideal position for the fluxgate compass is the forward bilge. It is well away from the engine and any other metal. Being so low down, it is protected in rough sea conditions. Once through the hatch, the fluxgate is mounted and lined up on the fore-and-aft line of the boat, with the arrow pointing at the bow.**

Below **The pump itself is mounted at the same height as the steering ram, well away from splash areas.**

pitch and roll so as to provide steady heading outputs. For steel boats, this is something of a conflict of interests as the only place away from large lumps of metal (in this case the boat itself) is up the mast. However, it does not need to be too high to clear the magnetic influence of the boat's steelwork.

The final consideration is the position of the autopilot control panel. This can be bracket or flush-mounted.

You should ideally include a switch and fuse in the power circuit, although these are not supplied with the kit as the switch looks better if it matches the rest of the boat's switches.

Calibrating the compass is the final part of the installation process. This stage varies between different makes of autopilot, but it generally involves accurately aligning the compass with the fore-and-aft line of the vessel. You should motor the boat along various headings and in full circles until the computer has calibrated itself.

The finished job is completed with only the control unit on show and the rest of the work hidden below decks.

Top right **When installing the control panel, simple black Perspex mount supports are assembled to tilt the control to an angle of 25 degrees, making it easy to read the display and carry out course adjustments. The brackets are made by cutting out Perspex pieces and assembling them with strong glue.**

Bottom right **An on/off switch and its related fuse are installed next to the main switch panel and fitted into another custom-made black Perspex panel. (The second switch is for another function.)**

LED navigation lights

Changing to LED navigation lights can enable you to fit brighter lights with a longer range, while considerably reducing power consumption. They are also inherently more reliable than traditional filament bulbs.

There are broadly two options for fitting LED navigation lights: you can substitute the existing bulbs for LEDs, or fit replacement all-in-one LED lamp units. The former is a fairly quick and easy option, but there are also some drawbacks.

The International Regulations for the Prevention of Collisions at Sea (COLREGs) specify exact angles for each colour of light. However, most replacement bulbs are a substitute for a hairline filament with a much larger and wider light source, which means the correct angles may not be maintained with the LED bulb.

Above **Changing your existing navigation lights to LED can make a significant saving in electrical power consumed, while also making the boat more visible at night.**

Below **LED navigation lights offer low power consumption and extremely long life. The LED lights need to maintain the angles specified by the COLREGs.**

Far left **An LED replacement bulb next to its traditional halogen filament equivalent – note the hairline filament on the right compared to the LED's wider profile.**

Left **A typical replacement LED bulb in a traditional navigation light fitting (left), with its housing (right).**

Warm white vs cool white

It's also important to select the correct type of white light for the replacement bulb. Early white LEDs were all 'cool' white, which included a large amount of blue tint. They therefore weren't suitable for use with the red and green lenses of port and starboard (or tricolour) lights, as these filtered out so much of the blue tint that the output was not sufficiently bright enough to be clearly visible.

More recently, the introduction of warm white LEDs has overcome this problem. Cool white bulbs can still, however, be used in white navigation lights: stern lights, anchor lights and steaming lights.

All-in-one units

All-in-one LED navigation light units are available from a number of manufacturers, covering a surprising range of prices. The more expensive are likely to have certification that they meet international standards such as those set by the US Coast Guard. In all cases the units must show the correct light sectors, with accurate cut-offs.

Most are sold as sealed units, which means they can be expected to remain watertight for many years.

They are generally sold with a short length of wire exiting from the unit, which should be soldered to the boat's wiring, then wrapped in heat-shrink insulation and wrapped with self-amalgamating tape to maximise the lifespan and reliability of the connection.

Apart from cost and the time taken to replace the existing light fittings, the other drawback of this approach is that a bulb can't easily be replaced. On the plus side, the inherent longevity of LEDs means the new units should be very reliable, although you can't just replace a bulb while on passage in the same way as you would with traditional navigation light bulbs.

Anchor lights

If you spend a lot of time at anchor, it's worth choosing an anchor light with a light-dependent switch. This will turn on automatically at dusk, when you may be ashore, and will switch off at dawn, when you may still be asleep. Even though LED lights draw comparatively little current, this still has the potential to save a significant amount of electrical power.

Right **An all-in-one unit replacement. LED navigation lights are expensive but are a neat solution.**

Underwater lights

If you want to light up the seabed, turn your rooster tail into a plume of 'fire', or just create your own underwater aquarium, submersible LEDs are the way to go. They are inexpensive to buy, easy to fit, low in power consumption and very durable. With a little imagination, they can turn your boat into a floating work of art.

Fitting underwater lights is proving increasingly popular, especially among motorboaters, and while there is some practical value in lighting up the surrounding sea, such as checking the seabed for obstructions or inspecting your stern gear, the main reasons are aesthetic. LEDs draw very little power, so are ideal for even the smallest craft, and

Below **LEDs are now available in a variety of colours, including some that can change on demand. This powerboat has chosen flame red for its rooster tail, but 'warp drive' blue is equally popular for the stern gear under way.**

by matching interior LED lights to the underwater lights, the whole boat and the surrounding water can be bathed in soft mood lighting. Better still, multicoloured lights are available that can be synchronised to music, allowing you to create your own underwater light show via a tablet computer.

At the heart of each underwater light is the hard-wearing and highly reliable LED, usually housed in a metal or polycarbonate fitting enclosed with a tough acrylic lens. These lights are invariably either 12 volt or 24 volt, and range from

the equivalent of 20-watt bulbs (producing 770 Lumen) to 250 watts (giving 12,000 Lumen). They draw anything from a few milliamps to an average of 0.2 amps each, so they won't drain the domestic power supply. Each unit emits a specific colour and intensity, while the top-end range can be multicoloured. The beams emitted can penetrate as far as 30m (98ft) in crystal clear water, with different colours suited for specific areas.

Smaller units are available for tenders, and a remote control unit can be used to flick on the

Far left **The smallest lights are often the simplest to fit, as they only require a small hole for the wiring. The rest of the unit is simply bonded to the hull with a powerful adhesive sealant.**

Left **Larger units such as these US-made Ocean LEDs will require a hole to be drilled in the hull, much the same as when fitting a seacock. The flange is coated with sealant for a watertight seal.**

underwater (and deck) lights of an anchored yacht to help identify it if you are approaching on a dark night after a run ashore.

Choosing the lights

Fitting underwater lights will involve drilling into the hull, although the holes themselves are not particularly large, usually around 9.5mm (³⁄₈in) for the smallest units to a maximum of 114mm (4½in) for superyachts.

There are a few things to consider before planning your system:

Location: On motorboats the most usual location is on the transom/ bathing platform area, although some owners ring the entire waterline with a halo of lights. As some bathing platforms extend a considerable distance from the transom, where the underwater lights will be mounted, allowances have to be made for the reach of the beams, and any shadows that may be cast by stern gear. The lights should be evenly spaced for best effect. If in doubt, use more lights.

Larger yachts also run lights along the outer hull near the transom. Floodlights give a wash of colour whereas beam lights look more dramatic.

Colour: The most popular colour is blue, as the shorter wavelength allows it to penetrate deep into the water. Apart from looking good, the blue light also excites natural phosphorescence in the sea, adding to the display.

White is ideal in very clear seas, where it brings out the natural beauty of the seabed. The LEDs usually give a very pure white light, but in murky or brackish water it will tend to look yellow or even brown. For these conditions, green is a much better choice, as it has excellent penetration and retains its colour the best, especially on lakes and rivers.

Multicoloured LEDs are perfect for creating light shows, and for mixing and matching the colour to suit the mood. Red, for example, can be used to give an 'after burner' effect in a sportsboat's rooster tail.

Right top **Green is the best choice in murky water.**

Right middle **White gives the best penetration in clear water.**

Right bottom **Blue is universally the most popular colour.**

Underwater lights 2

Having established the location of each light, and ensuring there is nothing on the inside of the hull that will get in the way, fitting will involve drilling a single hole right through the hull. On smaller units, this will be just for a power cable, as the light is held in place by adhesive sealant, but larger units use a threaded stem with a flange sitting flush against the hull. The fitting is secured using a large nut tightened down on a flat washer from inside the hull, with generous amounts of underwater marine sealant to make it absolutely watertight.

Some units may also use stainless steel screws to lock the flange in place. After that, connection is easy. Unlike ordinary bulbs, LEDs have a positive and negative terminal, and won't work if these are reverse connected, so a clearly marked red (positive) and black (negative) wire protrude through the stem for connection to each side of the lighting circuit.

On the metal units, usually bronze, a grounding lug is included so the light can be connected into the boat's anti-galvanic bonding circuit, but this precaution is unnecessary on polycarbonate bodies. It is a good idea to antifoul the exterior flange of each light; they are usually supplied with a masking template to protect the lens during the painting process.

Once deployed, the lenses will need a quick clean with a soft brush every six weeks or so to keep them clear of slime, although some clear silicone antifoulings have been successfully used to deter any marine growth.

The LEDs should last for up to 50,000 hours of continuous use, and as they are highly resistant to vibration, shock and sudden changes in temperature, they can used while under way at full speed with dramatic effects. Some designs allow the emitter unit to be withdrawn from inside the boat should the LEDs need replacing, although more usually the whole fitting will need to be changed.

Below **The lights are spaced about a metre apart, such as these on the transom of a Dutch-built motor yacht. Long bathing platforms may require more LEDs with a beam effect rather than a floodlight, to reach out from underneath.**

Complementing the lights

Many manufacturers are now offering packages where you can buy a series of LEDs for fitting all over the deck, and colour matched to the underwater lights – or complementing them in some other way. These decklights can be very practical, giving a useful guide when going up to the bow, lighting up the companionway steps, or bathing the cockpit in soft mood lighting.

Uplighters and downlighters are also used on spreaders to illuminate the sail, a useful extra warning to an oncoming ship, or for an impromptu rigging inspection underway at night. Underwater LEDs and matching decklights are regularly attached to a boat's tender, or even a personal watercraft, where the water plume telltale becomes a fountain of red or blue to match the mothercraft.

Some manufacturers have added lights in unexpected places, such as on the underside of deck handholds, or in a strip along the bottom of the boom over the cockpit. The boat's name can also be spelt out in a tube of LEDs bent into shape.

Prices are competitive and manufacturers are becoming ever more imaginative, so for a modest outlay your boat can be lit up, both inside and out, just like a superyacht. One thing is certain – when lit up like a Christmas tree, you're unlikely to be run into at anchor.

Below **LEDs can be placed under the boom to illuminate the cockpit.**

Above left and right **Placing LEDs on the spreaders of the mast is both attractive and practical, especially if they can be switched on wirelessly. They not only make the yacht look good, particularly when matched with the underwater lights, but they can also help with anti-collision measures, identification by shore parties and rig inspections.**

TIP

When making way at night with the deck and water aglow with your chosen mood lighting, remember that your statutory navigation lights must also be prominently displayed, even if they do clash with the colour scheme.

Lightning protection

Lightning strikes to boats are relatively rare, and usually cause damage rather than injury. While lightning can't reliably be discouraged from striking your vessel, a few simple additions will help to guide it safely away from anything vital if it does.

The coast of Florida, USA has the highest incidence of marine lightning strikes in the world, with an average of 1.5 hits per 1,000 motor boats, and five in every 1,000 yachts. Away from Florida's climate, the odds grow longer, but boats still remain vulnerable as they can act as a 'lead' for a ground charge, effectively shortening the distance a bolt has to travel to earth via the sea.

A great deal of research has been done over the years to protect ships and boats from the effects of a lightning strike, but there is still no perfect solution. Most defences involve providing the charge – which can be thousands of amps – with a safe route to ground. Unprotected boats could see the charge flash sideways between the mast base and the chain plates, or exit through grounded seacocks, which are promptly blown out of the hull.

The most vulnerable vessels are yachts, mainly due to their tall masts, with multihulls being the most likely to be hit and damaged. This is due to their large surface area, which acts as a platform for the lightning to arc through. The safest vessels, oddly, are large steel ships, as there is so much metal in contact with the water that the charge usually dissipates safely.

Lightning prevention

You can't physically prevent a lightning strike, but you may be able to lessen the chances of being hit. Part of the problem of being offshore is that the water also contains an electrical charge, and this literally climbs up your boat to the highest point and acts as a 'lead'. The opposing charge in the air above is drawn to this lead, and closes the

Below **Storm clouds gather across a Greek anchorage, emphasising the vulnerability of the yachts to a lightning strike.**

TIP

A domestic oven offers protection from massive electromagnetic fields by acting like a Faraday cage. This means it is a good idea to put sensitive portable electronics in the yacht's oven during a storm. Even a strike in the sea nearby can damage chip-based electronics if they are not protected. A customised metal box could be used in the same way.

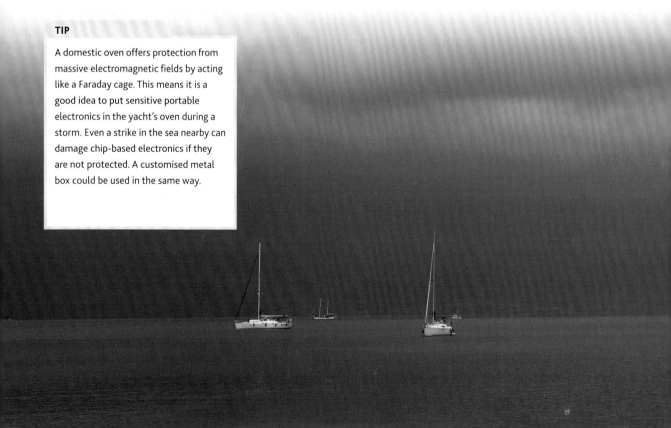

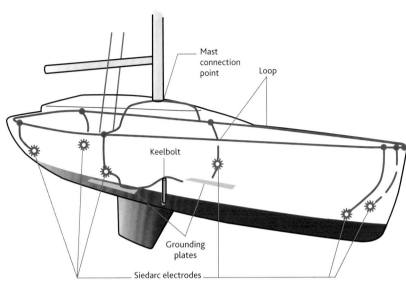

Mast connection point

Loop

Keelbolt

Grounding plates

Siedarc electrodes

Left **A pair of lightning lead diffusers on the top of a superyacht mast, stored in a yard awaiting repair. The idea is that the wire brush effect breaks up the lead of the charge that gathers at the top of the mast.**

Above **This system (from US-based Lightning Protection Inc.) guides the current outside of the vessel, rather than through it. A loop conductor around the deck is said to equalise potentials, and is connected to Siedarc electrodes and copper grounding plates at water level for maximum dissipation.**

circuit with a lightning bolt. The usual culprit is the VHF aerial which is not only the highest part of the rig, but also tapers to a point, which focuses the charge. If this lead can be broken up, it is possible the boat will be less likely to be hit. One approach is a wire brush type arrangement that is put on a post very close to, but higher than, the tip of the VHF, and so makes the boat less attractive to a strike.

Lightning deflection

Another approach to limiting damage or injury from lightning is to create a Faraday cage (or Faraday shield) around the hull. In 1836, the British scientist Michael Faraday observed that a metal enclosure would absorb electrostatic charges (and some kinds of electromagnetic radiation) and redistribute them around the external surface only. Anything inside the cage remains

electrically neutral due to the physics of opposing electrical fields.

The large-scale Faraday cage systems designed to shield an entire yacht work on much the same principle. Highly conductive lightning rods at the top of the boat are connected to a series of thick cables that run outside the hull, and then run to earth on submerged copper grounding plates. Each system is custom designed and installed by specialists. Great care is taken to steer the cables away from vital systems.

Direct path

A further solution is to provide any lightning strike with a direct path to earth by grounding the mast to the keel. Other systems rely on a grounding plate of at least 930cm² (1ft square) of copper connected without any sharp bends to the base of the mast to steer the charge to

earth. Similarly, the bonding system that links all the underwater components of a boat (propellers, stern gear, seacocks etc) is also connected to the grounding plate, and should steer the charge away from the crew while also preventing post-strike fires.

Unfortunately, lightning protection isn't an exact science and sceptics argue that any system designed to protect against lightning may also serve to attract it. Even so, a protection system should go some way to keeping the charge away from the crew by preventing dangerous side flashes.

Battery-charging inputs

If you are having battery problems, it's tempting to exchange the boat's batteries for those with a larger capacity. However, this may be dealing with just one part of the problem, and if you're not putting enough charge into the existing batteries, the issue may simply become worse with a larger battery bank.

There are a number of options available for boosting battery-charging inputs, and most boats will benefit from a multifaceted approach. While it's now more cost effective than ever before to add additional inputs such as wind and solar, or even a towed generator, it's still worth starting by optimising the main engine's charging system.

Alternator size

As a rule of thumb, the alternator size, measured in amp hours, should be around one third of the total size of the battery bank(s) being charged. This will enable the engine to be used to charge the batteries from 50 per cent charge level to 80 per cent in one or two hours. These figures are important – 50 per cent

Above **It's becoming ever easier to sail with the same conveniences as at home, but they tend to draw a lot of electrical power – make sure your system can keep up with the demands.**

Below **The further afield you venture, the more important it is to have robust charging inputs. A variety of systems will assist you if one of them fails. A combination of solar and wind power is an ideal option for many boats.**

Below right **A towed generator attaches to a pushpit with over 18m (59ft) of braided line attached to a propeller in the water. This creates electricity while sailing rather than relying on running the engine.**

is the lowest charge level that you can let batteries fall to without significantly reducing their lifespan, while it becomes progressively more difficult to cram the final 20 per cent of charge into batteries.

If your alternator is notably smaller than this relative to the batteries, it's worth considering replacing it for a more powerful model – a number are available that will fit popular marine engines. An alternative is to fit a second alternator, and many marine engines can easily accommodate this. This approach also has the advantage of redundancy, so if one alternator fails you won't experience a complete electrical failure.

Optimising engine charging

Many boats have battery banks that are charged via a split-charge diode arrangement, which allows one battery to be reserved for engine starting only, while the other battery (or bank of batteries) runs the vessel's lights and systems. The advantage of this is that it's not possible to use the engine battery for anything other than starting, so it cannot get drained by the systems to the extent that there is not enough charge left to start the engine.

On the face of it, this is an excellent arrangement. However, there is a downside – the diode will reduce the voltage that the alternator produces by up to one volt. This in turn reduces the current and therefore the total amount of energy that reaches the batteries.

There are two main ways to solve this: replacing the diode with a voltage sensing relay (VSR) or fitting a smart alternator regulator. The former is an inexpensive and easily fitted option, although you don't

Above **Relying solely on the engine for charging inputs is often not the most efficient arrangement, especially for today's power-hungry boats.**

Right **The regulator (the silver and black component positioned on the lower left-hand side of the back of this alternator), is vital in determining the rate at which the alternator will deliver current. Fitting a smart regulator can significantly boost output.**

get the benefit of the three or four stage charging functions of a smart charger, which helps to get the final 20 per cent of charge into the batteries.

Smart regulators measure the voltage at the batteries and modify the alternator output to ensure this stays at an optimum figure (usually 14.4 volts) while the engine is running. Most incorporate three-or four-stage functions that reduce the time needed to charge from 80 per cent to full charge.

> **TIP**
>
> As an alternative to upgrading batteries and charging systems, it may be more cost effective to pay attention to reducing power use by fitting LED lighting (see pages 122 and 196) and replacing an old fridge with an efficient, well-insulated model (see page 116).

Battery-charging inputs 2

While it makes sense to optimise charging via the alternator – there are now more alternative affordable methods of battery charging than ever before. For a boat that's used predominantly at weekends and for occasional holiday cruising, the battery bank may not need to be augmented if the batteries are 100 per cent charged at the start of every trip.

This is straightforward for boats that are kept in a marina berth with shore power – a three- or four-stage mains-powered charger will keep the batteries permanently topped up to 100 per cent. This regime is also good for the overall lifespan of the batteries, which can be expected to last noticeably longer.

Solar panels

The most cost-effective arrangement for boats that do not have access to shore power is usually a solar panel (see page 270). A modest-sized panel will replenish all but the biggest battery banks when the boat is not being used and will again help to prolong battery life. A panel used for this purpose does not need to be permanently installed – it can simply be propped securely on deck when the boat is not used, so the installation time needed is negligible.

A solar panel that's rated at less than 8 to 10 per cent of the battery's capacity does not need to charge via a regulator. However, larger panels must have a regulator to prevent the batteries becoming overcharged. These are generally compact and are easy to fit into the circuit between the panel and the batteries.

Long-term use

Longer-term cruisers need to think carefully about charging inputs and whether they have enough battery capacity for their needs. Wind power is often seen as being an attractive option, but in many cases it has now been eclipsed by solar.

When in port or at anchor the boat is, almost by definition, in a sheltered location, so there's less chance of the consistent and reliable wind that's needed for a wind turbine to generate a significant amount of power.

By contrast, the advantages of solar power can be enjoyed even in northern Europe, where the frequently cloudy skies may be offset by the long summer days. Solar panels also work better at lower temperatures than those of, for example, the Mediterranean summer, which helps the efficiency of solar charging in the more northern climates.

Right **A four-stage mains-powered charger is by far the best solution for any boat that's connected to shore power.**

Below **A small and inexpensive solar panel will repay its modest cost many times over by keeping batteries topped up while the boat is not being used.**

Above **Wind power has the potential to generate a lot of electricity in a strong breeze, but may not help much in a sheltered anchorage.**

Left **A fully installed diesel generator is still the preferred option for large yachts, but don't fit one without first considering the drawbacks.**

Generators

A fully installed and sound-insulated diesel generator has long been the favourite method by which larger yachts generate their electrical power. The advantages are obvious – usually unlimited electricity at the touch of a button, without increasing strain on the main engine.

However, there are a number of downsides, including additional weight, space required and maintenance. They are also expensive both to buy and install, which leads some people to choose a cheap portable petrol generator instead. These are noisy and can rarely be used at sea. A large quantity of petrol would also need to be carried on board in order to generate a significant amount of electricity.

A less obvious disadvantage of a portable petrol generator is that it's all but impossible to ensure the exhaust gases will blow clear of accommodation areas, hatches and ventilators at all wind angles, which creates a risk of carbon monoxide poisoning. Don't be complacent about this – people have died following a slow build-up of fumes from their generators.

Fuel cells (see page 282) are cheaper and easier to install than diesel generators, and don't have the drawbacks associated with portable petrol generators. Admittedly they are expensive if used heavily, but they can be an ideal solution for a 'top-up' generator on a boat where most of the power needed is provided by solar or wind power or the main engine.

Battery capacity

As electrical demands on board increase, the amount of battery capacity required also goes up. Installing additional or larger capacity batteries may help solve battery problems, but will add significant weight to the boat, as well as increase battery charging time and fuel consumption. A better solution is to improve the efficiency of the charging system, which will restore the capacity of the batteries back to what it was when the batteries were new.

While good quality, heavy-duty commercial vehicle batteries are ideal for boat use, many people prefer spill-proof, maintenance-free marine batteries. These offer very long self-discharge times and plenty of reserve power from a comparatively small case.

Common battery charging problems are sulphation, which takes place when batteries are left in a discharged state for long periods, and counter voltage, which occurs during charging and is caused by charge build-up on the surface of the battery plates before it can coalesce into the cells. This convinces the regulator that a higher rate of charge has been attained, hence the quick drop from high charge current into a heavily discharged battery.

After a short period of time, battery capacity becomes reduced by about 30 per cent when charged using an alternator with a regulator. This is the point where additional batteries are often fitted, instead of solving the real problem of lost

Above **The deep cycle batteries in the foreground have a higher capacity than the larger truck battery.**

Left **There are plenty of batteries on this boat, but 30 per cent of their capacity is wasted if they are left discharged for long periods causing sulphation of the plates.**

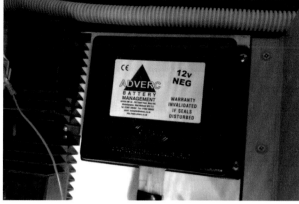

capacity. Fitting a specialised battery capacity sensor improves overall charging performance and, equally important, restores some of the batteries' lost capacity.

Regulators set the alternator output to approximately 14.2 volts, which is quite adequate for the simple charging needs of road vehicles. The lack of temperature compensation means car batteries are undercharged in winter and overcharged in summer!

Vehicle regulators use 'machine sensing' and detect charge voltage at the alternator rather than at the battery, which means the regulator cannot compensate for losses in the wiring between battery and alternator or the 0.9 volts customarily lost through a standard split charge-blocking diode (a device that splits the charge between batteries). With these losses, charge voltage reaching the battery may be reduced to around 13 volts, which is insufficient to overcome counter voltage. The regulator therefore 'thinks' that the battery is fully charged and cuts the charge to a trickle, leaving that 30 per cent capacity unused.

Fitting a specialised regulator

Specialised regulators convert the alternator to 'battery sensing' and detect voltage at the battery via an additional lead. They can compensate for losses in the wiring and through blocking diodes by adjusting the rate of charge to suit the actual needs of the battery.

The most visible effect of fitting an external regulator is the speed with which batteries are recharged. Charge drop-off into heavily discharged batteries doesn't happen and the batteries charge in about half the time without overcharging or gassing (the build-up of hydrogen within a battery). To ensure the batteries are charged fully and safely, a variable charging cycle is used. The effect of monitored

Above left **The specialised regulator has an additional wire added to allow the Adverc unit to control the alternator output. If the Adverc fails, the standard regulator will take over.**

Above right **Fitting the external regulator Adverc unit in a dry, protected area.**

charging control can be seen when the batteries are full and there is only a trickle charge being provided. If you switch on several high current draw items, such as engine room fans and bow thruster, the charge rate instantly rises to compensate for the current draw.

These systems are suitable for DIY installation and will not cost a great deal more than adding extra batteries, yet they will transform the electrical performance of the system.

Right **Swapping the internal regulator for the modified version that works with the external regulator.**

Shore power

Shore power means connecting to mains electricity. The benefit is that you no longer need to draw on the 12-volt boat battery to power equipment. Connecting to shore power involves installing a consumer unit, fitting plug sockets and dragging cables through the boat, all of which can be done by the average DIY enthusiast, leaving the connecting and checking to a professional electrician.

Above **A typical small consumer unit designed for harsh domestic environments. This needs to be installed in a dry protected position.**

The work divides roughly into two parts: installing a consumer unit and running the cables through the boat to the sockets and any mains-powered equipment. The system doesn't need to be any more complex than a couple of circuits protected by an earth leakage circuit breaker with suitable miniature circuit breakers to protect the separate circuits.

Your boat may only have one or two circuits. If a more sophisticated system is required then additional circuit breakers can be installed in the consumer unit. This system uses a 'harsh environment' consumer unit (which provides more protection), complete with two

miniature circuit breakers and an earth leakage circuit breaker. You always need to install all mains equipment in a dry and protected area on the boat, but the extra protection of some types of unit gives an added degree of safety.

In this case, the consumer unit is mounted beneath one of the lounge seats adjacent to where the shore power is fed in through a dedicated shore power socket.

Connecting up a mains supply

First, assemble the consumer unit, together with the circuit breakers ready for wiring. It is often easier to wire these small units before they are mounted on a bulkhead and

after the new cabling has been run through the boat. The unit can then be mounted in the chosen position. As each cable is run through the boat, number it with an indelible pen to aid identification during the connection phase. Note that for this installation domestic twin and earth cable was used. You should check on the regulations that apply in your country for installing cable – you may find it is mandatory to install multi-strand cable such as 'Arctic Blue', due to its greater resistance to vibration and mechanical damage.

The wiring connections within the consumer units are straightforward but if you are unfamiliar with them, then leave them to the electrician. Use domestic snap-lid trunking to protect and tidy the mains supply cables. You can mark the trunking with an indelible pen to clearly warn of mains current.

Left **The soleboards are taken up in the wheelhouse as the cables are run.**

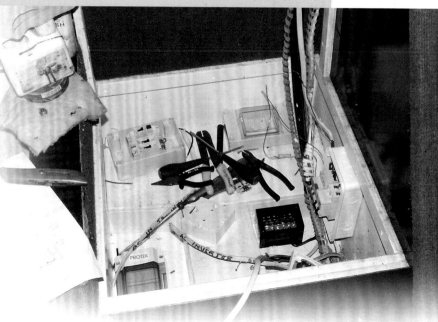

Above **Snap-lid trunking, which is normally available in white plastic or galvanised steel offers good protection for mains cabling and is held in position with ties.**

Electrolytic corrosion

One important point to consider when installing a shore-power system is electrolytic corrosion, which occurs when stray electrical currents flow between metals immersed in an electrolyte (sea water). A circuit can be made through the earth connection in the boat's shore power supply.

If several boats are connected to the shore supply, the connection between all of them is established through the earth cable and the immersed metal lowest in the galvanic scale on any boat in the circuit is the one that corrodes.

Where only one boat has a protective anode fitted on their hull, this may well be the lowest metal in the scale and the anode will protect all the other boats on the circuit – and possibly even the metal piles of the jetty. This is why an anode can sometimes be found to be wasting away far faster than normal.

To prevent this happening, an isolating transformer fitted in the boat's shore-power input will break the connection while still ensuring a safely earthed system. The galvanic isolator unit is installed

Above **Consumer units ready to be installed – in this case, beneath the lounge seating close to the shore-power socket inlet.**

between the shore power inlet and the consumer unit in a convenient location, such as on a secure bulkhead. This may only be necessary if several boats are continually connected to the shore power. If the power supplies are disconnected when unattended your boat may not need one.

Right **When using shore power, you are connecting boats electrically via the earth cable. The anode on vessel B protects vessel A (because it has no anode), but is wasted faster than normal. A galvanic isolator on vessel A would break the connection between the vessels.**

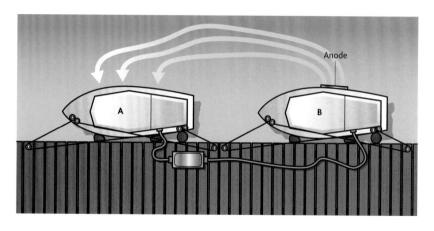

Inverters

When you are away from shore power (AC power) and you want to use gadgets that use AC power, you would normally need a separate on-board generator to power them. An inverter, however, is a device that converts the DC current from a battery into AC current, therefore providing access to AC power on board without a generator.

Above **A square wave inverter is ideal for running smaller power tools and phone battery charging.**

Devices that are 12 volt can be plugged directly into the boat's DC battery system. However, using an inverter means on-board AC gadgets can also be powered from the boat's batteries. Unless the devices are very power hungry, you won't need a huge inverter to do the job.

Inverters range from the very simple stand-alone types to complex systems, which are hardwired into the boat's mains power system. They are generally economical, low

Below **An inexpensive 500-watt square wave inverter running a standard mains-powered jigsaw.**

maintenance and relatively compact sources of AC power. However, some owners of inverters may also have a generator on board, as this provides extra power to charge batteries when there is high power demand.

Inverters share certain electrical components with battery chargers, which means that many models are available as combination inverter/charger units. Most automatically switch to battery charger mode when plugged into shore power, changing smoothly back to inverter mode when the AC power input is turned off.

Types of inverters

Inverters don't all produce the same type of current. The cheapest inverters supply square wave current, which, simply put, is rough not smooth. This is fine for basic items on board such as an icemaker, for example, but some televisions or laptops will not function well using

this sort of current or may become damaged. If you just want to charge a mobile phone or run light power tools then a square wave model would be ideal. A 500-watt inverter would be sufficient for the task, and simply clips onto a battery's terminals when needed.

The mid-range option is a modified sine wave, which is a smoothed out square wave, helping to make it more compatible with many everyday electronic devices. A 400-watt modified sine wave inverter would be adequate for a modern television as well as for charging up devices such as a laptop.

The ideal current is sine wave, which is smooth flowing, producing a better and cleaner current – all electrical equipment will run on it and it is less likely to cause harm to any devices that use it. A heavy-duty sine wave inverter is the most expensive type of inverter but it has the most uses. It could provide, for example, 2,000 watts of continuous mains power, plus fully automatic battery monitoring and charging when connected to shore power.

It could be run into the mains system to augment the shore power when away from the pontoon socket and run a standard electric kettle,

Above left **A 400-watt modified sine wave inverter is compatible with many devices.**

Above right **A 2,000-watt hardwired inverter/charger, supplying all the vessel's mains sockets.**

microwave oven, television, hairdryer and heavy power tools. Other heavy consumers, such as an immersion heater element in a calorifier, would be best run from a generator or direct shore supply.

Use of power

When choosing an inverter, you need to consider the amount of mains power you will need on board. Small inverters will operate one or two smaller appliances simultaneously, but if you want to run a number of devices together you'll need a larger capacity unit.

You also need to think about the total capacity of the on-board batteries and their condition. Inverters depend on adequate type, size and the number of ship's batteries for proper operation. In addition to your appliances, your batteries still need to keep pace with all the 12-volt DC uses such as lights, electric heads, water pumps, electronics and other systems.

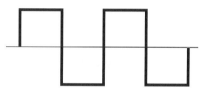

Square wave

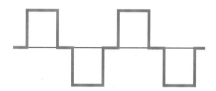

Modified (quasi) sine wave

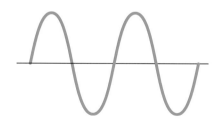

Sine wave

Above **Types of AC signals in inverter systems. Inverters affect the overall efficiency of the system by the amount of DC current that transfers to AC current. Loads on the inverter dictate what size of inverter to buy.**

Inverters 2

Installation

Once you have decided what type of inverter you need, the process of installation can begin. For those with older boats or no shore power system installed, the set-up must be designed to suit the individual requirements of the owner.

Installing a dedicated inbuilt inverter is not a job to be undertaken lightly. It requires a good knowledge of both the boat's electrical systems and that of mains power. It is important to carefully follow all the instructions provided by the manufacturer for the installation. Larger inverters can consume a significant amount of power at times, and the wiring must be as specified. You should also refer to the standards for the country where you are installing the equipment.

The layout of the equipment may be decided by the original equipment installation. In our example here, shore power consists of just two circuits, protected by standard circuit breakers. One circuit supplies the immersion element in the calorifier, the other supplies the socket outlets throughout the boat.

The inverter being installed in this case is a 2,000-watt hardwired inverter/charger to supply all the vessel's mains sockets, and a new consumer unit replaces the old one. For this installation, it is important to ensure that the inverter can never inadvertently be switched on to power the immersion heater element in a calorifier. This is because the heater draws too much power and would soon flatten the batteries.

It is possible to divide the systems so that when on shore power, the immersion heater element can be automatically energised, but when using the inverter it does not take in power. A changeover switch in the system makes it impossible for

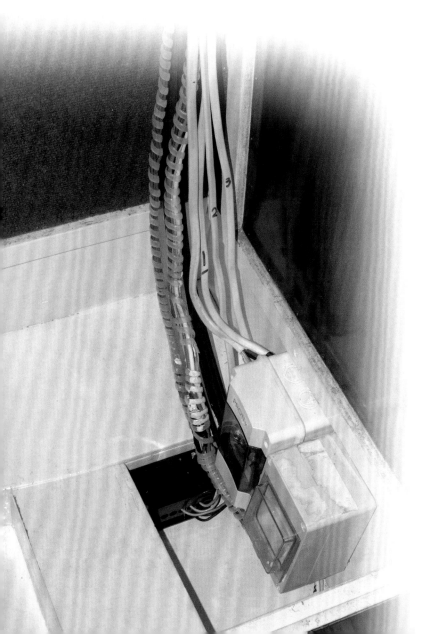

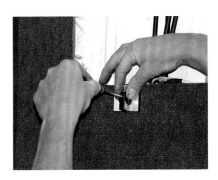

Above **Fitting the shore power/inverter changeover switch.**

Left **Twin consumer units for separate shore power and inverter input.**

the inverter to connect to the immersion, and this is linked into the system close to where the power comes on board to the consumer units.

The new 2,000-volt inverter directly replaces the old one on board. When installing an inverter you need to lift it carefully into place (it can be heavy), taking care not to damage any of the exposed components.

When you install an inverter

- Place it on a reasonably flat surface.
- Keep it away from the engine compartment.
- Place in a dry position, not exposed to rain or flooding.
- Keep it well ventilated, with clearance all round.
- Keep it away from heat and direct sunlight.
- Do not use it near flammable materials.

You can also install a multi-control panel for on-board regulation of the power supply.

When laying cables to the batteries, it is important to use the correct size of cable for the battery connections because the drain on full inverter power is quite substantial. The cross-sectional size recommended for this model is the largest standard cable size available. You should use a heavy-duty crimping tool for fitting terminals to the cables.

Right **Wiring layout that prevents the inverter from supplying the calorifier immersion element by use of the changeover switch.**

Above **Fitting the new 2,000-watt inverter/charger.**

Left **Remote control for an inbuilt inverter system.**

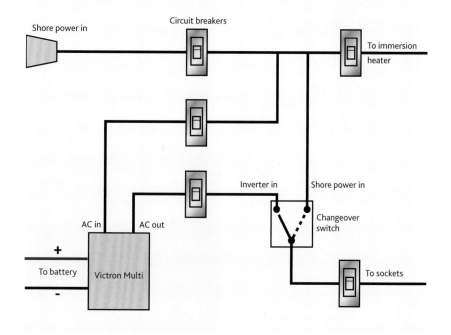

Electrical and systems tips

Electrical circuits are the mainstay of most modern yachts, so it pays to be able to make the best use of the power supply on board, and carry the right equipment to deal with the most common faults. Here are a few ideas from yacht builders and owners who have optimised their electrical systems.

The box of bits

A bulb or fuse will always blow at the most inopportune time, requiring you to hunt through numerous packets. So why not put everything you need in an organiser, with each compartment clearly marked so you don't need to squint at tiny bulb markings by torchlight?

Dedicated charging point

Nowadays there are so many different portable devices that need recharging that it makes sense to have a dedicated charging centre on board. Consider having a navigation station made up with a special locker that is packed with AC and DC outlets for various charging devices. This avoids a spaghetti of cables across the chart table or around the saloon.

Access to wiring junctions

Regular inspection or occasional fault-finding requires easy access, so many builders ensure that key junction points are fully accessible. Areas such as the main battery switching station are designed so all the connectors are easy to inspect. If refitting a yacht, ensure that access panels are easy to open.

Above **Clearly marked compartments are a useful way of storing essential small items.**

Below **This Oyster yacht has a fully accessible main battery switching station, making it easy to inspect.**

Right **The navigation station on this Discovery 67 yacht has a dedicated charging point. The shelf holds the devices while they are topped up.**

Above **A swing-out chartplotter, which can be accessed both from below deck and from the helm, can greatly assist with navigation on a small yacht.**

Above **The cabin of this Discovery 67 yacht has a mirror that doubles as a navigation screen. Note the controls by the bed.**

Swing-out chartplotter

On smaller yachts, locating a chartplotter near the helm can be a challenge, but creating a simple swing-out arrangement makes navigation easy. When inside the yacht, it can be used to plan routes from the comfort of the saloon, and when needed on passage, it simply swings out and locks within easy reach of the helm. While it can block the companionway, it also swings easily out of the way.

Navigate from your bunk

Check out this dual-purpose screen – a cabin mirror that can double as a navigation device. From a remote control console within reach of the headboard, the skipper can access all the navigational and domestic data available, and even plan the next voyage while relaxing. Once activated, the electronic display shines past the silvering of the mirror.

Below **The foot controls here are for a bow thruster, whereby pushing the port button will move the bow in that direction.**

Foot buttons for thrusters or windlasses

Fitting waterproof, foot-operated switches at the helm makes it much easier for the helmsman to control important electrical devices such as bow thrusters while still retaining full control of the wheel and throttle. The same principle could be used for an anchor windlass, as the helmsman often needs to manoeuvre quite tightly as the anchor is dropped, holding the nose into the wind and then reversing to dig the anchor in. A circuit breaker on the pedestal disarms the switches until needed.

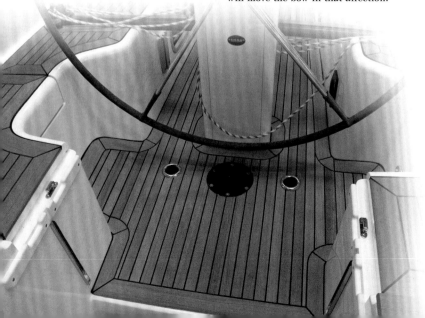

OTHER TIPS

Shore power supplies in some parts of the world can be a bit temperamental, so if your lights start to flicker or essential systems drop out, a voltmeter will tell you at a glance if this is due to a trough in shore power voltage or if your devices are at fault. A clear digital indicator can be set up in a control panel and wired into the shore power input.

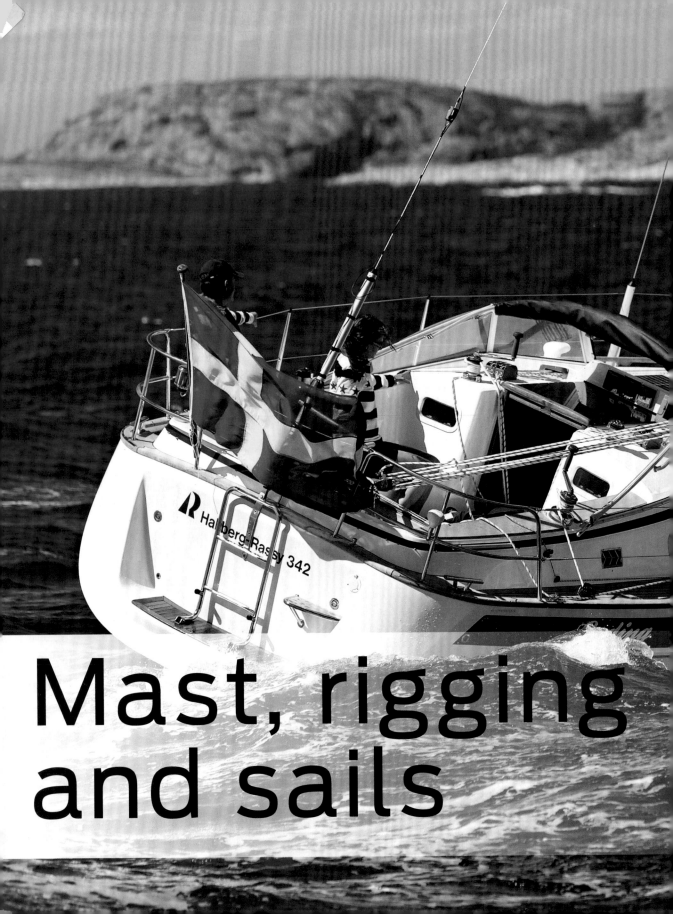

Mast, rigging
and sails

7

Rigging and sail-mending skills

Regular inspections are the key to keeping a boat's rig and sails in good order. However, there is always the possibility of more significant damage that requires repair.

As sails age, areas of stitching will chafe through well before the cloth becomes damaged, and a small area of broken stitching can quickly run along the entire length of a seam. Ideally, any badly chafed seams should be run through a sewing machine as a precaution, before the thread finally breaks. Most domestic sewing machines are capable of sewing through up to three or four layers of sailcloth, provided an appropriately heavy-duty needle is used.

Alternatively, seams can be hand stitched – using the original needle holes makes this an easier process. Hand-sewing is, however, still a time-consuming task, so hand stitching is generally reserved for short-term repairs, such as oversewing both sides of a length of damaged stitching to prevent it unravelling further. Use double-sided tape to hold the two panels together in exactly the right place while it's being stitched.

However, long-distance sailors who don't carry a sewing machine on board may have to undertake a considerable amount of hand-stitched repairs as they sail. That's a very strong incentive to carry out repairs the moment damage is first noticed!

Small holes in sails can be repaired using self-adhesive sailcloth, providing the sail is cleaned of salt water and thoroughly dried before the patch is applied. Larger holes, or those in very high stress areas, in particular the leech, clew and near mainsail battens, will also need to be stitched to survive extended use in strong winds.

Below **A traditional rig built with modern materials. Rigging skills are useful whatever type of rig you have.**

Rig problems

If remedial work is needed on rigging at deck level – for example, to replace a damaged clevis pin, chain plate or bottlescrew – the mast can be supported by taking halyards down to secure deck fittings near the chain plate, and applying moderate tension to the lines. However, it may not be safe to climb the rig in this state, so if any standing rigging above deck level needs to be replaced, the mast should be lowered first. Before doing so, count the number of turns on each bottlescrew, so that the rig can be returned to its original tension and tuning.

Ropework

If a braided rope has significant chafe, there's little that can be done to remedy it, short of creating two much shorter lines from it. Historically, such remnants of three-strand ropes were spliced together to form another line that was only marginally shorter than the original. Splices are also used to create eyes in the ends of ropes. Splicing is easiest with three-strand lines, but is also possible with braided ropes such as those used for halyards.

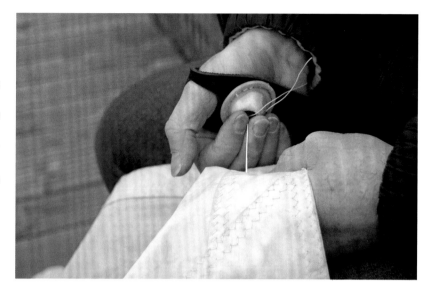

Above **Carrying out a small sail repair using a sailmaker's palm (this is similar to using a dressmaker's thimble).**

Below left **Removing the mast makes it easier to work on the standing rigging above deck level.**

Below right **The correct way to adjust rigging screws, using the right sized spanners.**

Lazy jacks

Lazy jacks create a cradle of ropes into which lowered or reefed sails can be collected, and are a very useful piece of running rigging for short-handed crews.

Relatively simple to retrofit, lazy jacks are a useful piece of running rigging for any boat, which can make reefing or furling mainsails an easier task. Particularly useful for singlehanded sailors or short-handed crews, lazy jack systems are made up of two lines that are attached to the mast, either at or above the spreaders, from which a series of additional lines run off to the boom, forming a cradle of lines into which a lowered sail can be caught. In heavy weather, when you need to shorten sail quickly and efficiently, and you don't want sails flapping, the usefulness of lazy jacks is particularly clear.

Disadvantages of lazy jacks

However, lazy jacks are not liked by everyone, and some sailors consider that their benefits are outweighed by their disadvantages. Extra rigging running from the mast and boom adds to the amount of windage that you have aloft, and if the lazy jacks are incorrectly set up (too tight), they can cause chafe or affect the set of the sails. If you have a fully battened mainsail, then the battens may also snag on the lazy jacks as the sail is hoisted, so you need to be careful about how you set them up, and also be prepared to tweak them a bit until they are correct. You may also need to make adjustments to your sail cover in order to make it fit around the lazy jacks.

Right **Stack pack-style lazy jacks make sail management easier for crews that are short-handed.**

Types of stack pack systems

Traditionally, lazy jacks were only seen on gaff-rigged boats, but in recent years, and particularly since the invention of stack pack-type systems, which feature integral lazy jacks with mainsail covers, they have become a regular feature on modern Bermudan-rigged yachts.

Above **Stack packs combine sail covers with lazy jacks.**

Right **Stack packs feature mainsail covers that are attached to the boom permanently, with lazy jack lines running off the top edge.**

There are a variety of names for these systems, but they are generally known as stack packs, which consist of a sail cover with integral lazy jacks. A sail cover is permanently fixed to the boom, and stiffened with GRP battens that run its entire length. Lazy jacks are attached to either side of the sail cover, and when the sail is lowered it falls within these. The sail cover can then be closed with a zip.

Fitting and setting up

There is a wide variety of ways in which lazy jacks can be fitted and set up, and you can either buy an off-the-shelf system from a rigging manufacturer or chandlers, or you can make your own. Some systems are fixed and very simple, others are more complex and can be tweaked and adjusted as required via a series of blocks and cleats. There are also versions that can be stowed away when the mainsail is raised so as not to create extra windage aloft when sailing.

Off-the-shelf lazy jacks

These are often the simplest lazy jacks to fit as they come as a complete kit of parts and with full instructions about how to fit them, so there will be no guessing about how much rope you will need or where the ends will be attached to the mast and boom.

However, they also tend to be the more complicated. Instead of just being made up of a system of ropes and eyelets, they feature blocks between the different lines, as well as a cheek block and cleat

on the boom. Although many of these systems allow the lazy jacks to be tweaked as required and also stowed, having extra blocks aloft, potentially rubbing against the sails and mast, can create excessive windage and increase the risk of chafe, therefore shortening the life of your sails. These systems aren't cheap either, and you'll need to be fairly adept with a pop-rivet gun to attach pad eyes to the metal spars.

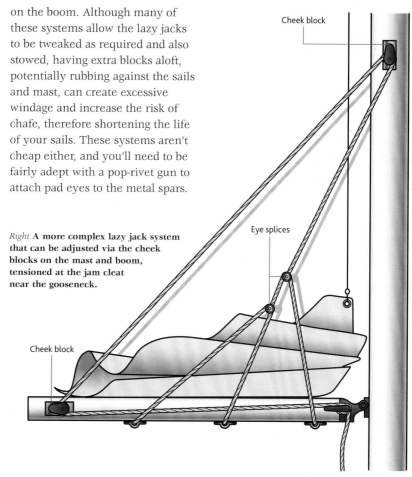

Right **A more complex lazy jack system that can be adjusted via the cheek blocks on the mast and boom, tensioned at the jam cleat near the gooseneck.**

Cheek block

Eye splices

Cheek block

Lazy jacks 2

Fitting your own lazy jacks

Fitting your own system of lazy jacks is not difficult, but it will probably require some research, experimentation and testing before you achieve the perfect set-up. However, if you opt to do this, it can be relatively inexpensive, because with a fixed system all you need is some rope along with some thimbles and pad eyes.

The hardest part of fitting your own system is deciding where you are going to run the lazy jack lines from and to so that they are efficient at collecting the sail, yet won't interfere with its hoisting.

To set up a simple lazy jack system:

○ Measure the length of your mainsail's luff, and then calculate 70 per cent of this. This figure is recommended as the best height up the mast to fix the lazy jacks.

○ You will then need two lengths of braided line – 6mm (¼in) in diameter – with a thimble attached to both ends of both pieces of line, and a third piece to feed through the thimbles. Stainless steel, galvanised or nylon thimbles can all be used, but stainless steel will last the longest. These should either be inserted into eye splices or eyes

that are secured with seizings. The rope needs to be long enough for the thimbles to be located about halfway between the gooseneck and where the line is attached to the mast.

○ Attach one end of each line to the point you have marked off on the mast. The most secure method for this is by pop-riveting (see page 254) a pad eye to the centreline of each side of the mast.

○ Feed a second length of line through the thimble on the line that runs down the port-hand side of the mast, underneath the boom, at about a third of the way along its length, and then back up through the thimble on the starboard-hand rope. Attach two more thimbles to either end, so that the ends finish above the head of the mainsail when it is lowered in its track.

Left below **A simple lazy jack system provides a cradle into which a sail can be dropped quickly and efficiently.**

Inset **The top of the lazy jacks should be fitted to pad eyes on the mast. They can either be fixed directly or, as in this case, the line can be run back down the mast to a cleat to make them adjustable.**

TIP

If the lazy jacks snag on the ends of your spreaders when running downwind, attach a small length of shock cord to one lazy jack near the spreaders. Run the other end around the front of the mast and attach it to the other lazy jack, so that the cord is pulling them away from the spreaders.

Far left Attach nylon thimbles to both ends of the lines that run down from the mast. These should either be inserted into eye splices or eyes that are seized in place.

Left To prevent the lazy jacks moving along the boom, use a line underneath the boom to hold them in place. Eyelets or loops in the line can be used, or here the lazy jacks have been passed through strands of the line.

✿ With a third length of line, feed one end through the lower port-hand thimble, underneath the boom, at about two-thirds of the way along its length, and then back up through the thimble on the starboard-hand line. The ends can then be joined together to make a continuous length, or thimbles can be inserted and they can be attached via pad eyes to the boom. If the lazy jacks are to be fixed, leave enough slack in them to allow for the shape of the sail when under way.

✿ If you want an adjustable system, you can fit a cheek block and cleat to the boom so that one end of this line can be cleated off. The other end should have a thimble put in it and then be attached to another small pad eye on the other side of the boom.

✿ To prevent the lines from slipping along the boom, you will need to run a length of line underneath the boom, from the gooseneck to the end, with either loops or small eyelets fitted at the correct positions through which the lazy

jacks run. Alternatively, you can split the line underneath the boom and feed the lazy jacks through the strands of the line.

✿ It is a good idea to hoist the sail during installation to check that the lazy jacks are the correct length. When you first raise the sails, check that the sail raises and lowers smoothly and that it flakes neatly between the jack lines.

Above A new lazy jack stack pack-type system almost completed. Final adjustments need to be made, including cutting the cord to the correct lengths.

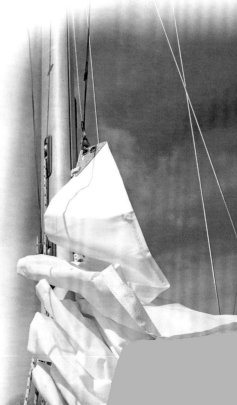

Right The sail is dropped and flaked inside the sail cover, and closed with a zip.

Headsail furling

The ability to deploy, reef and stow the headsail from the safety of the cockpit has been a great innovation for cruising yachtsmen. Fitting the necessary hardware to a forestay is relatively easy, but does need some careful measurements.

The development of roller reefing means that a large foresail can be carried permanently hoisted, and quickly and easily deployed when needed. This is because the genoa is rolled up around a foil, and can be pulled in or out depending on how much sail area is required.

Most roller-reefing systems work to the same principle. The forestay is enclosed by length of foil, usually made from aluminium that is free to rotate. (This shouldn't be confused with roller furling, where the sail is rolled up around a rope, and can't actually be reefed as there is too much twist.) At the base is a drum with a light line attached, and at the

masthead end is a swivel. To attach the sail at the start of the season, a halyard car runs up the foil and pulls the specially adapted luff of the sail into a groove in the extrusion. Once the sail has been hoisted, the tack is attached to the drum. A line on the drum is pulled out and the foil rotates, wrapping the sail evenly around the foil for stowage.

Above **The main difference between roller furling and roller reefing is to do with the forestay and drum gear. This version of roller furling features a rope forestay with a continuous line to a flat drum (on the left of picture), whereas the roller reefing has an aluminium foil over a wire forestay and a larger drum.**

Below **Roller reefing allows for the quick furling and deployment of a very large headsail from the safety of the cockpit. It can be deployed manually or by the use of electrics (as in this picture) or hydraulics.**

Above **Electric and hydraulic systems are available that are fully sealed against the elements, and make furling even the largest foresails touch-button easy.**

To deploy the sail, you release the drum line and pull on the downwind (leeward) sheet and the sail unwinds, often helped by the wind. To reef, you release the sheet and pull the drum line in to reduce the sail area.

The invention of roller reefing meant that yachts no longer have to carry a large sail wardrobe in bulky sailbags, as the largest sail can be adjusted to suit every wind condition. Nowadays, high-tech alloys, rugged bearings and precision components have made this concept almost standard on most cruising yachts, while smaller versions with lightweight foils are available for dayboats and dinghies.

Retrofitting or simply upgrading an old system is well within the realms of the DIY enthusiast with some basic tools, and most systems are supplied as a made-to-measure kit with illustrated instructions.

Buying considerations

When looking for a supplier the buyer on a budget has to know what to look for when choosing the ideal set-up. The robustness of the build, the ease of installation and any ongoing maintenance requirements will all be factors in the final choice.

Aesthetics can also play a role, as some systems are attractively finished with polished stainless steel drums, whereas others are robustly functional. Electronic and hydraulic upgrades are also available.

KEY BUYING CHOICES:

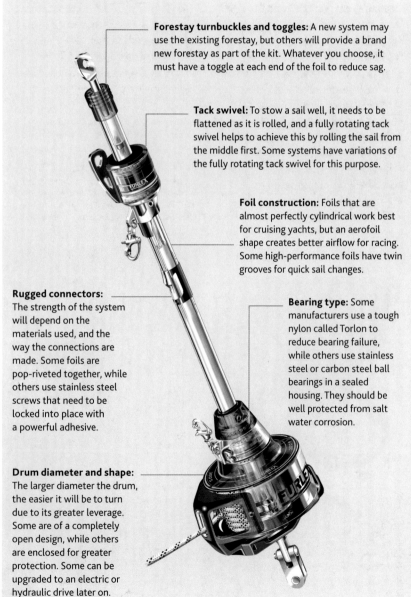

Forestay turnbuckles and toggles: A new system may use the existing forestay, but others will provide a brand new forestay as part of the kit. Whatever you choose, it must have a toggle at each end of the foil to reduce sag.

Tack swivel: To stow a sail well, it needs to be flattened as it is rolled, and a fully rotating tack swivel helps to achieve this by rolling the sail from the middle first. Some systems have variations of the fully rotating tack swivel for this purpose.

Foil construction: Foils that are almost perfectly cylindrical work best for cruising yachts, but an aerofoil shape creates better airflow for racing. Some high-performance foils have twin grooves for quick sail changes.

Rugged connectors: The strength of the system will depend on the materials used, and the way the connections are made. Some foils are pop-riveted together, while others use stainless steel screws that need to be locked into place with a powerful adhesive.

Bearing type: Some manufacturers use a tough nylon called Torlon to reduce bearing failure, while others use stainless steel or carbon steel ball bearings in a sealed housing. They should be well protected from salt water corrosion.

Drum diameter and shape: The larger diameter the drum, the easier it will be to turn due to its greater leverage. Some are of a completely open design, while others are enclosed for greater protection. Some can be upgraded to an electric or hydraulic drive later on.

Fitting a unit

A basic roller-reefing unit can be fitted in a day, provided you have taken all your measurements correctly. You don't even need to drop the mast, so long as you can safely support it with a temporary line. Some systems don't even require the forestay to be modified, as they use split components and telescopic foils.

The correct sizing of your headsail system will be based on the length of your forestay, the maximum diameter of the wire and clevis pin, and the size of the turnbuckle. After receiving this information, the manufacturer will provide you with a kit containing all the essential components. There will also be detailed instructions, so we will only look at the key stages here. Before starting, you will need a few basic tools for the fitting, including hacksaws, pliers, spanners and screwdrivers, but nothing specialist.

A critical component is the forestay. If it is more than four years old it should be replaced as part of the conversion, but it's a good idea to replace it anyway because you won't be able to inspect it once it is hidden inside the foil. A professional rigger can fit the new forestay with the terminals needed, but a DIY enthusiast can successfully reuse the original forestay with terminals such as the Sta-Lok or Norseman brands.

Below **A close up of the top connections to the mast, shown on a mock-up. The lead of the halyard is important to avoid the foil being snagged, or putting too much strain on the bearings. This display shows a roller furling (red line) and roller reefing system on the same mast.**

✪ With the mast braced and the forestay detached from the boat, the wire can be laid out on the pontoon for the roller assembly.

✪ If reusing your existing forestay, you will need to ensure you cut it according to the manufacturer's requirements, using a fresh hacksaw blade.

✪ The foil is supplied as a series of sections, which are connected with pop rivets or bonded screws. It is essential that these connections are well made.

Above **Roller reefing is supplied as a kit, with everything you'll need for the installation apart from some fairly basic tools. Some manufacturers will also supply you with a new forestay already modified to suit their system.**

VARIANTS ON SELF-FURLING FORESAILS

The ability to furl and unfurl sails without having to reef them has led to some much simpler systems where the sail is only used either fully open or fully stowed. Typical variants are:

Hanked-on sail furler: The sail is hanked onto its own forestay, which is rotated by a small drum at the base with a swivel at the top. It is ideal for dinghies, dayboats and small catamarans, where dropping the headsail under way would be a precarious operation. This type of system is not designed for reefing, only for stowing, and avoids the expense of having to convert the sail.

Code zero furler: Used for the loose-luffed asymmetrical spinnaker design called a 'code zero' and for a gennaker (a cross between an asymmetrical spinnaker and a genoa), this type of furler uses a no-twist torsion rope threaded into the sail.

Top-down furler: An alternative to the snuffer; the top-down furler is used for asymmetrical spinnakers, and requires less luff torsion than the code zero arrangement. The wrapping, as the name suggests, starts at the top.

The foil is then fed over the forestay from either the top or the bottom, depending on the system being used.

☙ The final section of foil may need to be cut to length, before being connected to its end swivels.

☙ With the drum and foil attached, the final task is to lead the control line aft through pulley blocks on the stanchions. Adjusting the backstay will provide the final tensioning of the foil, or by making small adjustments to the lower foil section.

Above **Critical to the installation is how the turnbuckle at the base will attach to the bow. This Solent rig system has used the central flange of the anchor roller to anchor both drums. Note that the foremost one is slightly smaller than the rearmost one, as it carries a smaller sail.**

Ongoing maintenance should consist of a regular washdown with fresh water, frequent checks of the terminal connections, and the occasional 'feel' of the bearings to ensure they aren't rumbling.

Right **When assembling the foil, it slides over the forestay and is isolated from it by nylon bushes. This older system is due to have a new forestay as it has been in operation for more than four years, and cannot be inspected when hidden behind the foil. Wire rigging should ideally be changed every eight to ten years or so.**

Far right **The foil section, showing how it wraps around the wire forestay. Joining the sections is usually achieved with small grub screws that are locked into position with a dab of specialist adhesive.**

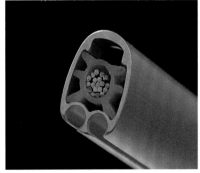

Additional forestay

Most small- to mid-sized sailing sloops will have a single forestay, often supporting the foil for a self-furling headsail. However, many cruising yachtsmen like to add an additional forestay for extra security, to aid goosewinging or for flying a storm jib.

The forestay is the only piece of standing rigging on the average yacht used to carry a sail and, by its very nature, has to withstand additional strain and wear. Many dismastings have been attributed to the forestay parting under load, usually through excessive wear of a terminal fitting.

As such, cruising yachtsmen like to have another forestay available, either ready for use at a moment's notice, or permanently in position to reinforce the standing rigging.

The extra forestay offers several advantages. It:

✪ Enables two foresails to be hoisted together and opposite each other, allowing for poled out 'goosewinging' for long downwind passages, such as a trade wind Atlantic crossing.

✪ Acts as a spare forestay, should the furling gear fail (so long as a sail with hanks is carried).

✪ Can be used to carry a storm jib, taking the strain off the furling headsail system.

An additional forestay is usually fairly easy to fit. Masthead rigs often have a spare sheave in the top box for running a second halyard, and special fittings can be bought to allow for detachable forestays to be fitted further down the mast.

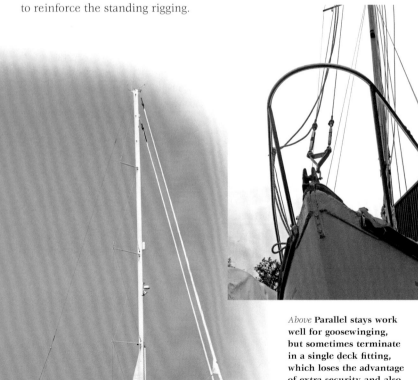

Above **Parallel stays work well for goosewinging, but sometimes terminate in a single deck fitting, which loses the advantage of extra security and also compromises tensioning.**

Above **The stay (see arrow), shown here in the 'redundant' position off to one side, is using a dedicated in-mast sheave for the halyard. This forestay could also be used as an emergency shroud.**

Left **The Solent rig is a popular solution to having an extra forestay, as it uses the mast's original backstay for support. It is particularly useful on long downwind passages, when both foresails can be poled out.**

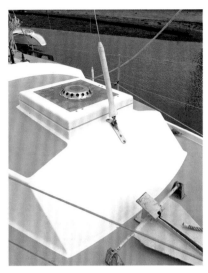

Far left Detachable forestays use a quick-release lever to slacken the stay for relocation. This one on a Moody 44, shows the substantial hook through a U-bolt.

Left A baby stay, as seen on this Westerly, is there to supplement the standing rigging, and is not really intended for flying a sail.

Choosing the right set-up

The extra forestay will be one of two types – permanent or detachable.

If it is to be permanent, then its location will be critical in terms of additional standing rigging. On a masthead rig (where the forestay starts at the top of the mast), the second forestay should be no more than 500mm (20in) below it, or about 10 per cent of the total mast height. If it is any lower, then there is a risk that the mast could distort, or 'de-column', when the extra forestay is under load, as there will be no counter force behind it. This means running backstays will be needed, so it's best to keep the second forestay very close, and parallel, to the first one.

Ideally, the second forestay will be in line with – and in front of – the main forestay, and made from wire one gauge smaller. This is so the rearmost forestay becomes the main load bearer and can be tensioned properly. If roller reefing is fitted, the additional, thinner forestay is usually placed in front of the foil,

so it won't foul the sail, but will allow an additional sail to be hanked on for downwind work. The Solent rig has two identical forestays set up, usually each with a furling headsail.

Parallel forestays

Some yachts fit identical forestays side by side, which is a workable solution but gives tensioning problems on either tack. The best set-up, if running side-by-side forestays, is to have them both terminate independently on deck, usually to each side of the stemhead fitting. On some smaller yachts, the forestays end in a single terminal, which still allows for goosewinging. Others have roller reefing and a standard forestay side by side.

Detachable stays

Detachable stays are usually found behind the forestay, as they will probably only be used in extreme conditions when the genoa will be furled, or for a long downwind passage when the genoa will be poled out.

Detachable forestays should start at (or very close to) the masthead, unless running backstays are acceptable, and usually have a quick release lever that can be adjusted for the right tension. When the forestay isn't needed, it is clipped to a U-bolt in the deck near the shrouds. When deployed, it is moved to another U-bolt on the foredeck and clipped on. The halyard usually works from a built-in mast sheave, or to a pulley attached to an eye riveted to the mast.

Another type of extra forestay is a 'baby' stay, which is a small wire that leads from the first set of crosstrees and terminates quite a long way back from the bow. This stay is used to support the mast, rather than flying a sail. However, some yachtsmen have been tempted to beef up this baby stay to take a very small storm jib, as it brings the centre of effort a long way aft and nearer the mast, although it's not something riggers recommend.

Backstay adjuster

Many modern boats have fractional rigs that respond readily to changes in backstay tension. This can have almost as much effect on depowering the boat as the first reef in the mainsail and can be done in seconds. An adjustable backstay can also help a more traditional masthead rig by reducing forestay sag when sailing close-hauled.

Increasing backstay tension increases fore-and-aft mast bend, which in turn flattens the mainsail. In terms of sail mechanics, this has a depowering effect on the boat as it affects the flow of air around a curved sail. This is most pronounced with fractional rigs (where the forestay terminates below the top of the mast), but will also have an effect on masthead-rigged boats.

A second benefit is that increased backstay tension will tend to reduce forestay sag, which helps to produce a more efficient sail shape and allow you to point closer to the wind.

In the past, adjustable backstays frequently meant expensive hydraulics, or cumbersome levers to turn a bottlescrew under load. However, modern rope technology and the improvement in blocks means systems are now much simpler and are easy to fit.

Cascade systems

Today a cascade system is used in most installations. Typically this is in the form of a number of single blocks that 'hang' below each other, with each one doubling the purchase of the system.

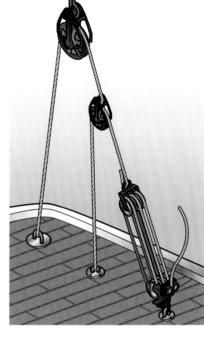

Above **A cascade system is an easy and cost-effective way to double or quadruple the power of a purchase system.**

Below **Adjustable backstays aren't just the preserve of racing yachts – they can help a cruiser to improve sail trim and upwind handling.**

Left **This backstay has a triple cascade, which increases the purchase by a factor of eight.**

Left **On boats significantly larger than 12m (40ft), backstay loads can reach a level at which hydraulics are still the preferred option.**

As few as four blocks can produce a powerful, yet simple backstay adjuster with a 24:1 purchase. Spliced Dyneema or Spectra line is generally used for the cascade and needs to be no larger than the diameter of the stainless steel wire used for the backstay. It must, however, be strongly secured to the boat and additional attachment points in the transom may be needed. These should be through-bolted with large backing pads to spread the load.

For smaller boats a 12:1 purchase may be adequate. However, adding an extra block to create a 24:1 system is an easy way to achieve more power, and will suit most boats of up to 12m (40ft). Above this size, it may be necessary to resort to a hydraulic system. A hydraulic backstay allows for quick adjustment of the rig and is pressure controlled.

Back-up strop

Installing an adjustable backstay would not be a step forward if it reduced the security of the rig. It is important to add a strop that will ensure sufficient tension is retained if the adjustable backstay tensioner is accidentally uncleated. This should run directly from a securely mounted fitting on the boat to the fixed wire part of the stay.

> **TIP**
>
> A quick and easy solution for a boat with split backstays is simply to attach a long sail tie to one side of the backstay, then lead it round the other side to pull the two parts together.

Above **The wire backstay back-up strop is a safety precaution. Its purpose is to prevent losing the backstay if the backstay tensioner is uncleated by accident.**

Jackstays

Fitting strong points to which safety harnesses can be attached, plus jackstays that run the length of the boat on each side so that crew can move around the deck without needing to unclip their harnesses, are big safety improvements.

Most safety harness lines are rated with a safe working load of 750kg (1,650lb), so strong points need to be attached securely to the vessel. Typically this means large U-bolts secured through the deck, with large washers behind, although a bigger aluminium-backing pad would be even better.

For a boat with a slotted toe rail, it is possible to shackle the jackstays directly to the toe rail, providing you check it is bolted through the deck – some are only screwed to the deck. Even with a through-bolted toe rail, it's worth seeing whether you are able to attach the jackstay close to a leg of the pulpit and pushpit, which will give additional security, as they are normally attached with large bolts through the reinforced hull-deck join.

Above **Reinforcement is needed beneath a strong point used for attaching a jackstay. A plywood pad plus large washers, will help to spread the load. A large aluminium or stainless steel backing plate is also a good alternative.**

Below **Jackstays are essential in heavy weather, as they allow crew members to move the length of the boat without unclipping their harness lines.**

Left **Securing a jackstay to a slotted toe rail – this can be a quick and easy option, providing you first check the toe rail is adequately secured, with through-bolts and large washers.**

Positioning jackstays and strongpoints

Jackstays should be routed so that it is possible to move the whole length of the vessel without interruption. The exact route will vary for each boat, depending on the layout of the deck gear, and may pass inside or outside of the shrouds.

You should also add extra strongpoints near the companionway and the helm position. The former enables crew to clip on from a position of safety below decks before going outside in stormy weather, while the latter means the helmsman's safety line need not interfere with that of other crew members when they are moving around the boat.

Material choices

The most common materials used are stainless steel wire or heavy-duty webbing. The advantage of webbing is that it will stretch when loaded, thus reducing the maximum load that the system, or the man

overboard, will experience. Also it will not roll under your feet, creating a slip hazard.

On the downside, webbing deteriorates in sunlight, so should be re-stitched at five-yearly intervals and replaced every ten years. These periods should be halved for boats that are kept in a hot, sunny environment, but can also be extended if the jackstays are rigged only when the vessel goes to sea.

Jackstays are best attached to the strong points with a heavy-duty shackle, sufficiently wide to accommodate the full width of the webbing. Smaller shackles create ridges in the webbing that increase the point loads on the stitching.

Below **Another way of securing the jackstay is to bolt a strongpoint through the deck to which the jackstay can be attached.**

Deck gear

The past decade has seen a considerable amount of new thinking in terms of deck layouts, with the aim of simplifying the arrangement and minimising friction. Although these changes started in the racing sphere, cruising boats are now also gaining these benefits in increasing numbers.

The neat symmetrical rows of lines led aft to banks of identical clutches, which first became popular in the 1980s, are losing favour. This is primarily because each time the line is routed around a corner, the load in the line and the amount of friction in the system are dramatically increased. Instead, lines are now to a greater extent treated individually, with each one led in as straight a route as possible to a separate clutch or jammer.

The articulation of blocks is also important – to keep friction at bay and minimise chafe on the line they must be free to align precisely with the load. Rather than using metal shackles, this is increasingly done with line attachments using either a spliced loop or a soft (line) shackle. The strength and reliability of this

has now been proven by the most hi-tech long-distance racing boats, which have returned to the old methods once used on gaff-rigged working boats.

Choosing the right blocks

There has also been a big move forward in the technology used for blocks and pulleys, which are nowadays lighter and more compact, while also being able to handle loads of a size that might once have been taken to a winch.

Ball bearing or roller-bearing blocks are used to minimise friction in lines that move fast, such as mainsheets, while plain bearings are used to maximise strength for heavily loaded lines that move slowly, such as backstays and kicking straps.

Above **Halyards that exit the mast foot athwartships are notorious for increasing friction if they are led back to the cockpit, as the line has to turn through a full 90-degree angle.**

Left **Line attachment is cost-effective, allows perfect articulation, is lightweight and easily inspected for damage. Line attachment of mainsheet blocks allows each one to align perfectly.**

Updating efficiently

Don't worry about rerouting every line in an older style deck layout; this would be a time-consuming and expensive task and in any case most lines don't carry a high load. Instead, focus on straightening the lead of those that are the most difficult to handle – these are usually the main halyard and reefing lines.

It may be possible to reposition deck organisers to reduce the angle through which the lines are turned: this alone can reduce both load and friction by 30 per cent or more. However, this won't work for boats that have halyards exiting athwartships at the base of the mast, unless the most frequently used halyards are let through a new exit placed higher up the rig, then through a turning block that's free to swivel at the base of the mast.

This is easily arranged and can reduce friction by more than 50 per cent, making a sail much easier to hoist and lower.

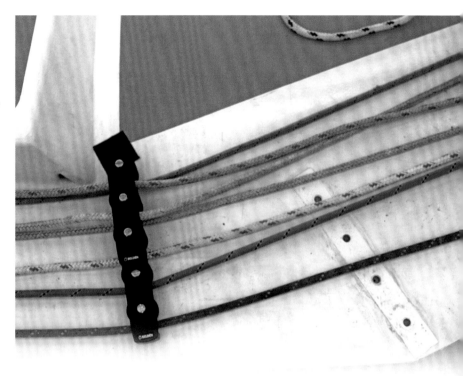

Above **The deck organisers have been repositioned to minimise the angle through which the lines turn, reducing friction by around 50 per cent. The holes of the original will be faired and painted to match the rest of the coachroof.**

MAKE A HALYARD EXIT IN THE MAST

Mark the position of the halyard exit, which is created by making several adjoining holes.

Drill the holes to create the exit, and file the edges of the aperture round and smooth.

Pull the halyard through the exit with a hooked piece of wire.

Leading halyards aft

Being able to lead all the halyards and reefing lines from the mast back to the cockpit can make a yacht easier to handle by reducing the need for the crew to go on deck in heavy weather.

Nowadays, most modern cruising yachts are configured to hoist and reef the sails remotely from the cockpit, rather than from where the halyards emerge at the base of the mast. But for those of you that may have an older yacht, it is relatively easy to convert the deck layout so that key control lines can be led aft. Adding an electric winch or two on the coachroof by the main hatch will greatly assist the use of these control lines, especially those with a heavy load.

Below **Leading the control lines aft, especially when used with electric winches, can make a large sailing yacht easily handled by just two people.**

Planning

The first task is to draw a sketch to identify each line, and where it emerges from the mast. Then decide which lines you actually want to lead back, and those that may be better staying put. Make sure there is logic to the selection. There is little point running the main halyard aft if you need to go back to the mast to free off the topping lift. On mid-range cruising yachts, usually around eight lines come aft, four each side of the companionway.

Too many lines will leave a lot of line in the cockpit, which may get in the way, so keeping the controls to the essentials is good practice.

Above **At the planning stage, looking at the set-up on similar boats will give you some ideas. This Southerly has the halyards vanishing under cowlings, and even into a hand rail.**

Lines to consider leading aft are: main halyard, topping lift, kicking strap, single or twin line reefing lines, spinnaker halyard, towable genoa car lines and genoa halyard (unless roller reefed).

The planning sketch will also help you identify some of the obstacles in the lines' path, such as hatches, dorade vents, hand rails and coamings.

Choosing the right hardware

Converting your boat to cockpit sail handling does add some friction to the rope runs, so it pays to invest in high-quality fittings with perfect articulation to minimise resistance. The hardware falls into four main categories:

1 Mast base blocks

Choosing the right blocks depends on how they will be attached to the deck. Your mast may already have swivel posts or a rail fitted to accept the shackle pins of blocks. If not, attachment points can be added, either as a special plate that goes under a deck-stepped mast, or with rails or eye bolts that are secured through the deck itself.

Plain bearing blocks are best for high static loads, as ball bearing types tend to squash the internal balls if heavily loaded in one position over a period of time. This results in a grating, uneven spin when in use. It is also best to use single blocks, as double blocks can tip over when two uneven loads are applied.

Spring-loaded, stand-up blocks are a good investment, as they deflect the line at deck level and both swivel and rotate to line up with the path of least resistance.

Above **Your mast may already have swivel posts, or a rail fitted, to accept the shackle pins of blocks. If not, attachment points can be added to the deck.**

Fixed pulleys with a crescent-shaped frame can also be used, and are bolted to the deck once they are perfectly aligned with the halyard's run towards the mast from the first organiser.

2 Deck organisers

These are strips of horizontally mounted pulleys that alter the direction of each line as it crosses the deck.

When feeding the lines to the organiser, the highest loads should be placed to the inside sheaves, the ones nearest the mast, as the shallower angle will reduce the stress on each one. For boats with a split-level cabin, specialist vertical organisers (or single blocks) are available to keep the line close to the deck as it follows the contour.

Below **Available as units of two or more sheaves, in tight spaces two shorter strips can be mounted on top of each other. The lead can be 90 degrees or more.**

3 Clutches or jammers

You'll need a series of rope clutches or jammers before the control line reaches the winch. This is so that tension can be held on a line indefinitely while the winch is used on another halyard. A high-quality clutch will be kind to the rope, while still allowing for adjustment, so is better for strong loads that may need quick release in safety.

An alternative is the spring-loaded jammer. When a line is under load in a jammer, it can be adjusted in towards the cockpit, but not outwards without fully releasing it from the mechanism, so they are best used for light loads.

4 Winches

The lines will terminate at a winch beside the companionway. Smaller winches than those used for the sheets can be used here, as the loads won't be as great. Some larger yachts with heavy sails fit electric winches if there is enough room under the deck for the motor. Self-tailing winches will be an advantage as you

Above left **Rope clutches come in several designs, and should be placed before the winch. Most can accept a label on the top for quick identification.**

can use both hands on the handle. Make sure you have enough swing room to operate the winch without catching the sprayhood (dodger in US) or companionway surrounds. You may be able to relocate the halyard winches from your mast rather than buy new ones.

Installing the hardware

Having selected your deck hardware, it is best to manually position them with the ropes fed through and tensioned if possible to ensure that there is no crossover or abrasion against protrusions. Once you are happy that the lead looks fine, mark where the organisers and other fittings will go, and then check that the bolts won't interfere with an internal bulkhead or with any wiring conduits.

Above right **Self-tailing winches are the best as they can be used two handed. Make sure there is enough room to swing the handle. These ones are electric.**

A final check is to try out the various components, and to work backwards from the rope clutches to the base of the mast. This will ensure that each critical turn is as finely orientated as possible so that the organisers and blocks can run freely. Fitting the deck hardware will mean that parts of the headlining may have to come down. Bed down the hardware with silicone sealant and use large stainless steel washers and Nyloc nuts on the bolts, with enough clearance for the headlining to go back.

The jammers should be a minimum distance of 200mm (8in) from the winch to minimise friction, and you may need to angle them upwards slightly with an insert underneath for the best lead. You may also need to raise the organisers on strips of hardwood to clear a cockpit breakwater (coaming), if fitted.

The halyards will probably need to be lengthened to reach all the way back, so may need replacing. This will be a good opportunity to choose a different colour or pattern for each one if you want to. Stickers are available to identify each clutch or jammer, but nothing beats 'pull the red one' in an emergency.

With sealant applied to the organisers and jammers, and everything bolted down, the final touch is to add some rope tidies in the cockpit – either detachable canvas bags, a purpose-built GRP or wooden bin, or specialist clamps with loops of elastic.

Or convert your boat back...

Some yachtsmen prefer not to bring the lines back to the cockpit, but keep them at the base of the mast. The main reasons are the extra rope ends that can clutter the cockpit, the lines running across the deck that could form a trip hazard, and the extra friction on the system that can slow the lowering of sails.

However, today's predominance of cockpit control as standard on so many production boats does suggest that while it may be more costly and create more friction, this is a more popular set-up.

Above **To feed in your new halyards, use a sailmaker's needle to make a small bridle in each, and use the old halyard to pull the new one through.**

Below **You will probably have to buy new, longer halyards to reach back to the new winches, but this is a good chance to colour code them.**

TIP

When laying up a boat for the winter, placing wooden blocks under the halyards will keep the lines off the deck, and prevent dirt and algae from accumulating beneath them.

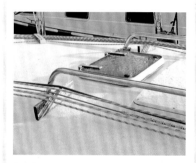

Sheeting points

With so much deck hardware available, it is now possible to fully upgrade your deck equipment, and also relocate it with minimal disruption.

Many older sailing boats are still fitted with their original deck equipment, and while fully serviceable, it normally requires a lot more effort to work than modern equivalents. On a few boats, the lead of the sheets may be wrong, or need rerouting due to additional deck equipment or a change of rig design.

Changing the genoa and mainsheet tracks and cars is very straightforward, helped by good design for the retrofit market. Many kits can use the bolt holes left by the original equipment, which greatly simplifies the job. If you want your genoa track curved or customised in some other way, many suppliers will be able to oblige, meaning you have endless possibilities to improve your sheet control.

Fitting towable cars

The correct sighting of the genoa car is essential to make full use of the cut of the sail, and many older yachts were fitted with two or more tracks each side to accept a wide range of hanked-on sails. Nowadays, where roller reefing is the norm, one

Below **Fitting a towable genoa car, as seen in operation here, will allow complete control of the sheeting angle from the safety of the cockpit.**

Above **Old deck layouts may have more than one track of the 'plunger pin' variety, which may be feeling its age and be in need of replacing.**

track is usually enough, especially as it can be fitted with a 'towable car'. This is an advance on the lockable 'plunger' car, where the crewman has to ease the loaded sheet, then kneel on deck beside the track, lift the locking plunger, move the car to a new position, and then drop the plunger again. Now you simply pull on a line from the cockpit and the car moves easily to a new position, to be held there by the line locked in a jammer.

Because there is some discrepancy between metric and imperial measurements used for tracks and the dimensions of various cars, it is usually best to start from scratch with all the components sourced from one manufacturer to ensure compatibility. Some types of track feature a groove that will allow you to simply slide it along the bolt heads of your original system using washers. However, you might want to move the new track either further inboard or outboard, or even to a different level (such as the toe rail) so new holes will be required.

If you are relocating the track, you will need to seal the existing holes in the foam or balsa core with epoxy, finished with gel coat filler. Countersinking the holes will help when filling.

Types of cars

Two types of cars are available; the cheaper ones feature roller bearings, while the more expensive ones have ball bearings. Sealant is applied around each bolt hole, and the track tightened down. Any excess sealant is cleaned up with a plastic scraper and white spirit. The cars are slid on (following the manufacturer's diagrams for the correct orientation) and then the end pieces attached.

When the sheet is under load, the towline holds the car against the gradient. However, in light airs, a piece of elasticised line is an optional fit that will draw the car rearwards for readjustment.

Similarly, if you have a fixed mainsheet point, or a dated lock pin horse track, upgrading to a fully adjustable car will allow you to tweak the curve of the mainsail for optimum efficiency. The ability to finely tune the cars from the safety

Above **Upgrading the hardware may also open up new location possibilities. Here, the genoa track has been moved off the deck and onto the cabin top.**

of the cockpit and prevent wind spillage can add a knot or more to the average cruising speed. On a long passage, this could reduce the time at sea by 20 per cent, so it's a good, practical investment.

Right **The fully adjustable horse car on this home-completed Van De Stadt design allows the skipper to fine tune the mainsail for maximum drive in all conditions.**

Single-line reefing

The ability to reef a boat from the cockpit has a number of advantages – it's safe, convenient and quick. With a well-planned system, one person should be able to tuck a neat reef into the mainsail of most boats under 15m (49ft) in as little as 60 to 90 seconds.

The speed and convenience of single-line reefing has benefits beyond the obvious safety factor of quick and easy reefing. When a sail is allowed to flog or flap in a strong wind it causes a disproportionate amount of damage. An efficient reefing system will therefore help to recover its cost over time.

It will also mean that you're more likely to be able to achieve a neat reef that gives a flat sail shape. An untidy reef, by contrast, results in a sail with a deep shape that's inefficient and causes additional heeling, making the boat more uncomfortable and more difficult to steer in strong winds.

Alternative methods

There are two main solutions to creating an efficient reefing system. One option is to rig separate reefing pennants from the luff and leech of the sail for each reef, which are then led aft to the cockpit. Strictly speaking, this is not single-line reefing, but it still achieves the goal of being able to reef the sail easily from the cockpit.

The obvious disadvantage of this system is that it introduces additional lines to handle and to keep tidy. On the positive side, friction is kept to a minimum, which reduces the overall effort needed and makes it easier to shake out a reef when the wind strength reduces.

The other solution is a system with reefing pennants inside (or outside) the boom that pull the luff cringle down first, before applying tension to the leech cringle. On the face of it this is a neater system – you can simply let the halyard down to a predetermined mark and then winch the reefing pennant in to pull the reef down. It also minimises the amount of additional deck hardware that's needed.

Left **The ability to reef the mainsail quickly from the cockpit helps to make sailing in strong winds easier.**

The downsides of this solution are additional friction and the long length of reefing pennant that is needed. This also means this system is not suitable for the third reef, which must be handled with separate luff and leech pennants, as described earlier, or you will need someone at the mast to hook the luff cringle over the ram's horn at the gooseneck.

Which system to choose?

Generally, fitting separate luff and leech pennants for all reefs may be the best solution for a boat that is frequently sailed with a full crew of competent sailors; if they are well coordinated, a reef can be pulled down very quickly with this method. It will also work well if the boat is occasionally sailed short-handed and has the additional benefit that the mainsail luff cringles don't need to be repositioned.

A single-line reefing system is ideal for a boat that is predominantly sailed short-handed, or where there are frequently non-sailing guests on board and reefing will usually need be to undertaken by one person.

Above **Reefing with a single-line system: if the halyard is marked at each reef it can be quickly lowered to exactly the right spot, before winding on the reefing line.**

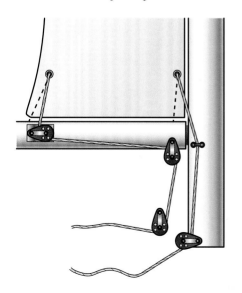

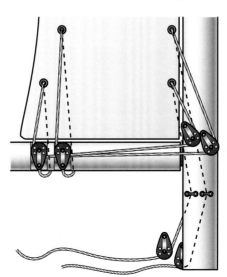

Far left **A two-line reefing system. There are two lines per reef (one single reef shown).**

Left **A full single-line reefing system in which there is only one line led aft to the cockpit per reef (two reefs shown).**

Single-line reefing 2

Although systems in which only one line is pulled to reef the sail are universally called single-line, this is a misnomer. One end of the line is attached to the luff of the sail, which is then routed into the boom, where it terminates at a sliding car that's also attached to a separate leech reef pennant.

Most modern booms are designed for such systems to be fitted easily, and it's also possible to retrofit a similar system in many older booms, although in the latter case you may need to create the system yourself from component parts. In this instance, you should take good care to ensure it works smoothly in order to avoid the various elements snagging against each other.

Not all booms are fitted as standard with the sheaves that are necessary for the luff pennant at the forward end, but modern spars should have provision for you to be able to fit this easily. You then attach the other end of this pennant to the car that's inserted into the after end of the boom, once you have removed the end cap.

Finally, you will need to reposition the luff cringles on the sail – they typically need to move aft by around 50–75mm (2–3in) to give the correct lead to the sheaves in the front of the boom. In most cases this will take a sailmaker a little less than an hour to do each reef.

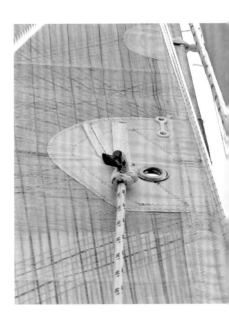

Above **This sail has been modified for single-line reefing by stitching a webbing loop for the luff pennant over the original reinforcing patch.**

Left **A block fixed to the mast near the gooseneck will give an optimum lead for the third reef's luff pennant, or for reefing arrangements with separate leech and luff pennants.**

Adding luff reefing pennants

Many boats already have the reefing pennants from the leech led back to the cockpit. If so, it's just a case of tying suitable pennants to the luff of the sail and leading these back to the cockpit. The most efficient way is usually to fix additional blocks to the side of the mast, just ahead of the gooseneck. This avoids needing to move the luff reefing cringle on the sail from its standard position.

You will then need to lead the lines to turning blocks fixed to the deck at the mast base, before guiding them aft to an additional clutch. Most deck layouts preclude taking the lines back via a direct lead, but a neat way of doing it is to use 'double decker' deck organisers that will fit on top of the existing ones.

Right **If necessary, deck organisers can be stacked to allow additional lines to be led aft.**

Below **A modern boom with additional sheaves retrofitted for the reefing line that leads up to the luff cringle.**

TIP

On many older booms the end cap may be corroded in place and be immovable even after drilling out the fasteners. If this is the case, start by tipping a kettle of hot water over it to remove any stubborn salt, allow it to dry, and then heat the outer metal with a blowtorch – this should expand the outer metal, allowing the end fitting to pop out. If this doesn't work, soak it in easing oil for two or three days.

Cruising chute

Many cruising sailors spurn light weather sails, possibly scared off by scenes of racers who come to grief after pushing too hard in strong winds. However, the real benefit of a cruising chute or spinnaker on a cruising boat is additional speed in very light airs, enabling you to sail instead of resorting to the engine.

An asymmetric cruising chute, tacked either directly to the bow or from a short bowsprit, is ideal for increasing speed on reaching courses in light airs. The equipment needed is minimal: two lines that will work as sheets, a tack line that can be led aft to the cockpit, and a halyard. The sheet turning blocks are normally located well aft, a little ahead of the pulpit; they are the same ones that would be used for a conventional symmetric spinnaker.

If your boat does not have blocks in this position, they can be shackled directly to a slotted aluminium toe rail, or to a U-bolt that's secured through the deck with a backing pad underneath. It's worth checking the vessel's manual to see whether metal plates are already bonded into the deck for this purpose. If so, you can tap a thread for the bolts, without needing to disturb the linings beneath the deck.

Below **Adding a cruising chute is a quick and easy way to boost light airs performance when sailing on a reach.**

Below **Whether or not you have a bowsprit fitted, the tack line at the bow should be led aft for adjustment from the cockpit.**

Above A double turning block with a jammer like this one enables the same winch to be used for more than one sheet, reducing the number of winches needed.

Right The sheet can be led from a block near the toe rail near the back of the cockpit to a primary winch.

Are additional winches needed?

Many owners are deterred from adding a cruising chute because they assume additional winches are required, which adds to cost and complexity. However, a double turning block with built-in jammers enables more than one loaded line to be used with the same winch.

In any case, it's only racing crews that need to make slick hoists and drops when rounding a mark. Cruising sailors, by contrast, can approach setting a cruising chute in a more relaxed fashion, furling or lowering the headsail before deploying the cruising chute, which then frees up the primary sheet winches to be used with the cruising chute.

Recent developments in furling gear for cruising chutes further improves their ease of use and means the sail can be hoisted before it is deployed. It can also be furled for gybing, which greatly simplifies the manoeuvre.

Benefits of a bowsprit

The extent to which your boat would benefit from a bowsprit from which to fly the sail depends much on the layout of fittings at the stemhead. If the forestay attachment is behind the stemhead and you're able to place a block for the tack line ahead of the pulpit, forestay and furling gear, then the only advantage would be in having a larger sail and being able to gybe more easily.

However, if the forestay is right on the stemhead and the pulpit significantly overhangs the bow, it may not be possible to set the sail without fouling it on the pulpit. Even if this aspect is not a problem, gybing the sail may be impossible without the pulpit getting in the way. A short bowsprit – the proprietary retracting type is okay for most cruising boats – will also give more room for furling gear to be attached ahead of the forestay.

Above A roller-furling chute set on a short fixed bowsprit makes the sail very easy to handle.

Spinnaker

Symmetrical spinnakers set from a pole tend to be more stable and efficient for running dead downwind than a cruising chute. For many boats it makes sense to carry both sails; the cruising chute for reaching and the spinnaker for running.

In most cases the same blocks used for the cruising chute sheets (see page 248) can also be used for the spinnaker sheets. Boats of less than around 11m (36ft) should have 'tweaker' lines – a block that runs along the sheet with a line led to the widest part of the boat. The tweaker line of the windward sheet (or guy), which leads through the outboard end of the pole to the clew of the sail, is normally pulled tight as this guides the line at an angle to the pole, helping to make it more stable.

On boats of more than about 11m (36ft), lifting the pole across the boat when gybing becomes challenging. Larger race boats, therefore, tend to be set up with separate sheets and guys for each clew of the sail, instead of the tweaker lines described above. This enables

Below **While a cruising chute is at its best on a reaching course, a spinnaker is often best for sailing dead downwind.**

Above **A tweaker line is used on this boat to move and help to pull the guy downwards from the outer end of the pole. It can be seen just above the toe rail on the right-hand edge of this photo.**

dip-pole gybes in which the inboard end of the pole remains attached to the mast. Larger cruisers can follow this example or, for a simpler arrangement, drop the spinnaker (or pull the snuffer over the sail), gybe the mainsail and then reset the spinnaker.

Mast fittings

Mast fittings will be needed for the inboard pole end. At their simplest on boats of less than around 9m (30ft), these can just be a couple of stainless steel rings attached with heavy duty rivets, enabling the pole to be set at different heights for reaching and running. However, it's neater to use a ring on a length of track that allows the pole height to be adjusted to the exact height needed while the sail is set.

Above and inset **Ideally the pole is attached to a ring on the mast that can slide up and down on a track, but on a smaller boat a simple eye securely fixed to the mast may suffice (inset).**

The pole will also require a topping lift – it may be necessary to add an additional sheave in the mast for this if there is not already provision for one – and a downhaul that should be led aft through blocks on the foredeck so that it can be adjusted from the cockpit.

Additional winches

Some boats will need additional winches in order to use a spinnaker, especially if you plan to race. However, cruising boats that don't need to carry out super-slick manoeuvres can usually get by without extra winches. For instance,

when the spinnaker is hoisted you can bear away directly downwind to put the spinnaker in the lee of the mainsail. This means you can furl away the genoa before hoisting the spinnaker, freeing up the primary winches to be used for the spinnaker sheets.

It's also arguable that a halyard winch is not needed, apart from on the largest of boats. Just make sure you don't pull the sheet in until the halyard is secure, and you don't let the halyard go until the sheet is free and the sail has been depowered.

Mast steps

Fitting a set of robust steps to your mast will greatly aid routine rigging checks and maintenance, as well as offering an elevated lookout position for piloting in clear, shallow waters.

Mast steps are available in two basic forms, folding and fixed. They are attached to alloy masts with pop rivets, and to wooden masts with bronze or stainless steel screws. There are several retrofit models available from chandlers or rigging shops, and some owners even make their own.

A set of correctly spaced steps will allow a member of the crew to climb the mast with relative ease to inspect various fixtures and fittings, to change bulbs in navigation lights, or to retrieve lost halyards. An elevated position for a lookout while approaching tricky anchorages is also a great safety feature when it comes to pilotage and, as such, some yachts only have steps as far as the first set of crosstrees. Here, a crew member can sit comfortably during an approach, calling directions to the helmsman below, or using this temporary crow's nest for a spot of photography.

While mast steps provide a good way to get up a mast, it is strongly recommended that any crew member aloft is also attached to a halyard via a harness, with another crew member below keeping some tension on the line. It only takes an unexpected roll of the yacht for a member of the crew to lose his grip, and it's a long way down.

Mast steps are a good alternative to the more traditional bosun's chair, although a downside is that both hands are needed during the climb. To stop and work on any part of the mast in safety, the crew member will need to secure himself to the mast with a belt around his waist or chest to free up his hands.

Right **Mast steps greatly aid maintenance and inspection of the mast. Here a rigger has climbed to the crosstrees using home-made steps. The steps were constructed from sections of stainless steel bar cut and bent to shape.**

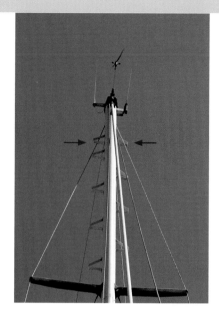

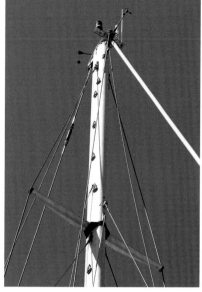

Far left Steps are attached from the top of the mast downwards. Notice that the first two are side by side (see arrows), at chest height to the masthead, to allow a good position for a crew member to work on the fittings.

Left Folding steps fit neatly against the mast, but offer less lateral security. They also need to be deployed by hand during the climb.

Fitting steps

The steps are best fitted with the mast down, and are often added during a rigging change. Things to consider are:

- Choose steps that can take a significant amount of weight. Some fixed step designs are very uncomfortable for bare feet, so look for designs that allow room for a sandal or deck shoe.
- Work from the top of the mast downwards. Place the first two steps side by side, so an average crew member can stand comfortably and will be chest-high to the navigation lights and fittings at the top of the mast. This will make them easier to work on.

TIP

Tying a thin cord between the steps and the outer shrouds above the crosstrees will prevent the mainsail from billowing through this gap on a dead run, improving its set and reducing chafe. An example can be seen in the photo opposite.

- Place the rest of the steps evenly apart, making sure that your legs don't have too much of a stretch. About 400mm (16in) between each tread is fairly common.
- Allow for the standing rigging. If a step seems to interfere with a shroud, the step can be rotated a little further around the mast to clear it.
- The crosstrees can be used as one of the steps if it falls where a step would be needed.

Folding or fixed?

Folding steps are neater as they stow flush against the mast and minimise interference with the rigging or sails. However, they have to be opened and closed on the ascent/descent, and don't offer much protection against lateral motion, so they are more easy to slip from. As such, they are usually only used in a marina or during a flat calm. Some yachts will have a combination of fixed and folding steps, with the folding versions around the base, avoiding the winches.

Above top Folding steps fold out to present a serrated edge for good grip, but are uncomfortable for bare feet. Other fold-out designs can be more forgiving on the sole.

Above A typical design for a fixed mast step, made from aluminium with a hard plastic base. Note the three 6.25-mm (¼-in) rivets that hold it in place.

Pop-riveting

Pop rivets, or 'blind' rivets, to use their technical name, are a means of securing two pieces of metal where it is difficult to access the reverse (blind side) of a structure. This makes them ideal for applications on masts. Pop rivets are easy to use, strong and very versatile.

The blind rivet is a way of joining two thin layers of material together, but its use is now widespread for a number of fixing applications.

Types of pop rivet

A pop rivet is available in many sizes and types, but essentially it is a short tube of malleable metal with a shaft called a mandrel through the middle. At the top of the tube, the mandrel flares out slightly, rather like the head of a nail. The pop rivet is inserted into a pre-drilled hole of a specific diameter, and then a special tool is used to grasp the protruding mandrel. As the trigger on the tool is worked, metal teeth grab the mandrel and pull it out, forcing the innermost end to compress and mushroom inside the mast. At a predetermined pressure, known as the 'blind setting', the mandrel snaps off, leaving the rivet locked firmly in place.

This method of securing items to an aluminium mast is widespread, especially as pop rivets are available in small increments in size, making them very versatile. They come in a number of materials, including aluminium, Monel, copper and stainless steel, although pop-riveting in stainless steel is very hard.

TIP

When making a number of holes for pop-riveting, use a cobalt-tipped drill bit. Although more expensive than standard drill bits, it remains sharp for much longer when drilling metal.

The shape and profile of the rivets vary widely, with some pop rivets having a secondary shell designed to peel back like a banana skin when joining lightweight or fragile materials. Mast applications tend to use the conventional rivet design.

Below **A riveting tool is placed over the protruding mandrel, before it is pulled back and the rivet 'popped' into place.**

HOW TO 'POP' A RIVET

Drill out the old rivet with a sharp drill slightly larger than the original rivet.

Clear away the debris, and insert the new rivet into the hole.

Attach the riveting tool, and start to pull the mandrel back until it snaps off.

The body has mushroomed on the 'blind' side, locking the fixing into place.

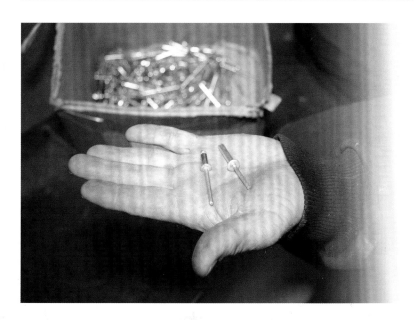

There are several different tools available for pop-riveting. For heavy-duty riveting, a pneumatic pop rivet gun is recommended. For smaller jobs, most riggers use a 'lazy tongs' hand riveter, as it is much easier on the hands.

Pop-riveting kits are inexpensive, and for mast applications it is recommended to use Monel rivets, due to the metal's greater strength and resistance to salt water. It is very important to drill a hole of exactly the right diameter as your rivet for a good fit.

Replacing rivets

The old rivet can be drilled out using a sharp drill bit of the same diameter as the original hole. This will break open the tube and cause it to fall apart. To replace the rivet:

- Make a new hole, by marking the mast. Mark the centre of the hole with a metal tool called a 'dot punch', then use a drill of the correct diameter to drill the hole.
- Insert the new rivet into the hole. The outer collar stops it dropping through.
- Insert the rivet gun over the mandrel, and then work it with a series of arm movements. The mandrel is held tight and pulled outwards, causing the flange at the top of the rivet to start crushing the tube as it moves along it. You can see the distortion on the blind side quite clearly. The mandrel snaps off flush with the outer collar, and the rivet should now last for many years.

Left **Two sizes of pop rivet. Those made from Monel last longer as they are more resistant to salt water.**

Windvane self-steering

For the voyaging yachtsman, wind-powered self-steering gear is a 'tireless helmsman', holding a course for days on end without requiring a single amp of electricity. It excels in heavy weather and some designs also double up as an emergency rudder.

Windvane self-steering is simply a self-powering autopilot that uses the force and direction of the wind to hold a yacht under sail on a preset course. Apart from making your yacht look like a serious ocean explorer, windvane self-steering is a very practical and low maintenance piece of kit that will helm on almost all points of sail. The tougher the conditions, the more effective it becomes. However, the windvane can only hold a course in direct relation to the wind, rather than to a compass heading (as with electronic autopilots), so if the wind suddenly changes direction, then so does the yacht.

Over the years, several types of windvane self-steering systems have been developed; some are more effective than others, and some better suited to specific kinds of yacht or multihull. The concept is particularly popular with boatowners who may be single-handed or short-crewed, but wish to undertake long passages without relying on complex and power-consuming electronic pilots.

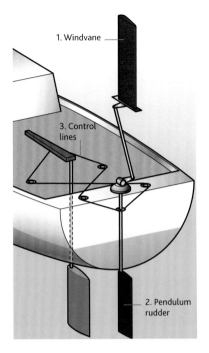

1. Windvane

3. Control lines

2. Pendulum rudder

Above **The windvane (1) is moved by the wind, making the pendulum rudder (2) rotate around a vertical axis. Water flows past the pendulum rudder so it swings sideways around a horizontal axis. Control lines (3) connected to the pendulum rudder and the boat's main rudder help the boat steer back to the correct course. The windvane returns to its initial position.**

Below **A self-steering system is ideal for small yachts planned for big journeys, such as this 22ft (6.7m) transatlantic Westerly Nomad. No power is required, and it is fairly easy to repair under way.**

Left **Most types can be made to fit any kind of transom. This Aries – its paddle and vane removed – has been adapted to fit a canoe stern. The more robust the vane design, however, the heavier it will be.**

Right **When not in use, the windvane can be removed and the blade swung out of the water, or it can be detached completely to prevent damage.**

Other types utilise a trim tab on the main rudder, and several can accept the connection of an electronic autopilot for use in light airs or when under power, too.

Pros and cons

When deciding whether to fit windvane self-steering gear, there are several considerations:

Pros:

- ✪ Requires absolutely no electrical power to operate.
- ✪ Low maintenance, and usually quite simple to repair.
- ✪ Very responsive, especially in strong winds.
- ✪ Excellent in heavy weather.
- ✪ Can be engineered to fit almost any hull shape.
- ✪ Ideal for singlehanded or short-handed passage making.

Cons:

- ✪ Can be heavy or bulky, depending on type.
- ✪ Only holds a course relative to the apparent wind.
- ✪ Takes a little 'getting to know'.
- ✪ Not very responsive in light airs or on a dead run.
- ✪ Adds vulnerable clutter to the stern.
- ✪ Can be expensive new.

How it works

The heart of each system is the windvane itself, which may use a horizontal movement (where it hinges at the bottom and is blown over by the wind) or a vertical movement (where it swings around like a weathercock). Once the yacht is settled onto its chosen course and the sails have been trimmed, the vane is pointed edge-on to the wind and the steering gear connected. When the yacht wanders off course, the vane detects a change in wind direction and triggers a response.

Some systems use the pressure of the wind alone to provide the necessary mechanical force to work a semi-balanced auxiliary rudder, while others harness the energy of the water rushing past the yacht to turn the main rudder. These servo-pendulum types are the most common and are also very powerful, with quick response times.

Compared with electronic autopilots that feature push-button operation and hidden mechanisms, windvanes are a bit more cumbersome and take more getting used to. They tend to be the preserve of keen, passage-making yachtsmen, although they will happily take over the helm at a moment's notice for coastal sailing. Many of the manufacturers are bluewater yachtsmen themselves, and have developed their particular system after thousands of miles of voyaging.

TIP

Some yachtsmen have found that kite-surfing rope makes for a very efficient control line, as it is thin and light, yet incredibly strong. This reduces friction in the system in light airs.

Fitting a windvane

Each manufacturer will have comprehensive instructions for fitting its system, and when it comes to the popular servo-pendulum models, most require the trailing blade to be sited along the yacht's centreline, using the backstay as a guide. Even a little way off-centre will compromise the unit's performance. Whatever the shape of the transom or the design of the rudder, struts can be engineered to support the mechanism in the ideal position.

Because windvanes are built in small batches, some on a semi-custom basis, there is a great deal of customer support available. Usually a boatowner will contact the supplier with details of the yacht, and the supplier may already have an archive of ideal solutions on similar vessels. Once the unit has been delivered, most often as a kit,

fitting is best done with the yacht moored stern-to in a berth, with spring lines attached to limit its movement. When the yacht is afloat it is easier to see where the yacht is lying to the waterline mark, as the amount of paddle that is immersed is critical to performance.

Any fixtures on the transom can interfere with the position of the system, but the suppliers insist that for best performance, priority should be given to the correct alignment of the steering gear, and other equipment relocated around it.

When fitting a windvane, take careful measurements and then centre the unit on the transom, supporting it with ropes from the pushpit or temporary gantry while you mark the drill holes for the supporting struts. Double-check inside the transom to ensure that the securing bolts won't interfere with any pipes, wires or access points.

Above **The customer has provided measurements and photographs of his boat for the vane gear manufacturer, who then builds the unit and the specific supports it will need.**

Right **The fitting is best done with the boat afloat, and in full cruising trim. Here it has been backed up to the pontoon for easy access.**

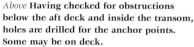

Above **Having checked for obstructions below the aft deck and inside the transom, holes are drilled for the anchor points. Some may be on deck.**

Once you have drilled the holes for the brackets, you may have to adjust the length of the struts so that the unit is sitting vertically in exactly the right position. Use sealant and backing plates for a solid, watertight connection to the transom.

With the frame bolted to the hull, attach the paddle, which will swing up when not in use, and then lead the control lines into the cockpit. For tiller-steered boats, cross these control lines over at the vane gear before leading them to each side of the cockpit and attaching them to a length of chain that will allow for correcting weather helm.

On wheel-steered boats, fasten a special attachment to the wheel. You can feed the lines in from the same side of the cockpit, if necessary, via a set of guiding pulleys. The last attachment is usually the windvane itself, and then the system is ready for testing.

Above **The transom supports are then cut, fitted with end caps and retaining grub screws, and then attached to the hull with through-bolts to backing plates.**

Using vane gear

The vane gear works best when the yacht is nicely balanced on its desired course. To deploy the paddle gear, it is often a good idea to slow the yacht down by rounding up into the wind for a few moments. With the paddle down and locked, get the sails trimmed just right, so that when the yacht wanders off course there is a natural tendency for it to correct itself. This means the vane gear doesn't need to exert too much effort to work efficiently.

Once sailing this way, attach the windvane and turn until its leading edge is pointing directly into the wind. Then connect the control lines, and monitor progress until you are happy that the vane gear is steering correctly.

Adjustments can be made for light airs by swapping to larger vanes, and this also works for the slightly more tricky downwind sailing when the breeze loses some of its power.

When not in use, the paddle should be pulled up and locked to avoid damage, and the vane itself taken off to avoid excessive wear on the system.

Above **The steering lines are cut to size, and attached to a length of chain. The links can be adjusted over the pin in the tiller to allow for weather helm.**

Tiller pilot

Tiller pilots tend to be used on smaller boats where it's not possible to install a below-decks autopilot drive system. They are available as either stand-alone units or as part of a system that integrates with the boat's electronics, including rate-sensing compasses, wind instruments and chartplotters.

Many of the considerations for specifying a below decks pilot also apply to tiller pilots. It's important to remember that cutting back on the size of a tiller pilot is invariably a false economy – as well as having reduced thrust, a smaller model will move the helm more slowly. This will be fine in calm conditions, but in testing weather it will result in more movement of the tiller, which will put the unit under unnecessary stress and consume noticeably more power.

It's also worth bearing in mind that many older craft, the type most likely to have tiller steering, were built with thicker laminates than the designer originally specified and may well be significantly heavier than the figures quoted by the boatbuilder. In addition, even boats of a modest size tend to collect a significant amount of extra gear, supplies and crew weight that can easily add a further 20 per cent to the total weight of the boat, which must be considered when the pilot is specified.

Installing a pilot

Most tiller pilots are designed to be mounted 450mm (18in) from the rudderstock and use fittings that are interchangeable between the majority of brands, although it's important to check the specifications for your unit in this respect. Most can also be mounted on either side of the boat. If possible, avoid putting it on top of a cockpit locker; this may immediately determine the side of the boat on which it is placed. If not, try to minimise wiring runs – the shorter these are the less power will be lost as heat in the cables.

Below **A tiller pilot is a big help to a short-handed crew and the best types are capable of steering a good course.**

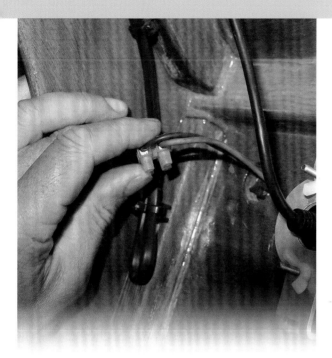

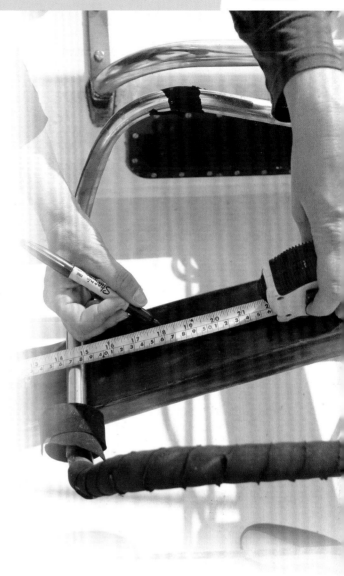

All manufacturers offer a wide range of fittings so that the unit can be installed horizontally at the correct distance from the rudderstock. These include various extensions for the unit's arm and brackets that can be added above or below the tiller.

Installing the mounts

As tiller pilots are installed close to the rudderstock, loads are much higher than will be experienced by a human holding the end of the tiller. The mountings on the boat and on the tiller must therefore be fitted in a secure manner that will withstand many thousands of load cycles over several years.

The key to this is to make sure you set the fastenings in epoxy resin. The socket for the pin at the boat end also needs to have a wooden backing pad glued underneath the deck, strengthened accordingly.

Above left **Keep wiring runs short and use a heavy-gauge wire so that energy is not lost as heat – the pilot may be one of the most power-hungry items on board, especially when steering in big seas.**

Above right **Measuring to fit the pin on the tiller – most need to be placed 450mm (18in) from the centre of the rudderstock, but check the manual to find the recommended distance for your system.**

Right **A wooden backing plate may need to be epoxied in place below the deck to ensure the deck fitting is securely located – it takes a lot of load.**

Electric winches

There are three key reasons to fit electric winches: convenience, safety and health. The latter is an important consideration that is frequently overlooked, yet a worrying number of boatowners have suffered heart attacks after a heavy session working winches.

Any boat over about 10–11m (33–36ft) has the potential to benefit from adding electric winches, particularly if the key crew members need some extra assistance or if you are sailing singlehanded. This is particularly true for boats with large genoas that require a lot of winching after a tack, and for boats with modern double taffeta laminate mainsails, which can be considerably heavier than other materials.

Which winches to convert?

The answer to this will depend on both your boat and the crew with whom you generally sail. For a modern design with a mainsail-dominated fractional rig and relatively small jibs, it's most likely that the biggest benefits will be gained from converting one of the halyard winches. This will also make reefing more straightforward, particularly if single-line reefing is fitted (see page 244).

Below **Fitting an all-electric winch system to this Nautor Swan 92 has allowed the owner to sail a large and fast boat with a minimal crew.**

Right **These push button controls for electric winches are found alongside the winch itself. They can be operated by the lightest of touch.**

On the other hand, if sheeting in the genoa after a tack or after partially reefing the sail is the most strenuous activity on board, then it will make more sense to convert the primary winches to electric power.

Drawbacks

The most obvious drawback of electric winches is increased power consumption, especially if the genoa sheet winches are powered. It will therefore be important to monitor the charge level of the service batteries while on passage. Although quite a bit of electrical power will be required to hoist the mainsail up the rig, this is usually undertaken before turning the engine off. However, wiring runs must be carefully considered so that they are kept as short as possible to reduce power being lost as heat in the wiring.

A further drawback is the space needed for the motor, which can detract from headroom in quarter berths or in the heads compartment. If this is likely to be a particular problem for your boat, it's worth seeking out a model with a low-profile horizontal motor.

Finally, the system will inevitably require additional maintenance compared to a boat with only manual winches. All the major winch manufacturers have service procedures for each model on their websites. Be aware that the watertight buttons used for most electric winches degrade rapidly in sunlight. This means they should be replaced at least every four or five years, and failure to do so may mean it becomes impossible to stop the electric motor turning, with potentially serious consequences.

Above **This electric sheet winch is operated from the cockpit for hoisting the main, making it very easy to work.**

Right **The underside of an installation. Note the space needed by the motor, which is usually horizontal to the winch base. A motor can also be hidden within a compartment.**

Electric winches 2

You can use existing manual winches as a guide to the size of electric winches that will be best suited to your boat, but bear in mind that in order to shave a little off the cost of the boat, most boatbuilders fit the smallest winches possible.

If your existing winches require undue effort when hoisting or trimming a sail, it will be worth replacing them with an electric model of the next size up. An electric winch that's too small is invariably a false economy that risks premature failure of the motor.

Converting existing winches

Some larger sizes of winch that are currently in production are designed so that a motor can be retrofitted. This saves both time and cost, so is well worth investigating when planning the system.

Below **Some self-tailing manual winches can be upgraded to an electric winch with the addition of a motor and wiring components. Conversion kits are available for some models.**

Wiring considerations

Electric winches can take a considerable amount of current, albeit for a relatively short length of time. This means substantial cables must be run to the motor – don't be tempted to skimp on this aspect, as power will be lost as heat in the wires if they are too small. If in doubt, it's worth erring on the side of caution and choosing a larger-sized cable than that specified.

While an electric windlass will always benefit from its own battery in the forward part of the boat in order to reduce the length of wiring that carries high currents, that may not be necessary when fitting electric winches, providing your main battery bank is relatively close to the winches. If an additional battery is needed, it should be located as close as possible to the winches that it will power.

Above **Anatomy of an electric winch. The motor sits in the accommodation directly beneath the base, and is protected from the elements by a deck seal.**

Speed 1 Speed 2

Breaker

Control box

M1 M2

A1 C A2

Battery

Above **You will need heavy wire, two switches, a control box and a circuit breaker to set up this two-speed system. Match the size of the cable to the size of the winch, system voltage and cable length.**

Alternatives

Change from a genoa to a jib:

Although once fashionable, big overlapping genoas are no more practical than flared trousers. They are only efficient at a relatively small range of wind strengths and angles, so it's possible to change to a smaller jib – maybe 110 per cent of the foretriangle size instead of 140 per cent – with minimal loss of performance. The smaller sail will require much less effort to sheet home after each tack.

Use bodyweight to hoist the sail:

Halyards that exit from the base of the mast and are then led back to the cockpit often have a large amount of unnecessary friction. It's possible to form a new halyard outlet position further up the mast, allowing one person to use their body weight to hoist the sail, while someone else tails the halyard in the cockpit.

Use a longer winch handle:

This won't reduce the total amount of effort required, but it will reduce the rate at which you need to work – a 25-cm (10-in) handle will give 25 per cent more mechanical power than an 20-cm (8-in) one.

Service your winches:

Most boatowners are guilty of failing to service winches on a regular basis.

Above **Fitting low friction mainsail slides and modifying the main halyard outlet position so that you can use body weight to hoist the sail may be easier on some boats than fitting electric winches.**

If they are given attention twice a year, friction will be minimised and the effort needed to hoist or trim the sail can drop by up to 25 per cent.

Sails and rigging tips

A modern trend is for couples to sail increasingly larger yachts short-handed, so builders are at pains to make deck layouts and rigs very easy to operate, with power assistance a common option. Here we have some ideas that will help to keep the cockpit tidy, and the rig smooth to operate.

Shortened halyards

On a yacht fitted with in-mast furling and/or roller reefing, the halyards will get very little use. As such, they are rarely led back to the cockpit, but remain coiled at the mast instead. These coiled halyards mean a lot of redundant rope that needs to be constantly kept tidy and prevented from unravelling during the season.

One very neat solution is a tensioning track. The halyard is cut so that just a short length shows once the sail is fully hoisted, and also has a soft eye-splice put into the end. This eye-splice is connected to a length of track on the mast, allowing the halyard to be fully tensioned using a detachable line to a nearby winch. When the sail needs to be lowered, a longer line is tied to the soft eye, and the halyard released from the tensioning track. The halyard can now run back up the mast until it is needed again.

Above **Redundant line from a halyard can be shortened by means of a tensioning track.**

Above right **The genoa sheets on this Hallberg-Rassy are elegantly stowed to create a clear cockpit.**

Stowing sheets

An efficiently managed yacht has an uncluttered cockpit, so the ability to stow lines out of sight (and therefore no longer underfoot) is very important. If a self-draining cockpit is built into the design of the yacht, it could be one solution for holding sheets. This could be improvised in yachts that have some redundant coaming space. Alternatively, a small bag on the outside of the cockpit could keep the ropes stowed until needed.

Stowing halyards

Another built-in design idea for halyard ends is an angled fibreglass rope bin. Crafted into the cockpit design, it not only captures the rope ends for the halyards, it also doubles as a comfortable backrest when lounging in the cockpit. There is a deep drainage channel underneath.

Right **A fibreglass rope bin is another cockpit solution for halyards on this Discovery 67.**

Rope ladder up the mast

An alternative to mast steps or a bosun's chair is a mast ladder. Essentially a rope ladder, it is hoisted on a main halyard and tensioned, allowing a crew member to climb to the top of the mast in settled conditions. It remains vital to his safety that he is connected to another halyard, with a crewman taking up the slack on a winch.

Rope shackles on large blocks

Consider the benefit of a block without a shackle. Instead, by attaching large sheet blocks to the boom with braided rope, the blocks have far more articulation, and a slight 'give' when the tension comes on. This reduces wear, making them quietly efficient.

Ready to cut

While rigging is generally highly dependable, a dismasting could threaten the safety of the hull in a seaway, so it is important to be able to cut away the rigging quickly. As such, many yachts have made provision to hack away at hard and soft rigging with appliances such as fire axes, knives and bolt croppers kept readily accessible for such a situation.

Above left **A mast ladder is easy to climb and gives you a stable and comfortable position to work from.**

Above right **An idea from a Nautor Swan 90 yacht is a shackleless block, which provides more 'give' under tension.**

Right **A fire axe stowed in the companionway is ready for emergency use.**

Eco upgrades

8

Solar energy

Solar panels are becoming cheaper as world production increases. Even the smallest panel will make a contribution to your energy independence, but positioning them effectively may need some imagination.

Solar panels, also known as photovoltaic (PV) panels, are now seen everywhere, from calculators to household rooftops. Most people are familiar with how they work – daylight falling onto a grid of encapsulated silicon semi-conductors excites electrons, which then move as a direct electric current (DC). On boats, this current is harvested and stored in deep-cycle batteries.

A well-made solar panel will give up to 25 years of 'free' energy and require almost no maintenance apart from the occasional wipe down and a visual check. The marine versions are usually ruggedly made from corrosion-resistant materials, and can often be manually tilted towards the sun.

Solar panels are available in several distinct types: rigid, rigid but semi-flexible and flexible. Many long-range yachts will have a combination of the two, allowing charging to be boosted on good solar days. Flexible panels can also be permanently mounted onto a curved surface, such as a hatch housing or cabin roof. Others are kept loose with a long cable so that they can be readily moved around the deck to catch the most direct sunlight.

Wiring in a solar panel or several linked panels (an array) is very straightforward, and with the current flow managed into multiple batteries by an inexpensive regulator, some yachts find they need little else to power all their domestic needs. For blue water yachts, however, the solar panels are usually part of a suite of recharging options that can supply power around the clock.

Below **Two large monocrystalline solar panels on an articulated frame. An array of 200 watts can usually supply most of the domestic requirements of an average yacht – when the sun shines.**

TYPES OF SOLAR PANEL

All solar panels are currently made from two thin layers of silicon constructed as a sandwich. The silicon was initially supplied as a by-product of the electronics industry, and prices continue to fall as new production techniques are discovered.

Monocrystalline silicon (rigid): The most efficient but expensive panels are made from large, thin slices from a single block of silicon. Monocrystalline panels are often identified as a series of squares with the corners rounded off.

Polycrystalline silicon (rigid but semi-flexible): Almost as efficient, and a bit cheaper due to the lower production costs. Polycrystalline panels are made from many smaller slices of silicon.

Amorphous (CIGS – flexible): Used primarily in flexible and folding panels, but not as efficient as rigid panels and have a shorter working life. Recently efficiency has risen to around 20 per cent from an average of 6 per cent.

Calculating energy demands

You will need to find out how much power each 'off grid' electrical device will consume when working (or in standby mode) and for how long that current will be needed. This demand will change according to how the boat is being used, so a helpful benchmark is the maximum draw your boat will need at any one time.

Above **Some owners dedicate a single solar panel to maintain the battery of one high draw item, such as a fridge or windlass.**

The power demand for each device is expressed in watts, a measure of energy calculated by multiplying the voltage (volts) available by the current (amps) being drained. This is then divided by the number of hours each day it is likely to be used. For example:

- A boat has a 12-volt battery supply, and runs a fridge that draws 4 amps. The fridge will cycle on and off as the thermostat kicks in, and runs for an average of 10 hours in every 24.
- Our calculation would be: 4 (amps) x 12 (volts) x 10 (hours) = 480 watt hours.
- To convert this into amp hours (Ah) to help us calculate the size of battery needed for the fridge alone, we divide the watt hours by the voltage; 480/12 = 40Ah. Left uncharged, the battery will drain in one hour.

There is a big difference between when the yacht is at sea, and when it is at anchor. The battery bank should be capable of supplying that demand without being drained by more than 50 per cent of its total rated capacity, and also have a recharging system capable of replacing more than that in average conditions. If the panels can virtually match that drain, then the batteries will be shallow-cycled, and so will last a lot longer.

Finally, you can now decide how much you want to replenish from renewable sources. Most long-range cruising yachts have a combination of charging systems – perhaps large wind generators for use in the northern hemisphere and solar panels in tropical waters, using wind generators as a supplement.

Solar energy 2

Maximising efficiency

The energy produced by a solar panel is quoted in watts (W), and is based on peak power production under optimal conditions, namely peak sunlight producing 1,000 watts per square metre at an air temperature of 25°C (77°F) and an air density of 1.5kg/m³.

However, the number of panels that need to be carried depends on how much energy is required on average and dull days, and the capacity of your battery bank to absorb it. Solar panels will be part of a wider rechargeable system that also includes wind and engine generation, and this will also determine the power you will want from the sun alone.

A 50-watt panel, for example, should provide 50 watts an hour in perfect conditions. In reality, it will be much less. Factors that affect a panel's performance are:

❂ **Direct sunlight:** The amount of direct sunlight each panel receives, ie the hours per day when it is fully exposed to the sun. Limiting factors are the angle of the sun, the length of the day and the amount of cloud cover.

❂ **Temperature:** If solar panels get too hot, their performance falls off, which is why they should be vented underneath, if it is at all possible.

❂ **Partial shadow:** Just a small area of shade can cause a big fall-off in performance, as the individual cells that don't have sunlight will draw power from those that do.

❂ **Damage:** Some panels, especially the flexible versions, may suffer some damage over time and fail to deliver their best output.

❂ **Cable resistance:** A long run of relatively thin cable can build up resistance, thus reducing the amount of current arriving at the batteries. Poor connections can also introduce inefficiencies.

The most accurate way to calculate the output from a panel is to multiply the rated output by the number of hours it will be exposed directly to the sun, and then assume an 85 per cent efficiency (or 75 per cent for northern latitudes).

Below **A large, partially articulated solar panel, such as on this guard wire, can be dropped down and lashed to the stanchion when not needed.**

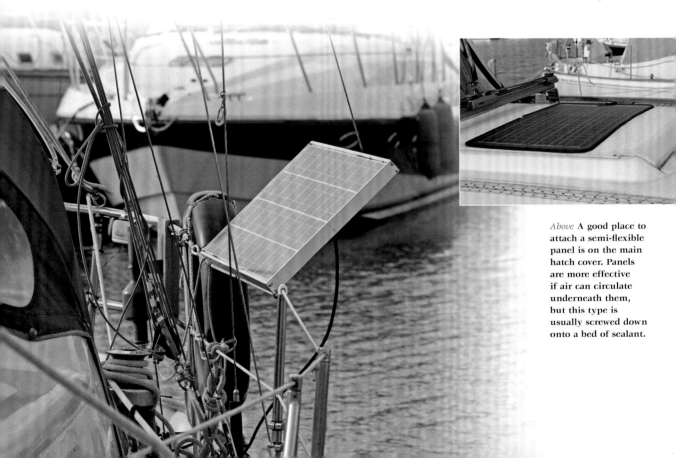

Above **A good place to attach a semi-flexible panel is on the main hatch cover. Panels are more effective if air can circulate underneath them, but this type is usually screwed down onto a bed of sealant.**

For example, a 10-watt panel exposed for 4 hours will produce: 10W x 4 = 40W x 0.85 = 34Wh (watt hours).

Choosing and using

With the cost of solar panels falling, it makes sense to carry the biggest panels you can, especially if sunlight is limited. Apart from providing as large a surface area as possible, there is more you can do:

- Articulate the panels, so they can be positioned to face the sun.
- Try to locate the panels where shadows won't be a problem.
- In hot climates, encourage a good airflow above and below the panel.
- Fit an intelligent regulator system (to balance the cells) to make the best use of the energy being created, and keep the battery system well maintained.
- Use the correct gauge of wire for long cable runs. With an increase in length, resistance causes a drop in voltage that can be fixed by using a larger gauge wire than would normally be needed.
- Supplement your fixed panels with flexible ones on long wires that can be moved easily to unshaded areas of deck.

PANEL MOUNTING IDEAS

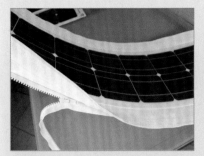

Manufacturers are offering extra options to their semi-flexible panels to make them easier to fit. Here a Solbian panel has been fixed to a canvas cloth with a pre-installed zip for attaching to awnings.

Semi-rigid panels are also available with pre-drilled holes with reinforcements already attached, or with pre-installed push studs. This makes temporary mounting in good weather very easy.

Lightweight panels can also be attached to the sprayhood, or in this case on a separate hoop over the top of the bimini. This design allows good air circulation underneath, but in bad weather these flimsy panels could be quickly detached and stowed.

Even small panels can be fully articulated. Here a pair has been mounted on a simple pivoting arm. The friction is adjusted with stainless steel knobs. Note the diode box on the back.

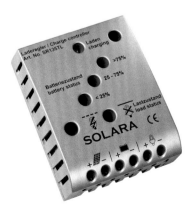

Left **A solar regulator is an important but inexpensive piece of equipment, and can monitor several panels at once. It carefully controls the flow of current entering the batteries, and prevents them from being overcharged. Note the simplicity of the connections.**

TIP

When fitting a solar array, bear in mind that if you fit a large controller from the outset (allow 15A rating per 200 watts) you will always be able to add to the area of panels on board as your power demands increase.

Wind power

Wind-powered generators are easy to fit and virtually maintenance free. They work tirelessly day and night to recharge the batteries whenever there is more than a gentle breeze.

Wind-powered generators are available in two distinct types, horizontal and vertical, but all work on the same principle. The force of the wind acts on a rotor, which in turn spins a coil of copper wire through a magnetic field. This generates an electric current, which is usually modified, before being fed into the batteries.

Choosing which system will work best on your boat will be a process of comparing prices, quoted outputs, design and user feedback. Some are quiet apart from a slight 'whoosh', but others can whine as the wind gusts. Many designs are well proven and all manufacturers can give advice and provide their own compatible ancillary systems, such as regulators and monitors.

Wind turbines do have their drawbacks, in that they put a lot of weight aloft and are less efficient on a long, downwind sail. However, once installed, they provide free, clean power whenever there is more than a few knots of wind.

Above **The most common type of wind generator is the windmill design, which can rotate through 360 degrees. This unit will typically produce 4.25 amps at maximum output.**

Right **Vertical wind generators are easy to install anywhere on board, especially on the mast, but their output is low and really only intended for trickle charging. This Forgen will produce about 1.5 amps at maximum rated wind speed.**

Generator types

There are three main types of generator used in the turbines, which may affect your buying decision. Each type has its own set of advantages:

Permanent magnet: Positioned around the spinning copper coil to provide the magnetic field, it is lightweight, has no brushes and very little maintenance is required. The downside is that the output can be limited compared to other types.

DC alternator: This type of generator uses an electromagnetic coil to generate the magnetic field. The whole system becomes more efficient as the speed increases. It requires little maintenance except to replace brushes.

Brushless alternator: Similar to a DC generator, the magnetised field coils are made of wire, so there are no brushes involved. These generators are more complex and so more expensive to replace or repair.

Above **The higher a wind generator can be installed above the deck, the cleaner the airflow it will encounter, making it more efficient. This one is on a mizzen mast, but some owners will install a wind generator at the masthead.**

Right **On smaller yachts, placing the generator on a pre-shaped pole, as shown here, will keep it away from the crew and clear of the rigging, without making the unit too top-heavy, or shading solar panels.**

How much output?

Manufacturers rate their generators at the maximum output before the system governs itself. This will be the wattage just below the level at which the generator will burn itself out if left unchecked.

Directly related to this output is 'rated wind speed'. Because of the battery voltage that the turbine has to supply, as well as resistance in a long travel of wire, very few produce any worthwhile current below about 6mph (10kph). Most produce their peak output around 25–28mph (40–45kph), with some type of brake cutting in above that.

Output is also directly related to rotor size. The bigger the rotor area, the more wind it can catch. Also, the more blades a wind generator has, the more torque it can produce, and torque is needed to spin the rotor from stationary. However, conversely, the fewer the number of blades in a rotor, the more efficient it becomes when spinning.

Two blades can 'chatter' when inertia combines with a yawing movement, unless the rotor uses a modified spring-loaded head. This chatter can be transmitted down the mast and into the hull as vibration.

Vertical wind generators generally have two or three opposing vanes. They have limited output and are generally used as trickle chargers.

They can be mounted almost anywhere on board as they are unlikely to cause any real harm if the rotating vanes are touched.

TIP

The larger the rotor blades, the more dangerous they can be, so allow plenty of clearance between the rotor tip and any part of your body, especially raised hands. If mounting onto a yacht's mast, ensure the blades are also well clear of standing and running rigging.

Wind power 2

FITTING A WIND GENERATOR

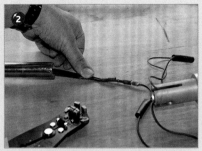

A new wind generator is usually supplied as a disassembled head unit kit, like this Rutland model. The blades have to be inserted correctly and bolted down, along with the tail fin.

The simple wiring to the battery regulator is run up the supporting pole, and connected to the corresponding wires from the generator with staggered connections. Note the plugs are heat-shrinked to seal them.

If mounting the unit on the stern, you can buy a pre-made radar mast that will take the wind generator, or you can have a pole custom-made. Some designs incorporate the pole into the gantry.

Controlling output

The maximum output of a wind generator is set to the top end of average wind speeds likely to be encountered, and some produce a current at a very low rotation speed. If the wind blows hard for many days, the generator can then be taken out of usage with a simple string attached to the tail, allowing the rotor to be swung across the wind so that the blades stall.

The ability to stop the current electronically depends on the type of alternator fitted. Some have thermal cut-outs, while others have an electronic brake to slow the blades to a virtual stop.

Whatever wind turbine you choose, especially if buying a second-hand unit, it's important that there is some sort of protection against overcharging.

Wind and water generators

Water-powered (or 'towed') generators are very efficient as the torque from water flow when a boat is under way is powerful and relatively consistent. Some units combine both wind and water generation capability from the same alternator, allowing the skipper to select the most useful force at play during a long passage.

There are two types of water-powered generator on the market, and you may also spot a few home-made ones as well. One type is on a hinged pole that is raised vertically to catch the wind, and after a quick swap from rotor to propeller, can be dropped into the sea and dragged along underwater. The system then continues to work when the yacht anchors in a tidal flow, as the propeller continues to spin.

The second type tows a spinner along on a length of multiplait rope that is connected to the alternator unit, secured in a bracket on the stern or hung from the pushpit rail.

The cable spins the armature in the usual way. The alternator, usually enclosed in a drum-like casing, can also be placed on top of a pole and fitted with a wind rotor and tailfin instead.

Below **A combined wind and water unit utilises the same generator, but has a propeller on the end of a pivoting submersible pole. This arrangement also works when anchored in a strong tidal stream.**

The towed generators can produce a significant amount of energy very quietly and are particularly useful on a long downwind passage. They are often used at night to run items such as navigation lights, autopilots, chartplotters and radar sets.

Combined wind/water generators are usually more expensive than their wind-only counterparts, and require more consideration when it comes to their brackets and fixtures, but they are also among the most efficient means of providing a steady flow of current on long passages.

TYPICAL OUTPUTS

Water-powered generator

Sailing speed	Output*
3 knots	2 amps
4 knots	3 amps
5 knots	5 amps
6 knots	6 amps

(*Manufacturer's figures for the DuoGen)

Wiring in a wind generator

Most generators will be outputting a DC current using two wires, positive and negative. A blocking diode is also integrated into the rotor head, although sometimes they are added further into the stem. A fuse should be placed as near to the battery as possible. Some systems will incorporate a dump resistor, which allows the regulator to dump unwanted energy into a heating coil so as to prevent battery damage.

Solar panel 30W max

Rutland 500

Blocking diode 3A

Solar regulator

Ammeter

Battery 12v

Alternator

Left A typical wiring diagram for a combined recharging system using a Rutland wind generator, an engine alternator and a solar panel. Note the blocking adiode on the solar array, the position of the ammeter, and the central role of the solar regulator.

Below The unit can be swung out of the water, a wind rotor and steering tail (not deployed here) attached, and then the whole thing raised vertically for use as a wind generator.

Below A lightweight mounting for a three-bladed wind generator on a mizzen mast. This type of mounting also helps minimise windage.

Go electric

Imagine being able to cruise silently from your berth under electric power, and then replace the charge from renewable energy sources while sailing. The fully electric boat has become a reality, although diesel-hybrid versions that combine thermal and electric engines still remain the installation of choice.

Electric propulsion has been used on boats since the Victorian era, but ever rising fuel costs, the advent of the hybrid car and greater environmental awareness has given the technology a welcome boost. Electric propulsion is becoming increasingly popular for mainstream craft, and a number of companies now offer retrofit electric motors to complement, or even replace, the boat's petrol or diesel engine.

Below **Electric outboards have evolved in leaps and bounds, as demonstrated by this remarkable high-performance Torqeedo outboard powered by efficient lithium-based batteries.**

Having an electric drive system makes a good deal of sense, particularly a hybrid version, coupled to a conventional thermal engine. Not only does the electric motor provide silent and pollution-free propulsion, it can also improve the power supply on board by doubling up functions as an engine-driven generator.

Charge can be put back into the batteries, too, while sailing. A combination of wind generators, solar panels and even harnessing the freewheeling propeller will all restore significant amounts of energy. Shortfalls can be made up later by running the engine or plugging into shore power.

While electric propulsion is quiet, fume-free and efficient, it has its drawbacks. Range continues to be a challenge without a heavy weight penalty in batteries. Pure electric drives also usually lack the power to punch into a head sea, which is why so many owners opt for a diesel-electric hybrid system instead. Even so, a well-planned electric drive system is free from the noise and pollution of a diesel/petrol engine.

Installing an electric drive

It's best to source all the components through one specialist, to ensure total compatibility. Some companies also utilise Controller Area Networks (CAN-bus) data systems, so every key component communicates with the others for maximum energy efficiency. A specialist will consider:

- What are the boat's dimensions – hull length, width, draught and hull shape? Some hulls are more easily driven than others, which is a key factor in deciding on horsepower.
- What is the desired speed and range – lakes and rivers, or coastal, too? Range is directly linked to how many batteries can be safely carried.
- Will the customer be attempting to recharge away from shore power (or 'off grid'), or have access to mains power?

Above **The advance of lithium battery technology has led to a new generation of power storage that is not only incredibly light, but also able to deep cycle to 80 per cent of capacity without damage.**

The next step is to calculate the battery capacity required, as well as where it can be placed in the boat to complement the ballast and avoid upsetting the trim.

Battery power

The usual choice is a bank of thin-plate pure lead (TPPL) traction batteries, whose design allows them to be deep-cycled on a regular basis without harm. For inland waterways, ordinary wet-cell, 'milk float' batteries are usually the best option, but for offshore work, sealed TPPL gel batteries are recommended.

Where space may be limited, a good solution is to use a collection of tall and very slim gel cell batteries, each of 2-volts, and connect them in series, as most electric motors operate at either 24 volts or 48 volts. Some slim-profile gel batteries can also be installed flat. Advances in lithium technology have led to a new generation of lightweight, very deep-cycle marine batteries that are highly efficient, although expensive.

Battery capacity is quoted in amp hours, so in theory a 100Ah battery will provide 1 amp for 100 hours, or

TYPES OF ELECTRIC DRIVE

Electric motors don't need air to operate, so can be fully immersed. This gives a much wider range of installation options and reduces the down-angle of the propeller.

Outboard: With no gearbox, electric outboards are lightweight and efficient. Some draw power from an external battery bank, while others run from an integrated lithium ion battery. Some very powerful models are now available.

Pod: Pod drives are fitted with strong seals and are designed to remain permanently submerged. When handling the boat, the wide arc through which a pod can rotate is a huge boost to manoeuvrability.

Saildrive: The electric motor is attached to the head of a conventional saildrive, with the gearbox emerging through the bottom of the boat. Saildrives are relatively easy to install and versatile where space is tight. The version shown here is a hybrid.

Shaft: A motor is placed in line with a propeller shaft. In a hybrid system, the thermal engine and the electric motor will use the same shaft and propeller, so the prop needs to be able to harness both 13hp and 130hp with equal efficiency.

10 amps for 10 hours. In reality, you can't drain all the power stored in a battery, even a deep-cycle traction version, without shortening its life. Although many are designed to be deep-cycled, most manufacturers recommend only dipping into 30–40 per cent of the energy

available to keep the cells in peak health. Usually, complex electronics integrated into the system will prevent any damage from exhaustive deep-cycling of the battery.

Go electric 2

Calculating kilowatt hours

To calculate kilowatt hours as amp hours, the more usual convention for battery rating, multiply the battery voltage by the rated amp hours to give watt hours. So, a 24-volt battery supplying 200 amp hours will give (24V x 200Ah) 4,800 watt hours. As a kilowatt hour is 1,000 watt hours, divide the watt hours by 1,000. The result is 4.8kWh. As you need 16.8kWh to run the motor for four hours, you will theoretically need three and a half of those batteries. However, only around 30 per cent is safely usable, so you will actually need three times the capacity to avoid damage. By rounding up, you will require 10 x 200Ah 24-volt lead acid batteries, which is a significant weight.

Hybrid drives

Because purely electric drives are limited on range, a hybrid solution is increasingly popular. The electric motor can be used for silently entering or leaving a port, and for enjoying motoring on calm days. The ability to bring the revs in gradually makes it ideal for manoeuvring, while savings of up to 30 per cent in fuel can be made on short passages.

There are two types of hybrid installation available – serial and parallel. In a parallel system, an electric motor is connected to the propeller shaft by a belt, or is positioned between the engine and the gearbox to form part of the drive train. When being spun by the engine or by the freewheeling propeller under sail, the motor becomes a powerful generator, topping up the batteries and providing domestic power. With the engine stopped and declutched, the electric motor can drive the yacht from the batteries.

A serial hybrid disconnects the engine from the drive train altogether, using it as a stand-alone engine generator to provide current directly to the electric motor, which in turn is permanently connected to the prop shaft. The serial hybrid allows a great deal more freedom with the internal design of the yacht, as the generator can be placed anywhere that is convenient.

BATTERY CALCULATOR

To size an installation, a typical battery capacity calculation for kilowatt hours (kWh) is shown below.

Boat: A 9-m (30-ft) round-bottom boat with low drag, weighing 3,000kg (3 tons) and powered by a 6kW electric motor. For 3–4 hours at cruising speed the calculation is:

✪ Lead acid: Motor power (kW) x 2.8 = battery capacity (kWh).

✪ Lithium ion: Motor power (kW) x 1.4 = battery capacity (kWh).

✪ The 6kW motor will therefore need (6 x 2.8) 16.8kWh from lead gel batteries or (6 x 1.4) 8.4kWh from lithium ion batteries.

Right **The battery capacity required for a day's cruising under electric power can be very large and heavy. Here, the batteries for a river launch are being made ready for connection. This bank will run the 4.5kW motor for about eight hours.**

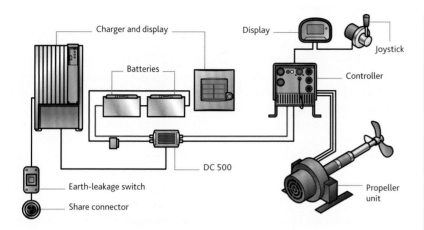

Charger and display

Display

Joystick

Batteries

Controller

DC 500

Earth-leakage switch

Share connector

Propeller
unit

This Steyr parallel hybrid features a
powerful electric motor sandwiched
between the engine and the gearbox.

On this Beta parallel hybrid, two electric
motors are held on brackets attached to
the engine itself.

Above **The wiring diagram for a Mastervolt
electric drive system. This design is based
on recharging from shore power via an
intelligent three-step battery charger. You
could greatly add to the recharging options
by connecting a large array of on-board
renewable energy sources.**

Both systems have their own
advantages, while the much larger
battery bank allows extended use
of the domestic items when lying
at anchor without having to run
the diesel engine or generator. The
most popular system is the parallel
hybrid, as it offers a spare motor
on the same shaft.

Power management

There are several controllers
available that will monitor the entire
system and balance the power levels
accordingly. Some can also take care
of energy being generated from
renewable sources and feed it into
the system. A clear display will show
the battery state, and the power

Right **Adjustable pitch propellers can be
turned into very effective turbines for
recharging under sail. Here, a Brunton's
EcoStar prop has the ability to angle its
blades to maximise the revolutions of
the freewheeling shaft, thus turning the
electric motor into a generator.**

being used or replaced. Also, an
'intelligent' battery charger will be
designed into the set-up to recharge
the batteries most efficiently.

Last considerations

Electric drives are improving, but
battery banks will need replacing
after about 1,500 deep cycles, after
which they will not perform well.
The larger electric motors continue
to need some kind of cooling system
and propellers must be carefully
matched to harness the output
across a wide horsepower range.
However, cruising under electric
power, with a full-sized generator
available, makes cruising much
more relaxed and
possibly entirely
self-refuelling.

Above **A serial hybrid on a 9.7-m (32-ft)
yacht. This generator is housed forward,
and connects to a bank of 6.4kWh TPPL
batteries (see page 279). Without the
generator, they supply two hours' cruising
at 6 knots.**

Fuel cells

Fuel cells are a direct means of converting a fuel's chemical energy into electricity. Fuel cells are a clean, quiet and efficient means of battery charging that is becoming more common aboard yachts and motorboats.

For shore-based applications hydrogen is the most common fuel, but hydrocarbons such as propane gas and alcohol can also be used. Marine systems frequently use pure methanol, as it's a relatively safe hydrogen-rich fuel that's easy to handle and store.

Below **The 6-m (21-ft) boats that race singlehanded across the Atlantic from France are completely powered (including electric autopilots and navigation lights) by fuel cells.**

Benefits of using fuel cells include a compact size, as well as ease of installation and operation. Most vessels use the automatic mode that constantly monitors battery charge, switching in when the voltage drops to 12.3 volts and charging until it reaches 14.2 volts. This mode means there is no danger of discharging the batteries below 50 per cent of their capacity, thus maximising their lifespan and ensuring there is always plenty of power available.

Choosing a model

Specifying the model of fuel cell is a different process from that of a generator – while most generators run for only a few hours each day, a fuel cell can run for 16 or more. Therefore the output power of a fuel cell can be significantly lower than that of a generator. After calculating your boat's average daily electrical power load, divide this by 12–15 to determine the output of the fuel cell(s) needed.

Above **Wiring the unit into the boat's electrics is usually straightforward and most are supplied with a display that allows you to monitor the state of charge.**

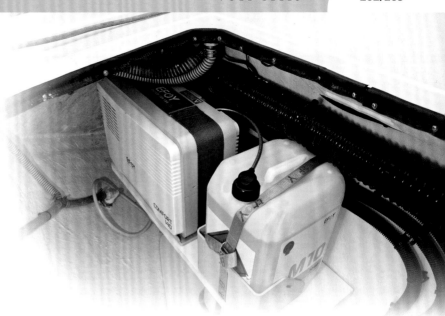

Above **The units are relatively compact and can be located in a cockpit locker, positioned so that there's easy access to change the fuel container when necessary.**

Fitting the cell

The unit can be fitted in a locker or under the chart table, provided an air gap of at least 100mm (4in) is available around the ventilation grill. This allows carbon dioxide to escape while ensuring there is an adequate supply of oxygen required for the chemical reaction.

Most units are supplied with a mounting kit that incorporates secure stowage for a bottle of fuel. The cell creates a relatively small amount of water, which can be drained to the bilge through a small pipe, or into a storage bottle that will need to be emptied occasionally.

Wiring the unit into the boat's electrical system is usually straightforward – a control panel is either incorporated in the cell or mounted separately. From this, two pairs of wires lead to the terminals of each battery bank. One pair is for the charge sensor; the other, with a fuse included, is for charging.

Current drawbacks

Balanced against the benefits of having a fuel cell on board, there are some drawbacks – including the high cost of the platinum catalyst, which has a typical lifespan of 5,000–8,000 hours, and a limited number of suppliers. The fuel needs to be exceptionally pure methanol, so it is also relatively expensive. However, fuel cells are subject to a great deal of research and sales are rapidly increasing. As a result, these disadvantages are likely to be eroded, with prices falling and the fuel availability improving. Additional research is expected to see the cost of the catalyst reduce, while further extending its lifespan.

Right **Most marine systems use methanol as a fuel, with carbon dioxide and water being the only by-products. An (expensive) platinum catalyst is used to promote the chemical reaction that produces electricity.**

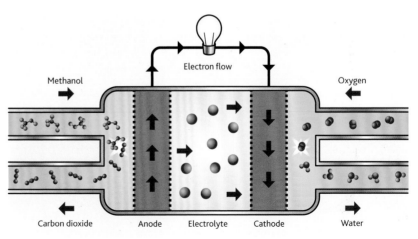

Better insulation

It is surprising just how much difference good insulation can make to living aboard, not only in retaining or reflecting heat, but also in deadening noise and reducing condensation.

The main purpose of insulation is to stabilise the living environment by limiting the effects of transmitted noise and changes in temperature. Directly connected to temperature difference is condensation, so good insulation can also help to keep a boat dry inside all year round.

Soundproofing

Many boatowners go to great lengths to suppress the noise of the engine, but completely overlook soundproofing in the rest of the boat. In the superyacht sector, where luxurious comfort is paramount, deep-fill insulation has become a major selling point and the solutions are quite ingenious.

Whatever the size of the boat, most engines have some sort of soundproofing. As there only needs to be a 10 per cent gap in the engine box to allow around 80 per cent of the noise to escape, most engines are well insulated. But sound also travels through the bilge and comes up between gaps in the floorboards. Noise is also generated from auxiliary equipment, anchor chains and rigging, and transmits through resonant surfaces and air ducts.

Properly soundproofing an engine means building the engine box right down into the bilge, or compartmentalising the area so that the sound is contained and can't migrate. If the engine still

Above **Specialist soundproofed plywood is available for floorboards and bulkheads. This contains a dense barrier layer, bonded into the centre of the laminate. Note the strip of blue anti-resonance foam.**

seems noisy, it may be time to re-soundproof, perhaps with an upgrade to modern materials. A wide range of specialised 'acoustic' foams and multi-layer barrier materials are available. Make sure that there are no gaps in the new soundproofing after application, and be suspicious of elderly engine mounts.

Below **Using insulating materials in a boat greatly improves the comfort of the crew by stabilising the temperature and suppressing transmitted noise.**

Above **Tanks or metal bulkheads can be covered in self-adhesive metal strips that work a little like placing a hand on a drum skin. They inhibit the ability of the surface to resonate.**

Left **Rubber is a good sound deadener, either as a sheet or as compressible seals to eliminate any air gaps. Here, a 3-mm ($\frac{1}{8}$-in) sheet has been glued to a floorboard. Quick-release catches can be adjusted.**

Soundproof checks

As noise may well be travelling beyond the engine bay, check that the floorboards are properly secured so they can't vibrate. Floorboards can be remade using soundproof plywood, or the existing boards can have rubber seals or backing sheets added as sound barriers. Noise often escapes through the engine's ventilation system, but the path it takes can be crossed with baffles.

- Even an outboard on a bracket can flex a yacht's transom like a drum skin, sending sympathetic vibrations right through the hull. Strengthening this area to reduce vibration will reduce noise.
- Securing loose items makes a big difference to noise transmission. This is why engines are usually supported on flexible rubber mounts, and cables and pipes are also clamped with rubber inserts.

- Metal structures, can be painted with a proprietary anti-resonance paint, while water and diesel tanks can also be insulated.
- Wet exhaust pipes and bow thruster tubes can be lagged, helping to suppress the noise that radiates when they are in use.
- Closed cell insulation on the inside of the hull helps to deaden noise from vibrating rigging and 'water chuckle', and reduce the reflected noise internally.

Soundproofing materials

Soundproofing involves the use of dense layers to absorb the energy from sound waves. Lightweight synthetic fibre is able to deaden high-frequency noise while also providing thermal properties. Because it is a very light material, there is a saving in extra weight over conventional 'barrier' soundproofing.

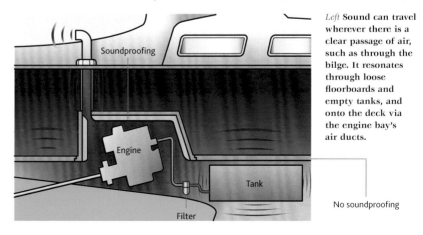

Left **Sound can travel wherever there is a clear passage of air, such as through the bilge. It resonates through loose floorboards and empty tanks, and onto the deck via the engine bay's air ducts.**

Better insulation 2

Closed cell foam or foil-wrapped rock wool can also be used. Denser materials tend to suppress lower frequencies, while lighter ones are better at stopping the higher ones, so soundproofing materials often contain a mix of the two.

Thermal insulation

Big differences in temperature can provide a number of problems on a boat, from discomfort for the crew to water condensing in the diesel tank. Simple thermal insulation is the cure.

Heat is transferred and lost in three ways; by convection, radiation and conduction. Boats are subject to all kinds of temperature zones, both inside and out. When the warm air from human breath or a fuel-burning heater moves around a cabin by convection and touches a cold surface, water vapour condenses as annoying drips. Good thermal insulation reduces temperature differences and so lessens the chance of condensation.

Another often-overlooked factor is hull colour. In hot climates, a dark hull will absorb radiation from both direct and reflected sunlight. This makes the outside skin very hot, and that heat will be conducted inside.

Good insulation will reduce the effects of this heat transfer, but a white or pale hull may be a better choice for prevention. A pale gel coat will help to reflect sunlight and keep the cabin cooler, although pure white may prove too dazzling. Creams and light greys are often a preferred solution.

Locations

On many early production boats, the space between the headlining and the deck was usually left as an air gap, so filling this void with silver-backed waterproof insulation will help keep the heat in and the hot sun out. You need to remove the headlinings (usually vinyl-covered hardboard) to place the insulation in the gap, and fix firmly with contact glue to eliminate voids where condensation could collect.

Silver-backed insulation acts as a moisture barrier and also radiates energy back from where it has come, so insulation with silvering on both sides is a good choice.

Taking the insulation right down the inside of the hull will further enhance the boat's thermal properties. You may need to remove all the panelling inside the boat to fix the material into place.

TIP

A pad made of insulation and inserted into the underside of a hatch will reduce heat loss at night. One made of bubble wrap will also allow light to enter for daytime use. Similarly, some liveaboard boats have temporary secondary glazing that can be attached during winter months, creating a large air gap behind the cabin windows.

Left **Insulation on a vertical bulkhead in a luxury steel boat. Note the silver backing that is on both sides of the material. There should be no air gaps between the material and the hull to minimise condensation there.**

Thermal gradients

In many boats, fuel and water tanks are located under the bunks. The heat difference between a sleeping body and the tank can be enormous, causing the bunk to 'sweat', and condensation to form in the tank. If the tank contains fuel, then this could encourage the diesel bug that lives in the fuel/water interface to form. Insulation, usually in the form of a jacket designed for domestic hot water tanks, drastically reduces the problem for both the sleeper and the fuel.

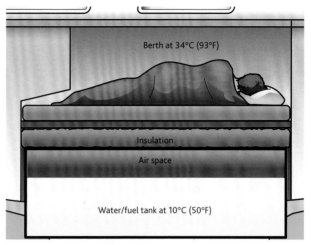

Berth at 34°C (93°F)

Insulation

Air space

Water/fuel tank at 10°C (50°F)

Left Insulation between the service tanks and a berth helps to mitigate difference in temperature between the two. This reduces condensation and so helps prevent mildew and the formation of the diesel bug.

Above **When using domestic insulation, be sure that the material is impervious to moisture. Exposed edges may need sealing with specialist tape.**

Right **Reflective solar film applied to the windows will make a big difference to the amount of radiated heat that can enter the cabin. Solar film is also useful on hatches, but it's fiddly to apply.**

Thermal insulation materials

Generally, the greater the air trapped in a material, the better it thermally insulates. Ideally, marine insulation should be fire-retardant, water resistant and fume-retardant. There are several marine foams available. These are supplied as either self-adhesive rolls and sheets, or for use with compatible spray or brush-on contact adhesives. Surfaces to be glued must be clean and dry, and if applying to bare fibreglass, the surface should be wiped with a solvent such as acetone first. The sheets will be hidden by panelling.

Reflective insulation

Cabin insulation greatly reduces radiant energy entering via the superstructure, but in hot climates this isn't always enough. Adding thin, reflective solar film to the insides of a boat's windows helps reduce the temperature while also aiding daytime privacy.

Many yachts have large clear hatches on the cabin roof, allowing the sun to penetrate and turn the interior into a greenhouse. A lightweight windscoop (see page 76) would allow light and air to enter, keeping the interior cool.

Holding tank

Holding tank systems are becoming more and more common as pollution awareness increases. Apart from their obvious necessity on inland waterways, they can also be very convenient in a marina to avoid an early morning stroll up to the facilities! Many owners virtually commute from marina to marina, so having a small tank is not a problem as it can be emptied between marinas.

For this installation you can use the Jabsco all-in-one system, which comprises a tank, a macerator pump and a level indicator in one compact unit. The tank also incorporates a deck pump-out facility so that it can be cleared by vacuum pump when required.

Additional equipment needed to complete the installation includes the hoses for connecting the heads to the tank, the tank to the outlet skin fittings and for the deck pump-out. Also required is the deck pump-out fitting and an anti-odour vent filter. Installing a system with separate components is not very different. However, the macerator pump will need to be bolted down separately and the level indicator will need to be fitted either before or after the tank is installed.

The installation

The first job is to plan the tank and pipework layout. The tank should ideally be located below the level of the heads and near to the heads compartment, although this may not be possible in a smaller boat,

Above **The hole for the pump-out fitting can be cut with a hole saw.**

Below **The tank is secured in position.**

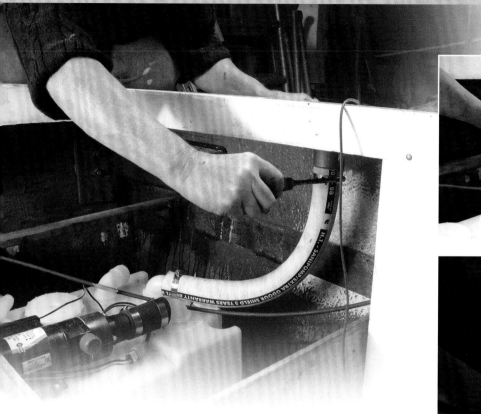

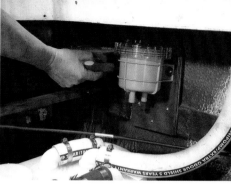

so a compromise may be required. Wherever the tank is mounted, it needs to be securely fastened. Once it is in, the pipework and ancillary fittings can be installed.

To start with, the pump-out fitting position is marked on the deck and a suitably sized hole saw is used to cut the opening. The fitting is then sealed and secured into position. Thanks to the location of the tank, the pump-out pipework is very short, making the pump-out extremely efficient. All hoses for this installation are high-quality, wire-reinforced, sanitary PVC, making them very odour resistant and highly flexible.

The anti-odour filter is the next item to be installed and connected to the tank. This is similar to a raw water filter except that it contains charcoal elements to avoid any

unpleasant smells from the tank vent. A simple 18-mm (³/₄-in) bracket sealed with wood sealer is fixed to a beam support inside the hull and the filter mounted onto the bracket.

The hole for the odour-filter outlet is drilled into the hull using another suitably sized hole saw. Sealant is then applied around the hole and the skin fitting placed in position. Next, the securing nut needs to be fitted internally and tightened. Remove any excess sealant from the outside of the fitting using paper towel and acetone. (White spirit would do the job almost as well.)

The connections from the tank to the filter and from the filter to the outlet are then made using the same high-grade sanitary hose, which completes the basic holding tank installation.

Above left **A short length of pump-out hose makes for a more efficient system.**

Top **The anti-odour filter is secured in position.**

Bottom **The vent outlet. Excess sealant can be cleaned from fittings using a rag and acetone.**

Holding tank 2

Having installed the holding tank, pump-out and anti-odour filter, the next step is to connect the rest of the pipework. The original heads discharge hose is disconnected from the outlet skin fitting, while the inlet fitting is left untouched as this side of the system doesn't need altering. The outlet hose on the heads must similarly be disconnected. If the age-hardened hose is difficult to budge, slice through it with a craft knife, which will allow it to come off easily.

Openings for the pipework are cut through the floor supports and the edges are sealed with resin. Once the resin has cured, the pipework is run through the boat. The hose from the heads to the tank inlet should now be connected, followed by the connection from the macerator to the outlet skin fitting.

The electrics

The electrics for the system are almost 'plug and play'! The power-in lead has a fixed plug and socket with positive and negative tails for extending as required to the fuse/circuit breaker board. A wire size table of data may be provided when you buy the electrics, showing the required size for any particular length of run. In this case a 2.5-mm ($^3/_{32}$-in) square cross section cable is needed. It also reminds us that the total length of cable run is from the battery to the equipment and back to the battery.

The cables are extended to the fuse board and negative bus bar using crimp terminals and heat-shrink covers, and the connection is made to a separate 16-amp fuse on the board. Similarly, the lead between the tank and control panel is 5m (16ft) long and has plugs at each end. This can slightly restrict

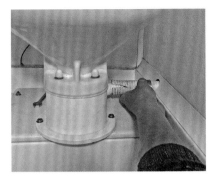

Above **After removing the hose clip, the age-hardened hose is sliced through to make removal easier.**

the position of the panel, but here the length is more than enough to mount the panel just where it's needed.

The panel includes a level indicator, which flashes when near the full mark, a press button to activate the macerator pump, which must be held for three seconds to prevent inadvertent operation of

Left **The new hose from the holding tank to the outlet skin fitting is run through the boat.**

Below **The hose connections at the tank, heads and skin fittings are all completed and double-checked for security.**

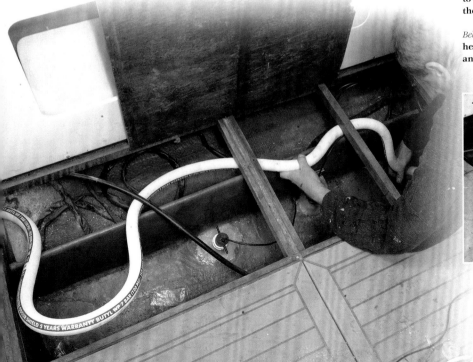

Above **This tank level indicator is fitted next to the heads-operating switch within the heads compartment.**

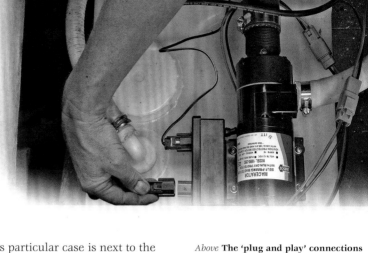

the pump, and a 'sleep' mode, which switches off the indicator for night use. The recommendation is for the display to be mounted in a prominent position, which is why the 'sleep' mode is provided.

However, it could also be mounted more discreetly in the heads compartment, although you would have to impress upon the crew the need to check the level before using the heads. The obvious position in

this particular case is next to the electric heads switch. A hole saw can be used to provide access for the socket on the back of the display, after which the display is then mounted and secured. Finally, the plug is connected into the back of the display.

This installation uses a simple system whereby the pipework is routed directly to the holding tank and then to the outlet skin fitting.

Above **The 'plug and play' connections simply plug together.**

If you want to have the choice of discharging the heads to either the tank or tothe skin fitting, you will need to use an additional 'Y' valve and 'Y' connector.

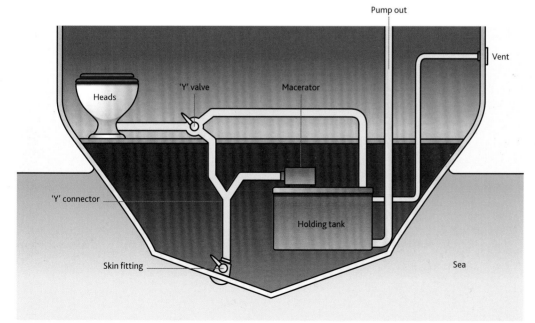

Left **A typical holding tank system with the optional direct discharge shown.**

'Greener' antifouling

The fouling of the hull below the waterline has been an age-old problem, but modern technology can keep the fouling away with virtually no adverse environmental impact.

Any boat afloat will act as free housing for all kinds of marine life, starting with slime, then weed, and finally barnacles, worms and mussels. Hormones secreted from established barnacles encourage others to join them, and the glue barnacles use is the most powerful in the natural world. Boats left in warm seas can quickly grow an entire ecosystem on the underside of their hulls, unless protected by a robust antifouling paint.

While modern antifoulings are very effective, they rely on the slow release of biocides in order to kill off any aquatic life that comes into contact with them. Despite being carefully formulated to be effective without causing too much collateral damage, these toxins only have a finite life.

TIP

Although copper conducts electricity well, especially in salt water, a layer made of tiny spheres of copper doesn't conduct electricity at all. Even so, it still pays to leave an 'anti-galvanic' gap of 25mm (1in) between the copper-based antifouling and any aluminium, steel or bronze stern gear, and to continue to use sacrificial anodes. Small tins of 'metal-friendly' antifouling are available to fill this gap.

As such, antifouling usually needs to be completely redone every other season, with touch-ups in between. Hulls have to be scrubbed clean, and then two new layers of antifoul paint reapplied. But what if there were some eco-friendly alternatives that relied on harmless technology to prevent barnacles and weed from getting a hold in the first place?

Copper resins

Copper has long been a component of antifouling paint, but several companies have found that by adding pure copper powder to porous epoxy resins, a boat can have a semi-permanent layer of natural antifouling that involves a lot less work once it has been applied.

There are two basic methods of application. One involves preparing the hull with a primer, and then painting on up to four layers of a pure copper suspension, with each coat chemically bonded to the next. Once dry, the final coat is abraded,

Left **Pure copper-resin antifouling sometimes needs light abrading to expose fresh material. The correct chemistry of the resin is vital, so DIY options don't always work.**

and the exposed copper turns to copper oxide to create a layer of verdigris that deters just about everything. Another version is to spray tiny beads of copper onto a sticky coat of pre-activated resin, trapping the copper on the surface like glitter on a birthday card.

The copper has to be applied carefully, and with the right resin, but once completed, all the boat needs is an occasional jet wash and light abrasion. It also has a negligible effect on the environment.

Natural products

Applications of silicone or Teflon provide a slippery surface. As a boat moves through the water, algae and other marine growth simply lose their grip and fall off. Silicone treatments are most effective on metal stern gear, including rudders, where any copper antifouling would have a galvanic reaction with the bronze or stainless steel. Frequent renewal is necessary.

Another natural product is lanolin, a derivative of sheep fat. It is used for propellers, shafts and rudders. Lanolin is applied to stern gear that has been gently heated first to aid absorption. Its life expectancy is only around two seasons, but it is easy to reapply and appears to be very effective.

APPLYING ULTRASOUND PROBES

The strategic section of internal hull where the flange will sit is wiped clean with acetone and lightly abraded.

Epoxy glue is mixed and applied to the outside edge of the flange, ensuring none gets into the threads.

Once the flange has been placed against the prepared hull, and the glue has dried, the transducer is screwed into it.

The transducer's cables are taken to the control box, which is wired into the boat's batteries. Current draw will be minimal.

Ultrasound

A transducer is placed on the inside of the hull and sets up a wall of ultrasound that causes tiny tremors in the water/hull interface.

The algae and larvae closest to the hull are unable to attach themselves. Spores and larvae can be so disrupted that they die and fall away. Ultrasound uses very little power, so is ideal for boats that spend quite a bit of time on a swinging mooring, and is fully effective when under way.

Left **Some systems use a very fine powder of spherical granules of pure copper, applied with low pressure air onto a layer of curing epoxy.**

Glossary

A

accumulator tank A water chamber that has a pre-pressurised internal air bladder.

adhesive sealant A type of sealant that has a very strong glue-like effect when cured. Some sealants are capable of holding steel plates together.

allen head A type of screw or bolt that has a recess that can only accept hexagonal Allen drivers.

alternator A device mounted on the engine that generates alternating current (AC) electricity, which it then converts to low voltage direct current (DC) to charge the batteries, and supply the boat's low voltage electrical demands. It is usually belt driven from the engine crankshaft.

anchor rode The chain, rope or a combination of both that connects an anchor to the boat.

angle grinder A very useful power tool that cuts by grinding at high speed (usually around 11,000 rpm). A number of attachments can be used to cut through fibreglass or stainless steel quickly, creating feathered edges in laminate, or removing rust from keels.

anode A sacrificial piece of metal, usually zinc, that protects other metal items in contact with water from galvanic corrosion, by eroding first.

antifouling Paint or coating applied to the bottom of a boat that will spend most of its time afloat, to prevent marine growth developing on the submerged areas of the vessel.

asymmetrical spinnaker A version of a spinnaker sail, but with a cut similar to a large genoa so that the tack is attached to the bow, or to a short bowsprit. Sometimes called an aspin or 'cruising spinnaker'.

athwartships The orientation of anything that runs from one side of a hull to the other, such as a thwart (seat) on a dinghy, or a bulkhead in a yacht.

B

baby stay Part of the standing rigging that gives fore-and-aft support to the mast. The baby stay runs from the centreline of the foredeck to the mast at the height of the spreaders.

backing plate A piece of wood, metal or fibreglass designed to fit under the deck beneath a fitting, and so spread the load of the retaining nut and washer.

backstay Part of the standing rigging that gives fore-and-aft support to the mast. The backstay runs from the back of the boat to the top of the mast.

baffle A barrier plate that partly blocks a tank or tube. Baffles slow down the movement of air or liquids to reduce noise or the effects of sloshing.

ball valve A ball-shaped valve that opens or closes with a single 90-degree movement of a handle.

batten The leech of most mainsails is strengthened by horizontal battens (usually made of fibreglass) that improve the sail's aerodynamic shape and increase its lifespan by reducing flapping.

belt polisher/sander A machine that can be fitted with different grades of glasspaper to progressively remove the rough 'as cast' finish of metal fittings.

bevel gauge A device consisting of two straight-edged lengths of metal or wood that can be set to any angle. It is used to establish the angle between two fixed points, such as the side of a frame and a plank.

biaxial glass roving A reinforcement material used with epoxy or polyester resins. The glass strands are woven in two distinct directions (two axis) for increased strength.

bilge Externally, the rounded part of an underwater hull. Internally, the flattest part of a boat's bottom where water usually collects for pumping out.

blind rivet Technical term for a pop rivet.

blocking diode A device that controls current flow inside photovoltaic systems and prevents electrical currents flowing back from a battery bank.

bosun's chair A device used to suspend a person safely from a line to perform work at the top of the mast.

bottlescrew turnbuckle A threaded device (made up of one left hand and one right hand thread), located between the wire rigging supporting the mast and the chainplates on the hull. Used to tension the rig.

bow roller A roller assembly used for guiding the anchor chain (or rope) over the bow of the boat.

bowsprit A pole (or spar) extending forward from the prow of the boat.

bulkhead A transverse full or partial 'wall' running across the boat, often used to separate different areas of accommodation. Bulkheads can be important structural members, especially on older boats.

bus bar A strip of metal that conducts electricity. This bar is where electrical connections are attached.

C

calorifier A vessel's domestic hot water tank. May be heated by engine cooling water, or by mains electricity via a shore power connection. It may also be heated by a diesel or gas fuelled heater.

capping rail A decorative trim, usually in hardwood, that goes over the top of a bulwark or set of stanchions.

centreboard A retractable keel made of wood, fibreglass, steel or other materials that pivots near its front edge. This allows it to swing upwards either directly under the hull, or within a case inside the hull.

chainplate The fitting that attaches the standing rigging (forestay, backstay and shrouds) to the vessel's hull and/or deck.

cheek block A sheave that is set against a boom or spar, and having just one outer cheek supporting the pin.

circuit breaker An automatic device for stopping the flow of electricity in a circuit.

clevis pin Typically a short pin with a large head and pinhold for a split pin. Most commonly used to join rigging components together. May be made of galvanised or stainless steel.

clew The lower or aft corner of the triangular sail.

close hauled Describes when a yacht is sailing very close to the wind, so the sails are hauled tightly inboard.

coachroof The cabin top, if it projects above deck level.

coaming A vertical partition around hatches or cockpits that prevents water from entering.

collet A two-part metal ring that fits around a groove on a shaft to hold it in place.

companionway The opening between the cockpit and the main accommodation, usually including an arrangement of steps.

compression joint A pipe joint consisting of a screwed coupling that compresses metal seals (olives) onto the pipe to achieve the seal.

contact adhesive A powerful glue that sticks upon contact with materials.

core Material that is used as a filler in a fibreglass sandwich laminate. Core material is usually made from lightweight materials, such as foam or balsa wood, and gives additional strength and insulation to a hull.

counter-bore A short hole of greater diameter than the main hole, to allow the head of a screw or bolt to e recessed.

cutlass bearing The aftermost bearing that supports the propeller shaft.

D

deck beam A transverse length of timber that supports the deck.

deck head The underside of a deck.

E

electro-hydraulic A hydraulic system operated by an electric motor, as opposed to manual effort, such as by a steering wheel.

Glossary

epoxy resin A type of resin that uses a hardener rather than a catalyst to promote curing. Epoxy resins have a far higher adhesive factor, and repel water far better than polyester resins, but are more expensive. They also need more precise mixing.

eye splice A loop that is formed at the end of a rope by turning the end back and splicing it to the standing part of the rope.

F

fairing The process of repeatedly filling and sanding a repair or other piece of work to create a smooth finish.

faux teak A generic term for artificial teak-effect extrusions.

fiddle A rail or batten around the edge of a shelf or table to stop items falling off.

flange The protruding lip of a hull or deck moulding that is used to join the two together. A rubber fenderstrip is often pushed over the flange to hide it.

float switch A device used to detect the level of liquid within a tank or bilge.

fluxgate compass An electromagnetic compass that uses small coils of wire around a highly permeable magnetic core. The reading is in an electronic form so it can be digitised, viewed remotely, and used for autopilot functions.

foot The bottom edge of a sail. Mainsails may be set loose footed, with only either end of the foot attached to the mast and boom, or the foot may be attached to the boom along its entire length.

forefoot The point at which the stem joins the keel.

forestay Part of the standing rigging that gives fore and aft support to the mast. It runs from the bow of the boat to the top of the mast.

four-stroke motor An engine in which there is only one power stroke for every four up or downward movements of each piston. Lubrication is via oil stored in a sump, as with all modern car engines.

G

galvanic corrosion The electrochemical action between two dissimilar metals that are in contact with each other or linked by a conductor, such as sea water. The more 'noble' metal (for example, bronze or stainless steel) will cause the less 'noble' metal (for example, aluminium or mild steel) to corrode. This can be avoided by isolating the metals, using plastic gaskets or an insulating compound, or, if they are below water, linking them to a sacrificial zinc anode, which will be corroded instead.

galvanising The process of coating mild steel with a protective layer of zinc. It is applied by dipping the steel component into a vat of molten zinc.

gate valve A valve with a 'gate' that is screwed into the pipework to block the flow of fluids. Not normally considered suitable for marine use, as it's not possible to tell visually whether the valve is open or shut.

gel coat Made from pigmented resin, gel coat is the smooth, decorative outer layer of a fibreglass hull.

gimbals A double-pivot arrangement allowing an item to remain level as the boat pitches and rolls. Also a single pivot-system that allows a cooker to stay level as the boat rolls.

gland A seal on a rotating shaft used to prevent oil or water leaking past.

glassing Used to describe laying-up or bonding in

fibreglass. A bulkhead would be 'glassed in' to a hull using resin and chopped strand mat (CSM) for reinforcement.

goosewinging Sailing with the mainsail out to one side, and the foresail out to the other. The term can also be used to describe twin foresails poled out on opposing sides.

grommet A soft rubber or plastic ring that protects wiring or piping from the sharp edges of a hole through which the wire or pipe passes.

GRP Glass Reinforced Plastic, or fibreglass.

grub screw A screw with no head that can be tightened into a threaded hole and have no projection outside.

gypsy A pulley with a pattern in its groove that grips the links of a chain – usually fitted to an anchor windlass. The chain and gypsy must be matched, because the wrong pattern size will cause the chain to jump off.

H

halyard Line used to pull sails up the rig.

headboard The top reinforced corner of a sail.

headlining The decorative material placed on the underside of the saloon roof or deck head.

heads A generic term used for a boat's toilet compartment, or sometimes the toilet itself.

heat exchanger Device used to transfer heat from one fluid to another. Most frequently encountered on a boat in the cooling system of fresh water-cooled engines.

holding tank Storage tank for toilet waste. In some places the toilet can only be discharged overboard at an authorised pump-out station.

hole saw A drill attachment consisting of a metal cylinder with a serrated edge to drill neat holes of a specific diameter.

I

impeller A rugged rubber paddle wheel with compressable blades that is used to pump water by spinning inside an elliptical casing.

inverter An electronic device that changes direct current (DC) to alternating current (AC).

J

jackstay A wire, tape or line running fore/aft the boat. A lanyard can be attached to it for safety on board.

jigsaw A portable electrically operated reciprocating saw with a short blade used for cutting shapes from sheet material such as wood, metal or fibreglass.

K

keel bolts Metal bolts that are used to secure a lead or cast iron keel to the hull of a sailing boat.

kicking strap An adjustable line lanyard used to stop the boom from rising (or 'kicking up') when sailing.

L

laid deck A deck where the planks of wood are laid onto the deck beams or sub-deck. On fibreglass boats, the laid deck is often used for cosmetic purposes.

laminate Usually used in reference to fibreglass construction, 'laminate' means the layers of fibreglass under the gel coat, while 'to laminate' is the process of laying-up a fibreglass hull with a series of wetted-out layers of reinforcement.

lazarette An internal storage area, often quite large, and usually located at the stern.

leech The back edge of a sail.

lift pump A small low-pressure pump used on diesel engines to deliver fuel from the tank to the high-pressure injector pump. Usually has a small lever allowing the pump to be activated by hand to bleed air out of the fuel system.

log A mechanical device, often using a paddlewheel or propeller, used to measure the distance travelled through the water by counting the number of revolutions the paddle wheel makes. This can be converted (by taking account of the time taken to travel the distance) into speed through the water.

luff The front edge of a sail.

M

macerator A device that chops up raw sewage into a liquid slurry before discharge overboard or into a 'holding tank'.

mandrel The shaft of an attachment that is inserted into the chuck of a drill. Also describes the shaft of a blind (pop) rivet.

marquetry A process in joinery where thin strips of wood are cut to a template above each other so they all form an intricate pattern on the same level.

mastic A flexible sealant made from a variety of substances according to use.

MDF Medium Density Fibreboard. A man-made material that is manufactured by combining wood fibre, wax and resin binder. The mixture is subjected to a combination of high pressure and temperature to form panels.

mildew A coating or discolouration caused by fungi in damp conditions.

mould A hollow shape in which a fibreglass component – from a hatch to an entire hull – can be cast. Moulds are usually made from a plug.

mouse An electrician's 'mouse' is made up of lightweight fibreglass rods that clip together and help to run cable in difficult-to-reach places.

mousing line The use of a light cord attached to a line (such as a halyard) temporarily when it's removed from the mast. Can also be used when replacing electrical wiring.

N

Nyloc nuts Nyloc is the trade name for nuts that have a nylon insert. This is designed to stop the nut from vibrating loose on a thread. Ideally, they should only be used once, as when removed the insert is compromised.

O

o-ring A small tubular ring, usually made of soft rubber, which acts as a seal.

olive A metal ring used to seal a compression joint.

outdrive Alternative term for stern drive.

P

palm A strip of leather that goes round the hand, which is fitted with a metal disc to provide reinforcement so a sailmaker's needle can be forced through sailcloth or rope when stitching.

pennants Lines used to reef a mainsail, especially for pulling the aft corner of the sail down to the boom.

Glossary

phosphorescence A blue-green luminous effect seen at night in seawater when some types of phytoplankton and jellyfish are disturbed by a boat's wake.

pintle The pin that forms the hinge on which a transom-hung rudder rotates.

plug A sculpted shape made from MDF, wood or some other soft material from which a mould is cast.

pod drive A method of propulsion where the vessel is moved through the water via an external pod and propeller.

pop rivet Generic term for a blind rivet.

pulpit The protective rail that encloses the bow of a vessel.

pushpit The protective rail that encloses the stern of a vessel.

Q

quadrant Fitting on a rudder stock to which the cables, rods or hydraulics for wheel steering systems are attached.

R

raw water The water in which a boat floats (for example, sea water), and used on board to cool the engine or flush the toilet.

reef point A reinforced eyelet in a sail. The reef points on some sails have short lengths of rope permanently attached, which can be used to tie down a reef when required. On other sails, a rope is threaded through the eyelet when the sail is reefed.

regulator (on an alternator) An electronic device for controlling the way in which the battery is charged by the engine.

relay An electrical device that converts a low power electrical signal into a more powerful one. It uses a low current to operate an electromagnet, which then closes a pair of contacts to allow a much larger current to flow.

retrofit A generic term to describe adding equipment to a boat that wasn't in the original specification.

RIB Rigid-hulled Inflatable Boat – typically a fibreglass hull with inflatable tubes.

rockwool The trade name for a type of insulation made from fire-retardant mineral fibres.

rope clutch A lever-operated device that a line passes through, which can be used to secure or release a line – usually a halyard – quickly.

router A power tool that can cut complex grooves in timber and other soft materials.

running rigging Lines used to raise and control sails or spars, such as booms and spinnaker poles.

S

saildrive A method of propulsion where the drive drops straight down from the motor and through the hull where it can pivot like an outboard motor.

scribe To mark a line on metal or wood by using a sharp instrument to show where it should be cut or a hole drilled.

seam The longitudinal gap between two planks.

shaft drive A conventional propulsion system where the propeller shaft exits the hull horizontally towards the rear of the boat, usually at a small downwards angle.

shear pin A weak link between the propeller of some smaller or older outboard engines and the propeller shaft. If the propeller strikes a solid object the shear pin breaks, thereby protecting the gearbox from damage.

sheave A grooved wheel in which a line runs, usually within a block or mast.

sheets Lines used to control a sail once it is hoisted.

shroud Part of the standing rigging that gives lateral support to the mast. Cap shrouds are the rig's longest shrouds, running to the masthead; lower shrouds run from the deck to just below the mast spreaders.

skiff A small boat.

skin fitting Through-hull fitting with a hole that passes through the hull from inside to outside. A valve must be fitted to through-hull fittings below the waterline, enabling inlet/outlet pipes to be sealed shut.

snuffer A tube of sailcloth that is pulled down a deployed spinnaker from the top to collapse it for lowering.

sole A generic term to describe the floor of a particular area, such as 'cockpit sole'.

solenoid An electromechanical device that converts an electrical signal into a mechanical motion using an electromagnet.

spars Collective term for masts, booms, gaffs, spinnaker poles, and so on.

splicing Joining two pieces of line or cable by weaving the strands of each into the other.

spline Thin strips of wood glued in the seams used as an alternative to cotton and putty.

spokeshave A tool used to shape and smooth wooden rods and shafts.

spreaders Struts projecting from the sides of the mast, which spread the angle of the upper shrouds.

stanchions Upright pillars or structures that support the guard wires around a boat's decks.

standing rigging The wires that support the mast, usually made of stainless or galvanised steel.

stem The foremost part of the hull that rises up vertically from the forward end of the keel.

stern drive A propulsion system where the drive unit on which the propeller is mounted passes through the transom at the rear of the boat. The drive unit is bolted to the engine/gearbox through the transom and can be removed for maintenance.

sternpost The vertical timber that rises up from the aft end of the keel.

stock (rudder) The rudder stock is the shaft that enters the rudder blade, with the upper end attached to the steering gear.

swaged terminal A fitting attached to the end of a rigging wire in a hydraulic press, using enormous force.

T

tack Bottom front corner of a sail.

topping lift A halyard attached to the rearmost end of the boom to hold it at a required height when the mainsail has been lowered.

topsides The hull above the waterline, but below the superstructure. Essentially, the sides of the hull.

torque wrench Calibrated wrench that measures the amount of force used to tighten a nut.

transducer A device that sends out sound waves in order to determine what is below the surface of the water.

transom A flat or gently curved surface that forms the stern of a boat. A transom can be mounted vertically or at an angle.

trim tabs These are normally two adjustable planes that are mounted on the transom of the boat. They adjust to changing conditions, improving efficiency and giving a smoother passage.

tweaker line This line is attached to the spinnaker sheet and is trimmed during manoeuvres keeping the spinnaker sheet closer to the deck and helping control the height of the pole. When on course, the sheet side tweaker is eased and the pole side is kept trimmed tight (almost to the deck).

V

veneer A thin decorative layer of material that is bonded to a substrate.

W

wetting out The physical application of activated resin to reinforcement material.

windage The amount of hull and top hamper a vessel carries that the wind can push against. A boat that carries a lot of windage will be more easily blown sideways when berthing.

windlass A mechanical or electrical device used to recover the anchor and chain or rope.

wiring loom The collective sum of wires required to operate an electrical device, or an entire vessel. Modern equipment is usually supplied with a 'plug and play', wiring loom or 'cable harness' where all the wires are pre-attached to a terminal block for easy installation.

Index

A

AC power systems 156
  and inverters 212–15
  watermakers 148
accumulator tanks 134–5, 137
acetic acid 68
acrylic canvas 72, 77, 83, 86
actuator, steering 192
air conditioning 120–1, 156
air flow, and ventilation 150–3
AIS (Automatic Identification
  System) 190, 191
alarms
  bilge pump 142–3
  carbon monoxide 106, 111, 155
  gas 154–5
alternators 204–6, 209, 275
aluminium fittings 48–9
amorphous solar panels 271
anchoring
  anchor lights 197
  chain 164
  chain counters 166–9
  windlasses 164–5, 185, 217
angle grinders 17
anodes 211
antennas, GPS 51, 52, 53
anti-odour filters 289
anti-syphon vents 141
antifouling 12
  greener 292–3
asymmetric cruising chutes 248–9
Automatic Identification System
  (AIS) 190, 191
autopilots 192–5
  calibrating 195
  electronic 257
  parts of 193
  positioning the system 194–5
  self-powering 256–9
  tiller pilots 260–1
awnings, cockpit 74

B

baby stays 231
backing pads, fitting 39
backstays 54
  backstay adjusters 232–3
bathing platforms 26, 35, 51, 62–3,
  99
  and underwater lighting 199
batteries
  access to 216
  alternator size 204–5
  battery capacity sensors 209
  battery charging inputs 204–7
  calculating requirement 280
  capacity 208–9
  checking state of charge 184
  deep-cycle 270, 279
  diesel-electric hybrid drives
    280–1
  electric drive systems 278, 279,
    281
  and electric water systems 133
  electric windlasses 164
  for fridges 116
  and fuel cells 282
  and generators 159, 207
  optimising charging 205–6
  and solar panels 206, 207, 271
  split charge systems 117

sulphation 208
  watermaker supply 148
  and wind power 206, 207
battery chargers 212
beeswax 104
bilge monitors 143
bilge pumps 142–3
  engine-driven 144–5
bilges, ventilating 151
biminis 74–5
blind rivets 254–5
blocks
  articulation of 236
  cascade systems 232–3
  choosing the right 236
  mast base blocks 239
bolts, removing stubborn 131
boom gallows 99
booms 247
bow thrusters 172–5, 185
  ensuring a good fit 174–5
  fitting the motor for 175
  foot-operated switches 217
  installing a tunnel unit 173–4
  soundproofing 285
bowsprits 249
British Thermal Units (BTUs) 120
bulbs 216
  LED 123, 196, 197
bulwarks 99
bunk cushions 68
  bolstering cushion foam 69
butane 154

C

cabin sides, faced-ply 40–3
cabin ventilators 151
cabling
  battery 215
  shore power 210
calorifiers 136, 213, 214
CAN-bus (Controller Area
  Networks) 278
canvas 72, 77, 83, 86
canvas work 66–89
  biminis 74–5
  cockpit cushions 70–3
  dodgers 82–5
  eyelets 84
  hatch covers 78–81
  hemming acrylic 83, 87
  lee cloths 86–9
  low-profile windscoops 76–7
capstans 164
carbon monoxide poisoning 106,
  111, 155, 207
cars, types of 242–3
carved nameboards 28–9
cascade systems, blocks 232–3
caulking, deck 44
central heating 108–11
chain
  chain counters 166–9
  and windlasses 164
charcoal heaters 106–7
charging
  battery charging inputs 204–7
  charging centres 216
  checking battery charge 184
chart plotters
  and AIS 191
  swing out 217

chimneys, positioning 106, 107
chisels 15, 19, 24
circuit breakers 185
circular saws 17
clamps and cramps 42
closed-cell foam 70–2
clutches 144, 236, 240
cockpits
  biminis 74–5
  cockpit floors 44–5
  cockpit tents 74
  cushions 68, 69, 70–3
  dodgers 82–5
  gratings 26–7
  tables 36–7
collector boxes 30–1
colour, underwater lighting 199
COLREGs (International
  Regulations for the Prevention
  of Collisions at Sea) 196
companionway
  handholds 38, 39, 98
  steps 26
  strong points 235
compression fittings 111
compressors, fridge 116–17
condensation 150
Controller Area Networks
  (CAN-bus) 278
cookers
  diesel 112–15
  gimballed 93, 94–5
  safety 93
cool boxes 116–19
cooling boats, air conditioning
  120–1
copper resins 292–3
Corian 101
corrosion
  deck fittings 48
  electrolytic 211
  stubborn fastenings 131
  unseizing corroded zips 68
counter tops 93, 101
counters, chain 166–9
covers
  hatch 78–81
  mainsail 222–3
cowls 30, 153
  guard rails 31
crimps 19
cruising chutes 248–9
cup stowage 127
cushions
  bolstering cushion foam 69
  bunk 68, 69
  cockpit 68, 69, 70–3

D

dampness on board 150
Danbuoys 51
davits 64–5
DC power, and inverters 212–15
deck gear 236–7, 239
  clutches 240
  deck organisers 237, 239
  fitting 240–1
  jammers 240
  mast base blocks 239
  replacing aluminium deck
    fittings 48–9
  winches 240

deck glands, installing 185
deck improvements
  bathing platform 62–3
  cockpit grating 26–7
  cockpit table 36–7
  davits 64–5
  deck handholds and footholds
    98–9
  deck lights 201
  dorade vents 30–1
  faux teak fore and side
    decks 46–7
  faux teak sole boards 44–5
  gantries and goalposts 52–5
  grab rails 38–9
  laying faux teak 46–7
  passarelles 32–5
  pulpits and pushpits 50–1
  replacing aluminium fittings
    48–9
  ventilation 152–3
  windlasses 164–5
deep-cycle batteries 270, 279
dehumidifiers 153
diesel bug 180
diesel cookers 112–15
diesel-electric power
  generators 157
  hybrid drives 278, 280–1
diesel power
  generators 157
  hot air diesel heating 108–11
  stoves 93
diffusers, lightning 203
dinghy hoists and davits 52, 64–5
displays, radar 188
diverter valves 149
dodgers 51, 82–5
dodgers (sprayhoods) 99
domestic improvements 90–127
  air conditioning 120–1
  charcoal heaters 106–7
  deck handholds and footholds
    98–9
  diesel cookers 112–15
  electrically operated heads
    140–1
  fiddle rails 100–1
  galley straps 96–7
  gas alarms 154–5
  general tips 126–7
  generators 156–9
  gimballed stoves 94–5
  hot air diesel heating 108–11
  hot water systems 136–7
  insulation 284–7
  iPods 124–5
  LED interior lighting 122–3
  manual water pumps 132–3
  pressurised water systems
    132–3, 134–5
  showers 138–9
  simple veneers 102–5
  stowage 127
  ventilation 150–3
  watermakers 146–9
dorade vents 30–1, 153
downlighters 201
drainage
  cockpit cushions 71
  showers 138–9
drills 17, 18

drip-feed diesel cookers 112
drive systems, electric 278–81
drums, headsail furling 226–9
ducting
    hot air 110
    insulation 111
dump resistors 277

E
eco upgrades 268–93
    electric propulsion 278–81
    fuel cells 282–3
    insulation 284–7
    solar panels 270–3
    water-powered generators 276–7
    wind power 274–7
electric anchor windlasses 164–5
electric bilge pumps 142
electric propulsion 278–81
    calculating kilowatt hours 280
    installing 278–9
    power management 281
    types of electric drive 279
electric trim tabs 179
electric water pumps 132, 133
electrical improvements 182–217
    AIS 190, 191
    battery capacity 208–9
    battery charging inputs 204–7
    electrical skills 184–5
    holding tanks 290–1
    inboard autopilots 192–5
    inverters 212–15
    LED navigation lights 196–7
    lightning protection 202–3
    Navtex 190
    radar 186–9
    shore power 210–11
    tips 216–17
    underwater lights 198–201
    waterproofing 185
electrician's mouse 187
electrolytic corrosion 211
emergency lighting 123
energy, calculating demands 271
engines
    engine-driven bilge pumps 144–5
    engine-driven watermakers 148
    oil changes 180
    optimising engine charging
        205–6
    soundproofing 284–5
    temperature alarms 181
    ventilation 152
epoxy resin 43, 58
exhausts
    diesel cookers 112–13
    diesel heating 108, 109
    soundproofing 285
expansion tanks 137
extension leads 16
exterior ply 40
eyelets 84

F
faced-ply cabin sides 40–3
fans, cooling 119
Faraday cage 203
fastenings, removing stubborn 131
faux teak
    decks 46–7
    sole boards 44–5

swage terminals 250, 257
fenders, stowage 98
fibreglass hulls, laying faux teak
    decks 46–7
fiddle rails 93, 100–1
filters
    anti-odour 289
    water 93, 149
fire-resistant board 114
fittings see deck gear
float switches 142
floodlights 199
floorboards
    faux teak 44–5
    soundproofing 285
flopper-stoppers 56
flues, positioning 106, 107
fluxgate compass 194–5
FM transmitters 125
foam
    bolstering cushion foam 69
    closed-cell 70–2
    reticulated 70–2
    waterlogged 68
foils 227, 228–9
foot pumps 93, 133
footholds, deck 98–9
foredeck, laying faux teak 46–7
foresails, headsail furling 226–9
forestays 249
    additional 230–1
    detachable 231
    headsail furling 226–9
    parallel 231
    reducing sag 232
fractional rigs, backstay adjuster
    232–3
freezers 93
friction, preventing in ropes 236–7
fridge-freezers 93
fridges 116–19, 156, 205
fuel cells 207, 282–3
    choosing a model 282
    fitting 283
fuel feeds
    for diesel cookers 113–14
    for stoves 93
fuel pumps, hot air diesel heating
    110–11
fuel systems
    fuel capacity 160–1
    fuel gauges 181
    fuel junctions 180
    and generators 159
    hot air diesel heating 110–11
    tank level gauges 162–3
furling gear
    cruising chutes 249
    headsail furling 226–9
fuses 185, 216
    fridge 116

G
G cramps 42
galley improvements
    counter tops 93
    diesel cookers 112–15
    fridge-freezers 93
    galley straps 96–7
    gimballed stoves 93
    handholds 38, 39
    ideal galley 92–3

rubbish disposal 93
sinks and taps 93
storage in 93, 127
ventilation 92
galvanic action 48
gangplanks 26, 32–5
gantries 52–5
gas bottles, rust-proof stowage
    of 126
gas systems
    gas alarms 154–5
    gas safety 155
gassing 209
gauges
    fuel 181
    tank level 162–3
generators 156–9, 207, 212
    installing 158–9
    output 275
    types of 157, 275
    water-powered 204, 276–7
    wind-powered 274–7
genoas 265
    and electric winches 262–3
    genoa cars 242–3
    halyards 239
    headsail furling 226–9
gimballed stoves 93, 94–5
glands, installing deck 185
glasses, safety 12
glasses, stowage 127
gloves 12
goalposts 52–5
GPS antennas 51, 52, 53
grab handles and rails 38–9, 98
granite, laminated 101
granny bars 98
gratings 151
    cockpit 26–7
grease, non-metallic 48
grommets 84
grounding plates 203
guard rails 31, 99
gypsy, winch 164, 166–7

H
halyards
    attachment points 98
    deck organisers 237, 239
    leading them aft 238–41, 265
    making an exit in the mast 237
    shortened 266
    stowing 266
hand tools 14–15, 18, 24–5, 130
handholds
    on deck 98–9
    down below 38–9
hardware, deck 236–7, 239
harnesses, jackstays 234–5
hatches
    handholds 98
    hatch covers 78–81
    insulating 286, 287
    and ventilation 151, 152
    windscoops 76–7
heads
    electrically operated 140–1, 213
    holding tanks 288–91
heads compartment
    handholds 38, 39
    manual water pumps 133
    showers 138–9

headsail furling 226–9
heating systems
    charcoal heaters 106–7
    hot air diesel heating 108–11
hit and miss vents 151
hobs, diesel 112–15
holding tanks 288–91
    installing 288–90
hose, for bilge pumps 145
hose clips 145
hot air diesel heating 108–11
    exhaust installation 108, 109
    fuel system and pump
        installation 110–11
    heater and wiring loom 109
    hot air ducting 110
hot water systems 136–7
hull improvements
    bathing platform 62–3
    bow thrusters 172–5
    davits 64–5
    dorade vents 30–1
    faced-ply cabin sides 40–3
    gantries and goalposts 52–5
    grab rails 38–9
    lightweight tiller 58–61
    nameplates 28–9
    pulpits and pushpits 50–1
    roll reducers 56–7
    stern thrusters 176–7
    trim tabs 178–9
    underwater lighting 198–201
humidity, measuring 153
hybrid drives, diesel electric 278,
    280–1
hydraulic steering 171, 192, 194
hydraulic trim tabs 179
hygrometers 153

I
icemakers 212
impact drivers 131
impellers, bilge pumps 144
insulation 284–7
    cool boxes 118, 119
    ducting 111
    reflective 287
    soundproofing 284–5
    thermal 286–7
interior lighting 185
    LEDs 122–3
International Regulations for the
    Prevention of Collisions at Sea
    (COLREGs) 196
inverters 212–15
    installing 214–15
    types of 212–13
iPods 124–5
isolating transformers 211

J
jackstays 234–5
jammers 240
Japanese back saw 25
jibs 265
    headsail furling 226–9
jigs 58, 59
jigsaws 17, 42

Index

K

kettles, electric 213
kicking strap 239
kilowatts, calculating kWh 280
knife racks 127

L

ladders 13
    rope ladders 267
lanolin 293
laptops 212, 213
laying up in winter 152, 241
lazy jacks 222–5
    fitting and setting up 223, 224–5
    off-the-shelf 223
    stack pack systems 222–3
lazy tongs 255
LCD displays 188
LED lighting 205
    bulbs 123, 196, 197, 200
    colour 199
    emergency lighting 123
    interior lighting 122–3
    navigation lights 196–7
    underwater lights 198–201
lee cloths 86–9
lemon juice 68
lettering
    applying to dodgers 85
    stainless steel 29
    vinyl 28
lifebuoys 51
lifting devices, davits 64–5
light emitting diodes (LEDs)
    see LED lighting
lighting 213
    bulbs 216
    colour 199
    deck lights 201
    emergency 123
    interior 185
    navigation 201
    underwater lights 198–201
    see also LED lighting
lightning protection 202–3
lines
    clutches or jammers 240
    deck organisers 236–7, 239
    leading halyards aft 238–41, 265
    line attachment 236
    sheeting points 242–3
    shortened halyards 266
    tweaker lines 250–1
liquid petroleum gas (LPG) 112,
    154–5
long-nose pliers 19
louvre doors 151
LPG (liquid petroleum gas) 112,
    154–5

M

macerator pumps 288, 290–1
mains power 156, 210–11
mainsails, and stack pack
    systems 222–3
mandrels 254
manifold 145
manual bilge pumps 142
manual water pumps 132–3
marine ply 40
marks, transferring 79
masthead rigs

additional forestays 230–1
backstay adjuster 232–3
masts
    granny bars 98
    making halyard exits in 237
    mast base blocks 239
    mast steps 252–3
    pop-riveting 254–5
    rope ladders 267
    spinnaker fittings 251
mats, rubber 26, 126
mechanical improvements 128–81
    bilge pumps and alarms 142–3
    bow thrusters 172–5
    chain counters 166–9
    electrically operated heads
        140–1
    engine-driven bilge pump 144–5
    essential tools 180, 181
    fuel capacity 160–1
    gas alarms 154–5
    general tips 180–1
    generators 156–9
    hot water 136–7
    manual water pumps 132–3
    mechanical skills 130–1
    pressurised water systems 134–5
    showers 138–9
    stern thrusters 176–7
    stubborn fastenings 131
    tank level gauges 162–3
    trim tabs 178–9
    ventilation 150–3
    watermakers 146–9
    windlasses 164–5
microwave ovens 213
mobile phones 213
mole grips 18
monitors, bilge 142
monocrystalline silicon solar
    panels 271
mood lighting 198
motorboats
    gantries 55
    trim tabs 178–9
    underwater lights 198–201
mould 150, 153
mouse lines, electrician's 187
MP3 players 124–5
multitools 130
multimeters 184
mushroom vents 30, 153
music, on board stero systems
    124–5
mustiness 150

N

names, boat
    dodgers 85
    nameplates 28–9
    LED lighting 201
navigation lights 201
    LED 196–7
navigation stations 216
Navtex (Navigational Telex) 190
noise
    and generators 159
    soundproofing 284–5
non-return valves 134, 194
nuts, removing stubborn 131
Nyloc nuts 49

O

oil changes 180
outboards
    electric 279
    outboard brackets 51
ovens
    diesel 112–15
    gimballed 93, 94–5
    safety 93

P

paint 13
palm sanders 103
panel saw 25
passarelles 26, 32–5
pedestals, steering
    and cockpit tables 36–7
    converting to wheel steering
        170–1
Peltier effect 118
petrol-powered generators 157
photovoltaic (PV) panels 270–3
planes 15, 19, 25
platforms, bathing 62–3, 99
pliers 18, 19
plywood
    applying veneers to 102–5
    cutting 42
    faced-ply cabin sides 40–3
    types of 40
polycrystalline silicon solar
    panels 271
polyurethane foam 70
pop rivet guns 18, 255
pop-riveting 254–5
portholes 151, 152
pot clamps 94, 95
power tools 16–17, 19, 213
pressure relief valves 136, 137
pressurised water systems 132–3,
    134–5
    accumulator tanks 135
    connecting 135
propane 93, 154
propellers
    bow thrusters 172, 173, 175
    stern thrusters 176
propulsion, electric 278–81
pulpits 50, 98
pumps
    bilge 142–5
    electric and manual sump 139
    electric water 132, 133
    engine-driven bilge 144–5
    hot air diesel heating fuel 110–11
    and pressurised water systems
        134
    water 132–3, 213
pushpits 51, 54, 98
PVC, reinforced 70

R

rack and pinion steering 171
radar 186–9
    connecting the cables 189
    fitting radomes 186–7
    installing the display 188
    radar masts 52–3
    radar scanners 52, 54
    trim angles 187
radio aerials 52
rails, grab 38–9

reefing
    leading lines aft 238–41
    single-line 244–7
reflective insulation 287
regulators 209
remote controls
    bow thrusters 175
    lighting 198–9
resin 13
reticulated foam 70–2
reverse osmosis (RO) 146–9
rigging improvements 220–5
    additional forestays 230–1
    backstay adjuster 232–3
    cutting 267
    jackstays 234–5
    lazy jacks 222–5
    leading halyards aft 265
    repairing 221
    sheeting points 242–3
    single-line reefing 244–7
    tips 266–7
rivets, pop 254–5
RO (reverse osmosis) 146–9
rode counters 166–9
roll reducers 56–7
roller reefing
    additional forestays 231
    headsail furling 226–9
rooster tails 198, 199
ropes and ropework 221
    arrangement on deck 236–7
    clutches or jammers 240
    deck organisers 236–7, 239
    leading halyards aft 238–41, 265
    rope ladders 267
    rope shackles 267
    sheeting points 242–3
    shortened halyards 266
    stowing halyards and sheets 266
rot 150
routers 42
rubbish disposal on board 93
rudder feedback sensors 194
running rigging improvements
    backstay adjuster 232–3
    lazy jacks 222–5
    leading halyards aft 238–41, 265
    sheeting points 242–3
    single-line reefing 244–7

S

safety 12–13
    gas 155
    safety harnesses and jackstays
        234–5
    stoves 93, 95
    tools 15, 16
saildrives, electric 279
sails
    cruising chutes 248–9
    headsail furling 226–9
    mending 220
    spinnakers 250–1
sanders 12, 17
    palm 103
saws 19, 25
scanners, radar 186
screens, dual-purpose 126, 217
screwdrivers 14, 15, 17, 18, 19,
    130

scuppers 99
sea water
 heads flushing 140, 141
 watermakers 146–9
seams
 double-rubbed 80, 83, 87
 repairing seams in sails 220
seating
 bolstering cushion foam 69
 cockpit cushions 70–3
 on pulpits and pushpits 50, 51
 repairing vinyl covers 68
self-levelling stairs 34
self-steering 54
 inboard autopilots 192–5
 tiller pilots 260–1
 windvanes 256–9
self-tailing winches 240
senders, fuel 162
sensors
 bilge pump 142–3
 chain counter 167–8
servo-assisted steering 171
servo-pendulum windvanes 257, 258
shackles, rope 267
shaft drive, electric 279
sharpening tools 24, 25
sheets
 cars 242–3
 sheeting points 242–3
 stowing 266
 tweaker lines 250–1
shore power 210–11, 213, 217
 and hot water systems 137
showers 138–9
side decks, laying faux teak 46–7
silicone antifoulings 293
sine wave inverters 213
single-line reefing 244–7
sinks 93
smart alternator regulators 205
sockets 130
solar energy 204, 270–3
 calculating energy demands 271
 choosing solar panels 273
 maximising efficiency 272–3
 mounting panels 273
 solar panels 270–3, 206, 207
 and watermakers 148
 where to mount 51, 52
soldering irons 19
sole boards, faux teak 44–5
solenoid valves 113, 114
Solent rig 231
solid-state sensors 142
solvents 13
soundproofing 284–5
 materials for 285–6
spanners 14, 18, 130
spinnakers 250–1
 mast fittings 251
 spinnaker halyards 239
 winches 251
splices and splicing 221
split charge systems 117
spokeshaves 19, 25
spot temperature handsets 181
spray dodgers 82–5
sprayhoods 99
square wave inverters 212

stack pack systems 222–3
staging 13, 21
stainless steel
 deck fittings 48
 lettering 28
stairs, self-levelling 34
standing rigging
 additional forestays 230–1
stays
 additional forestays 230–1
 backstay adjuster 232–3
 forestays 249
steel boats, davits 64
steering
 inboard autopilots 192–5
 lightweight tillers 58–61
 tiller pilots 260–1
 wheel 170–1
 windvane self-steering 256–9
steering pedestals, and cockpit tables 36–7
steps, mast 252–3
stereos, and iPods 124–5
stern thrusters 176–7
stoves
 charcoal heaters 106–7
 diesel 112–15
 gimballed 93, 94–5
 safety 93
stowage
 galley 93, 127
 halyards and sheets 266
straps, galley 96–7
strong points 235
sulphation 208
sump, draining the 138–9
switches, bilge pump 142–3
symmetrical spinnakers 250–1

T
tables
 cockpit 36–7
 veneering 102–5
tanks
 accumulator 134–5, 137
 expansion 137
 fuel systems 160–1
 holding 288–91
 tank level gauges 162–3
taps 93
teak 62
 decking ply 40
 faux 44–7
 teak-faced ply 40–3
 veneers 102–5
Teflon antifoulings 293
Teleflex cables 170, 171
television 126, 156, 212, 213
temperature
 engine alarms 181
 water systems 139
templates, materials for 41
tenders, davits 64–5
tenon saw 25
thermal insulation 286–7
thermoelectric cooler units 118
Thin Plate Pure Lead (TPPL)
 batteries 279
thixotropic contact adhesives 102
thrusters
 bow 172–5, 185, 217

stern 176–7
tiller steering
 converting to wheel 170–1
 lightweight tillers 58–61
 tiller pilots 260–1
 windvanes 259
toe rails 99
toilets *see* heads
tools 12–13, 14–19, 21
 general safety 15, 16
 hand tools 18, 24–5
 maintenance and care 14–15, 24, 25
 mechanical 180, 181
 power 16–17, 19, 213
 woodworking 19
topping lifts 239, 251
towed generators 204, 276–7
TPPL (Thin Plate Pure Lead)
 batteries 279
tracking systems, AIS 190, 191
transducers, ultrasound 293
trim tabs 178–9, 257
trucker hitches 89
TVs 126, 156, 212, 213
tweaker lines 250–1

V
varnish and varnishing 43, 104
veneers
 applying simple 102–5
 varnishing and waxing 104
 veneered ply 40–3
ventilation 150–3
 cool box 119
 cowls 30, 153
 dorade vents 30–1, 153
 during winter lay-ups 152
 engine 152
 fridge 117
 galley 92
 gas systems 155
 hot air diesel heating 111
 low-profile windscoops 76–7
 mushroom vents 30, 153
 on-deck 152–3
 static vents 153
 types of cabin ventilators 151
 types of on-deck ventilators 152–3
VHF aerials 191
 and lightning 202
vinyl
 lettering 28
 repairing seat covers 68
voltage sensing relay (VSR) 205
voltmeters 184, 217
VSR (voltage sensing relay) 205

W
walkways, articulated 32
waste systems
 holding tanks 288–91
 tank level gauges 162–3
water filters 93
water pumps 213
water systems
 heads 140, 141
 hot water 136–7
 pressurised 134–5
 pumps 132–3
 reducing consumption 132

showers 138–9
 tank level gauges 162–3
 watermakers 146–9
waterlogged foam 68
watermakers 93, 146–9
waterproof fabrics 70
waterproofing electrical systems 185
waxing, veneers 104
weather cloths 82–5
webbing 89
 galley straps 96–7
 jackstays 235
 sealing edges 97
wheel steering 170–1
 windvanes 259
winches 240
 for cruising chutes 249
 electric 238, 240, 262–5
 self-tailing 240
 servicing 265
 winch handles 265
wind power 204, 206, 207, 274–7
 controlling output 276
 fitting generators 276
 generator types 275
 how much output 275
 self-steering 256–9
 where to mount generators 52, 53
windage factor 173
windlasses 164–5, 185
 electric 264
 electrical connections 165
 fitting chain counters 166–9
 foot-operated switches 217
 kits 164
 mounting 165
windscoops, low-profile 76–7
windvane self-steering 256–9
winter lay-ups
 tips 241
 and ventilation 152
wire cutters 19
wiring
 access to wiring junctions 216
 diameters 185
 electric winches 264
 hot air diesel heating 109
 wind generators 277
wooden boats, ventilating 150
woodwork skills 24–5
 tools 19
work surfaces 93, 101
workbenches 16, 21
workshops
 foldaway 127
 portable 20–1
wrenches 130

Z
zinc chromate paste 48
zips 73
 unseizing corroded 68

Acknowledgements

The publisher would like to thank the following for their kind permission to reproduce photographs in this book. (Abbreviations key: t = top, b = bottom, r = right, l = left, m = middle)

Vanessa Bird 78–9, 80–1, 82–3, 84–5, 86–7, 88–9, 96–7, 150–1, 152–3, 222–3, 224, 225(t).

Peter Caplen 8(t), 13(tl), 29(b), 44–5, 46–7, 64–5, 102–3, 104–5, 108–9, 110–11, 112–13, 114–15, 116–17, 118–19, 124–5, 130, 134–5, 136–7, 140–1, 142–3, 144–5, 154–5, 160–1, 162 (except l), 163, 164–5, 166–7, 168–9, 184–5, 186–7, 188–9, 191, 192–3, 194–5, 208–9, 210–11, 212–13, 214–15, 288–9, 290–1, 296.

Nic Compton 220.

Sarah Doughty 12, 13(r), 14–15, 16, 173(m), 190, 221(t), 221(bl), 225(b), 233 (br), 294, 297.

Rupert Holmes 2–3, 9(tl), 20–1, 106–7, 122–3, 131(b), 132–3, 138–9, 196–7, 204–5, 206–7, 221(br), 232, 233(t), 234(t), 235, 236–7, 244–5, 246–7, 248–9, 250–1, 260–1, 263(t), 264(b), 265, 282–3, 284–5, 286–7, 299.

Richard Johnstone-Bryden 24–5, 40–1, 42–3, 62–3.

Jake Kavanagh 6–7, 8(b), 9(tr), 10–11, 13(br), 22–3, 26–7, 30–1, 32–3, 34–5, 36–7, 38–9, 48–9, 50–1, 52–3, 54–5, 66–7, 69, 74–5, 90–1, 92–3, 94–5, 98–9, 100–1, 120–1, 126–7, 128–9, 131(t), 146 (except br), 147, 148–9, 156–7, 158–9, 170–1, 172, 173 (except m), 174–5, 176–7, 178–9, 180–1, 182–3, 198–9, 200–1, 202–3, 216–17, 218–19, 226–7, 228–9, 230–1, 238–9, 240–1, 242–3, 252–3, 254–5, 256–7, 258–9, 262, 263(b), 264(t), 266–7, 268–9, 270–1, 272–3, 274–5, 276–7, 278–9, 280–1, 292–3, 295, 298, 304.

Pat Manley 17, 18–19.

Joe McCarthy 68.

Andrew Simpson 56–7, 58–9, 60–1, 70–1, 72–3, 76–7.

Picture agencies:
Alamy 28 ©Rob Walls/Alamy, 29(t) ©Imagebroker/Alamy.

Corbis 234(b) Ocean/Corbis.

i-stock 146(r) ©Paul Gregg/istock, ©davelogan/istock 162(l).

Shutterstock 4–5 ©Studivd/Shutterstock.

All illustrations by Peters & Zabransky (Stuart Edwards).

Author credits:
Vanessa Bird would like to thank Richard Oliver for his help with the canvaswork pictures.

Rupert Holmes would like to thank Landau Marine, UK, Marga and Busso Prillwitz of yacht Killani and Discovery Yachts, UK for their help with supplying images.

Jake Kavanagh would like to thank Discovery Yachts, UK; Furlex, the Netherlands; Hallberg Rassy Yachts, Sweden; Honda (UK); Hybrid Marine, UK; Landau Marine, UK; Lewmar, UK; Nautor's Swan, Finland; Ocean LED, USA; Steyr Motors, Austria; Sunsail, UK; Torqeedo Outboard, Austria; and Winner Yachts, the Netherlands, for their help with supplying images.

Jake Kavanagh would like to thank Bill Churchhouse, Ben Kay, Magnus Rassy, Gerrit van der Kleyn, Sarah Johnson, Denise Brehaut, Scott Turner, Grahame Hawksley and Paul Dolton for their help in researching this book.